TREASURY OF
NAME LORE

Also by Elsdon C. Smith
DICTIONARY OF AMERICAN FAMILY NAMES

TREASURY OF NAME LORE

By Elsdon C. Smith

HARPER & ROW, PUBLISHERS

NEW YORK, EVANSTON, AND LONDON

FIRST EDITION

LIBRARY OF CONGRESS CATALOG CARD NUMBER: 67-11352

M-Q

To My Wife
CLARE

PREFACE

Max Muller, the eminent philologist, said, "There is a petrified philosophy in language and if we examine the most ancient word for 'name,' we find it in *naman* in Sanskrit, *nomen* in Latin, *namo* in Gothic. This *naman* stands for gnaman and is derived from the root *gna*, to know, and meant originally that by which we know a thing." A name is a distinctive designation; that is, a word or sound or group of words or sounds by which a man is usually and regularly denominated or known.

For more than forty-five years I have been interested in the study of these personal names. During that time I have assembled a library of well over a thousand volumes in English on the subject, together with the principal works in other languages, and, with the help of friends, have accumulated seventeen bulging scrapbooks of newspaper and magazine cuttings. All of this has been helpful in compiling the present volume, and I am indebted to numerous authorities, unknown newspaper reporters, and writers. This work might be said to be the result of sweeping the onomastic (from Greek *onomastikós*, pertaining to names) edifice, a gathering of the onomastic tidbits stored here and there in hidden places. Light touches and anecdotes sometimes are used to illustrate some of the serious articles, and some articles are included only because they may be entertaining.

An appreciation of the complexities of the subject of personal names may be attained by a glance at the names of the officials attending a session of the United Nations General Assembly. No one man can even pronounce all of them correctly, let alone explain all of them in detail.

Much material has been gleaned from *Names*, the journal of the American Name Society. This society is composed of a group of onomastic authorities and others interested in place names, personal names, and other appellations.

Names are not consciously planned. Like the origin of language and the development of grammar, they are the results of the group thinking, or rather instinct or lack of thinking, of countless millions of people. This unconscious cerebral exercise is psychological rather than logical, and thus presents little formal regularity. In large, undeveloped countries such as China and India where communication between different parts is fragmentary and uncertain it must be realized that naming customs vary considerably from place to place.

The articles on the names of the people of different nationalities attempt merely to point out some of the more important characteristics of those names and their occurrence in the United States, and only a brief summary can be given. Only some of the unusual variations from the common name system in America have received attention. Typical and common names are frequently mentioned in order to give the reader a grasp or feeling for the names of that nationality.

The articles about the names of people of various nationalities are meant only to do two things: (1) give one an inkling of the sound or feel of the names and (2) indicate the ways they differ from our common names in America. The reader must remember that the emphasis of this work is not on linguistics but on social customs. The gradual growth of naming systems has been the chief subject of observation, rather than the etymologies of particular names.

The use or omission of numerous diacritical marks in foreign names has not been visibly uniform. In America suppression of the diacritical marks is quickly and arbitrarily enforced upon the immigrant. Many names that are not unfamiliar carried what has been casually referred to as "those hooks and curlicues" in the old country. In this work diacritical marks have been carefully retained only where they are necessary to reflect the flavor of various foreign names, or, in some cases, to call attention to the erudition of the author.

Specific books are cited at the end of some articles only when they are comparatively unknown and are strictly in point with the context of the article. Where there are many works in existence, as there are on surnames and Christian names, the reader must go to the bibliographies for further citations.

A book of this nature cannot be compiled without help from many authorities in the field of onomatology, and the author is happy to acknowledge the valuable aid received from the following: Dmitri A. Borgmann, Bennett Cerf, Jack A. Dabbs, Geart B. Droege, Wilbur Gaffney, Demetrius J. Georgacas, Augustin Maissen, Mamie J. Meredith, Gerald Moser, Julius S. Nyikos, Charlie Rice, Jaroslav Bohdan Rudnyćkyj, Alfred Senn, and H. J. van de Wijer. However these authorities cannot be blamed for the errors that may have crept in.

It is a particular pleasure to acknowledge the help of Merle Morrison who has aided greatly by reading the manuscript, and making valuable suggestions. Also the book owes a great deal to the inspiration and encouragement of my wife, Clare I. Smith, who has helped immensely by performing many tasks and indispensable services relating to the preparation of the work.

ELSDON C. SMITH

Evanston, Illinois
July 1966

with Gerald Abrams, James S. Wilkie, Charles Krow, Robert Wohlg, Robert S. ... J. Stout, and H. J. van der Velpe. However, these individual authors furnished for the company-wide enterprise to ... in a ... system to advance ... the field of scholarship, ... and added greatly toward the ... and making it valuable as ..., since the best ... a great deal in the import from many ... many of us ... Charles J. Styron was able to ... hard to bring about ... and profitable ... service relating to the population of the world.

Thomas C. Martin

Evanston, Illinois
August ... 195 ...

ABORIGINAL NAMES *See* AFRICAN NAMES; AMERICAN INDIAN NAMES; AUSTRALIAN ABORIGINAL NAMES; PRIMITIVE NAMES

ACQUIRED MEANINGS

Many names from the Bible have acquired the same connotations the world over. Thus we call a person an *Ananias*, a *Methuselah*, a *Moses*, a *Job*, a *Doubting Thomas*, a *Dorcas*, a *Judas*, a *Samson*, a *Delilah*, a *Jezebel*, a *Solomon*, or a *Jonah*, and everyone knows exactly what is meant. Indeed, almost all of the important characters in the Bible have been referred to over the years in connection with their character or actions as given in the sacred pages. Their names are imperishable.

Many who never lived outside of books convey by their names alone very definite meanings or attributes, possibly more than if they had actually resided on the earth. *Scrooge* brings to mind a tight-fisted, grasping, miserly, old man. *Shylock* is the wealthy, cruel, greedy, revengeful moneylender. *Svengali* is the sinister musician who forces people to do things they would not ordinarily do. *Dr. Jekyll* and *Mr. Hyde* are brought to mind when a hitherto respected and admirable person is discovered to have committed atrocious deeds. *Simon Legree* is any heartless taskmaster or overseer who drives others beyond their capacity. *Uriah Heep* points to humility. *Babbitt* is the average, middle-class man reaching for wealth with little concern for spiritual values.

Some names instantly bring some one thing to mind. *Rockefeller* immediately suggests wealth. *Longfellow* brings to mind poetical genius. *Barrymore* suggests brilliant acting, and *Webster*, authoritative meaning. *Toscanini* means superb musicianship. *Lincoln* typifies integrity. *Emily Post* is synonymous with etiquette. *Benedict Arnold* and *Vidkun Quisling* are synonyms for a traitor. *Socrates* means wisdom while *Houdini* means magic or anything that seems to defy explanation. *Beau Brummel* is the reflection of men's fashions. *Black-*

1

stone means law, *Baedeker*, a travelers' guide, and *Barnum*, fine showmanship. When one is compelled to meet every requirement or follow the rules exactly it is "according to *Hoyle*."

ACRONYMS

This term, coined in 1943, originally meant a pronounceable word formed from the initial letters or syllables of the successive parts of a compound term. Thus A.W.O.L. for one *a*bsent *w*ithout *o*fficial *l*eave is an abbreviation, while AWOL is an acronym. The meaning of the word has now been expanded to include abbreviations. CARE stands for Cooperative for American Relief Everywhere (formerly: Cooperative for American Remittances to Europe; Cooperation for American Remittances to Everywhere); UNESCO is United Nations Educational, Scientific and Cultural Organization; WAC means Women's Army Corps. Acronyms, far from being merely a dish of alphabet soup, are very useful as they make conversationally manageable terms for organizations with long cumbersome names. Business firms have appropriated the practice. One company named its new cereal WOB for Wheat and Oats for Breakfast.

The term could get out of hand. New York State in 1965 ordered construction of a nuclear-powered plant to produce fresh water from the ocean. The plant was not named SURFSIDE because it will be near the surf. SURFSIDE stands for Small Unified Reactor Facility with Systems for Isotopes, Desalting and Electricity. The man who put that one together must have been really acronym-happy.

See Acronyms and Initialisms Dictionary, Second Ed., Detroit, 1965
See also CODE NAMES

ACROSTICS

An acrostic is an alphabetic line, verse, or poem in which the initial or final letters, or both, of each line form the name or names of some place, thing, or person. They have been employed since remote ages in many nations. They are found in some of the Psalms, Proverbs, and in the Lamentations of Jeremiah in the Hebrew Bible, although they cannot be preserved in any ordinary translation. Ancient peoples were attracted to the acrostic form through their belief in the magical power of letters. Later development was stimulated through recognition of the acrostic as an aid in spelling, memory, and artistic expression. Many English literary men have scorned the use of acrostics.

One of the best-known acrostics is preserved for us in the form of a fish inscribed by early Christians on tombs of the first three centuries after Christ, and supposed to have a mystical reference to the name and attributes of Jesus Christ. The fish, long a symbol of ancient mysticism, was as a word in the Greek spelled ΙΧΘΥΣ. These Greek letters stand for the first letter of each of the Greek words for *Jesus Christ God's Son Savior.* The word is found in some English dictionaries as *Ichthys.*

An acrostic that is known to many is the simple:

North
East
West
South

A clever double acrostic is in the form of a guessing game, the answer being the English poet *Lamb* whose pseudonym was *Elia.* The words: (1) ancient Greek musical instrument, (2) a shoemaker's tool, (3) Italian poet, and (4) a fruit.

1. L yr   E
2. A w   L
3. M azzon I
4. B anan   A

In the time of Charles II in England there was a group of unpopular individuals in his ministry who were engaged in political intrigue. Since their names were Clifford, Ashley, Buckingham, Arlington, and Lauderdale, they were dubbed CABAL, through the use of the first letter of their names—aptly enough, because *cabal* means "secret plotters."

ADDRESSING STRANGE LADIES

How do you address strange ladies whose names you do not know? Some think *Ma'am* is safe ground; others consider it a slap in the face as it makes them seem old. At department store lingerie counters and in beauty shops some women call others *Honey* or *Dearie. Miss* is genteel for a young woman, as is *Young Lady.* For older ladies some say *Missis.* Then some become effusive and compliment them with

3

Doll, Sweetie, Girlie, Darling, Cutie, or *Baby;* anything indicative of youth or a glamorous personality is seldom resented.
See also CEREMONY OF EXCHANGING NAMES; ETIQUETTE OF NAMES

AFRICAN NAMES

Numerous tribes in Africa have little contact with others; so the naming customs vary a great deal. Some give a name immediately after birth, to be replaced with a second name when maturity is reached. Names are given with meanings although it is often difficult to learn the exact reason for the choice, especially as their mental processes vary from those in the more civilized countries. Because of the high mortality rate among infants, many names express in some way a hope for the child's continued life. Others in various ways reveal attitudes of fate and resignation. Some are connected with events happening at the time of birth.

Ghanaians and many other African tribes give meaningful names to their children which are bestowed in a ceremony at dawn of the seventh day after birth. The delay is to see if the baby will live. Besides an individual name each child has a birthday name indicating the sex of the child and the day of the week on which it was born. There is also a common nickname for the child for each day of the week.

Among the Ibo of Nigeria when a child is born, the families of the father and mother each propose a name, and it is a matter of prestige as to which choice is adopted. Sometimes no agreement is reached, and each family uses the name proposed by it. The matter of the name may lead to disputes between the parents and the families of each. Usually, however, the family enjoying the greater social prestige prevails.

Most of the names of the Ibo are short sentences, often, in the case of males, referring in some way to the child's birth, future, or hope of the parents. Examples for boys are *Aniweta* (Ani, a spirit, brought it), *Onolonye* (it has remained among us), *Dumaka* (help me with hands), and *Akubueze* (wealth is the king). For girls there is *Mgbuduumu* (one who supports breath), *Odosiaku* (one who takes care of wealth), and *Ekunaife* (do not say things). The exact connotation of each name is that in the mind of the giver.

4

As the various tribes have contact with Europeans, they tend to copy the European naming pattern, often substituting one or more common European names without regard to their significance and adding the father's name as a family name. Nevertheless, as nationalist feeling grows, some with European names revert to native names.

In 1962, Ethiopia by law provided that every family must adopt one surname and keep it, giving all the children only a new first name. Previously the custom had been for a son to be known by the father's names reversed. Thus, the son of a man named *Abebe Tadessa* would automatically be *Tadessa Abebe*, and the grandson would be *Abebe Tadessa*. A married woman does not take her husband's name, but retains her father's last name.

Among the Mashona in Southern Rhodesia the wet nurse often casually selects a name for the newborn connected with some event at the time of birth. No name at all is given for six months in some tribes. If the child cries continually, it is thought to be a sign that the name does not harmonize and another is selected, generally by the doctor who treats the patient. In some cases many changes are necessary. At maturity, or with girls when they marry, a new name is given which refers to the individual's behavior or character. Although they are not usually flattering and may point to bad manners, they are accepted and used without embarrassment.

The Lugbara, a Sudanic-speaking people of the West Nile district, often give their children names that call attention to unpleasant attributes or characteristics of the parents. They are generally given by the mother and are a means of calling attention to her husband's faults. Some are selected by the husband's mother.

See also PRIMITIVE NAMES

ALIASES

Criminals' Aliases

When a criminal chooses an alias to attain anonymity he almost always selects one that has some relation to his true name. The same initials are often retained. If he has initialed clothes, jewelry, or other articles, the same initials are a necessity. The chosen alias usually is about the same length and number of syllables and often contains the same letter groups or similar sounds as the real name. Thus *Harry Bartlett* may become *Henry Bennett*. *Henderson* may choose *Richardson*. Sometimes the name is merely Anglicized. The man may keep the first or middle name or use the family name as a middle name. Names of friends or relatives are appropriated. The man engaged in confidence games is likely to select a name which will tend to be impressive to his intended victims. This partial retention of his old name is an unconscious effort to retain his own "precious self." When he chooses an entirely new name he is likely to feel that he has left behind a part of his personality.

A Brooklyn cobbler, Frank Zakar, made and filed more than sixty false income tax returns to collect refunds during the years 1958, 1959, and 1960. He found it convenient to use names similar to his own like Zokor, Zahar, Zakor, and Zakore, in making out the fraudulent returns. A clerk going over the "Z" file was struck by the names used, and this brought about a disclosure of the fraud. This man was caught by his own name.

Crooks for years used various names to help conceal their malodorous work. But the practice fell somewhat into disuse by the establishment in Washington in 1924 of the National Bureau of Identification as a clearing house for fingerprint records. When identification could be easily established by fingerprints, a false name merely emphasized the intention to defraud.

Fugitives' Aliases

It has been observed that when fugitives change their names, about three out of five are likely to continue using the same first name. One out of five will merely take his middle name as his new first name.

Seeking a new surname, one out of five will choose his mother's maiden name. Most of the others will pick a surname with the same initial, sound, syllabic rhythm, or number of syllables as his original name. Thus Robert Bennett is quite likely to show up as Robert Fennet or Robert Benson or Robin Brownet. If he changes to something entirely different such as Henry O'Callahan or Ardrey Coffey, it will probably turn out that these are names closely associated with his past life—the name of a town or street in which he lived, a friend he admired, or a man for whom he worked.

In New Orleans, in 1955, the police picked up a man on a minor charge who gave his name as Davy Crockett. Becoming suspicious they checked up and found his real name to be Daniel Boone.

See also CHANGE OF NAMES; NICKNAMES

6

ALPHABETIC ORDER OF NAMES *See* Last Names Alphabetically

AMERICAN INDIAN NAMES

There are many different naming customs among the various American Indian tribes, and only a few representative ones can be outlined here. Some South American Indians give a child a hunting name when it is born while the father is hunting game. Upon return from the hunt the child is given the name of the animal killed, such as *Eruba* (spider monkey), *Tičasu* (pig), or the description of some experience the father encountered. One child was named *Tebu* (tick) because the tapir killed was covered with ticks. Indian children are generally not named after the parent. Each name is an individual one without any consideration for the way the father is known. Family names are not always used. After her marriage the wife continues to be known only by her own name.

Indian personal names have a definite significance. They describe the bearer in some way or tell of some event or action in which he took part. The meaning, however, is often not one which the white man understands. Personal names are often symbolic. They have implied meanings known only to those familiar with the circumstances attendant on the bestowal of the name. The brave named *Sweaty-Blanket* did not sleep in a filthy bed; the name indicated that he was a hard and tireless rider. Mr. *Two Belly* was one who provided so well for his family that his children were plump. *Big Mouth* was an effective tribal speaker. Many names when translated into English by clerks with little knowledge of the Indian languages come out as awkward phrases which conceal the real significance of the name.

Among American Indians names are given and changed at the critical epochs of life, such as birth, puberty, some notable feat, the first war expedition, elevation to chieftainship, and retirement. In some tribes each clan or group has its own set of names, in other tribes the names have nothing to do with totems. Many names given to babies are suggested by some dream of the father. Names may be loaned or given away. The Kwakiutl Indians have two sets of names, one for use in winter and the other in the summer. An American aborigine will almost never answer the direct question, "What is your name?" He will stand mute, but an obliging friend will usually answer for him. If none is present, he may turn to his wife, brother, sister, or anyone else and ask, "How do they call me?"

Those speaking the Muskhogean languages have a series of names approximately indicating age and social status. Boys and girls are given secret birth names, infancy names, early childhood names, later childhood nicknames, and puberty names. The secret names are sacred charms conferred at birth and revealed to the child after puberty. Calling an adult by a nickname is considered an insult. In addition, men receive civil titles and war titles after maturity, being commonly known by their paramount battle or puberty name.

Among the Shawnee the name of an individual, not descent, puts him or her into one of six name-groups: Rabbit, Turtle, Horse, Turkey, Raccoon, and Rounded-feet, the latter representing the dog, wolf, and other animals whose paws are ball-shaped. Bearers of the names are thought to have some of the characteristics or attributes of these animals and may be helped by them. Members of certain name groups are called upon for certain ceremonies. There is a definite emotional affinity and some competition between members of the same name group. Similar animal totem nomenclature exists in some other tribes.

Among the Indians of New Mexico the men have such names as (translated into English): *White Rock Mountain, White Cotton-Tree Bird, A Place in the West, Early Part of Sunrise, White Shells Kicking with Foot,* and *Jumping Bird.* Women bear such names as: *Yucca with Broad Leaves, Cloud When Dark, Flowers of the World, Looking-Glass Yellow, Flower of the Middle of the Day,* and *Water Jumping on Top of Log Looks like a Flower.* In Oklahoma there have been found such Indians as James *Red Nose,* Doty *Lump Mouth,* Jr., Elbert *Short Tooth,* Joe *Yellow Eyes,* Tom *Night Walker,* Esther *Medicine Bear,* and Joe *Little Crow.*

Among the Blackfoot Indians of Montana are found such names as *Drygoods Woman, Many-Tail-Feathers, Croweyes, Hellos Twice, Long-Time-Sleeping, Looking-for-Smoke,* and *Many Hides.* Names of some present-day Crow Indians of Montana are Harry *Rising Sun,* Myers *Black Eagle,* George *Real Bird,* Sampson *Bird in Ground,* Jr., Joseph *Mountain Pocket,* Jr., Frank *Grasshopper,* Guy *Old Bear,* Cyril *Not Afraid,* and Frank *Falls Down.*

On some reservations the Indians seem to be discarding the nature names like *White Cloud, Laughing Water,* and *Running Fawn.* Taking their places are names which indicate the influence of the white man, such as *Charley Goodnurse, Harry-Drive-Jeep,* and *Henry Make-wings.* Some Navahos, prominent in their communities, are *Tall Singer, Big Silversmith, Black Cattle,* and *Little Medicine Man.*

The Indian agents at various times decreed that those under their charge must adopt English-style names in place of the long, awkward names, such as *He-Who-Walks-Silently-in-the-Snow.* In some out-of-the-way places where there were few white men the Indians had trouble choosing names especially as some they encountered were difficult for them to pronounce. In one line an Indian hit upon *Harper,* the name of a Hudson's Bay factor. It was easy to say and all those in the line behind him also selected that name until the agent stopped it. Others selected names from the labels on packages. Since there were few white women known to the Indians, they had a particularly difficult task selecting names for girls. One named his first daughter *Flora* after a missionary's wife. By the time the eighth daughter arrived the family had exhausted its supply of available names, and the girl became *Kotuck Flora,* which in English is "Again Flora."

Many Indians were given European names, particularly in the Eastern part of the country, by settlers with whom they had direct contact. In 1678, Algonquian Indians in New York were receiving Dutch names. The army, not being able to find out the names of Apaches in the latter half of the nineteenth century, gave them numbers. A wealthy rancher, R_{14}, had a peak in Arizona named R_{14} after him. When the Indian service moved in, the Apaches were still unwilling to tell their names, and many were quickly given English surnames from the pages of a New York directory. Indian names have for years been gradually conforming to Spanish and Anglo-American naming practices.

The Indians are very casual about their names in their relations with modern industry. Many have worked sporadically on the Union Pacific Railroad. An Indian may work once under the name of *Crippled Boy.* After payday he disappears. Applying for work a few weeks later he may admit that he formerly worked under the name of *Lame Man,* and research finds that he was called *Man Who Walks Funny.* Confusion arises when these names are sent to the Railroad Retirement Board. *Charles Many Goats* may later return to work to work as *Chief Many-goats.* The first time he is listed under *Goats,* the second time as *Many-goats.* This careless habit of the Navahos taking one job under one name and another with another employer under a different name has created a real problem for social security officials.

9

New names are often bestowed on an adult at some tribal assembly after some act of physical courage known to his associates. Throughout life an active, able leader may receive several such honorable names, each one replacing his former name. Alice C. Fletcher, the authority on the Plains Indians, narrates a Pawnee old-time naming ritual in which there is a eulogy to the gods and the attributes of the hero of the moment are extolled. All this is intoned in a loud voice while the man receiving the name stands in full view of the assembly. The ceremony concludes with the impressive pronouncement (as translated):

Attend! Once more I change his name!
Harken! Riruts'katit, it was
We used to call him by, a name he won
Long days ago, marking an act
Well done by him, but now passed by.
Harken! Today all men shall say—
Harken! His act has lifted him
Where all his tribe behold a man
Clothed with new fame, strong in new strength,
Gained by his deeds, blessed by the gods,
Harken! Shaku'ru Wa'rukste shall he be called.

People marvel and make snide remarks at Indian names translated into English, such as *Peter One Skunk, Jessie Bad Looking, Thomas No Water,* and *Mary Bull Eye,* but are they different from some of our common names when translated into English? We have *Kennedy* (Big Head), *Campbell* (Wry Mouth), and *Cruickshanks* (Crooked Legs). There is *Adolph* (Noble Wolf), *Herman* (Army Man), *William* (Resolution Helmet), and *John* (Gracious Gift of God).

The possible development of Indian names (as well as all other personal names) is really well illustrated by the joke told of the Indian who introduced his family to a paleface with the words, "I am *Brave Eagle;* this is my son, *Fighting Bird;* and this is my grandson, *Four-Engined Bomber.*" Would a great grandson be *Mighty Rocket?*

There was the Indian *Shrieking Loud Train Whistle* who changed his name to *Toot.*

The story goes that the Indian went to court to get a white man's name, saying that he was sick of Rain-in-the-Face. "What name do you want?" asked the court.

"Drizzlepuss," he proudly replied.

AMERICANIZATION OF NAMES

The United States, the melting pot of the world, has received all the surnames of the world and has altered most of them to fit the sounds and spelling of the American language. Many immigrants are often known to their English-speaking neighbors by one name, a corruption perhaps of the real name, and to their compatriots and family by the original native name. Many names used by those of foreign nationality are not found even in the old country; they are American corruptions of the original name. Most early immigrants had no definite ideas as to the correct spelling of their names. All names, indeed, are American names. American family names differ from English surnames because of the many nationalities who have come to America and have altered their surnames for easier spelling and understanding. The nation is composed of people from everywhere (except the moon and Mars, as of this writing). Only the Indians are original Americans; yet their influence on personal names has been negligible.

Many more people in the United States have English names than might be expected from the proportion of people of English nationality compared with the other nationalities. The reason is that English is the common language, and when other nationalities changed their names they often took strictly English names or made their names appear to be like English names. Most Negroes selected English names after being freed from slavery. But not all immigrants adopted English names. In the lower Mississippi valley German names were altered to French forms, while in the Shenandoah and in the valleys of North Carolina and Tennessee many became Scottish and Irish.

In the Southwest the Spanish influence has been marked. Spanish-American names have suffered little change from their original forms. The phonetic character of the Spanish language and the fact that it is one that English-speaking people find relatively easy to learn have tended to keep the names in their original form. The ten most prevalent Spanish surnames in southwestern United States, in order of popularity, are: *Garcia, Martinez, Gonzalez, Lopez, Hernandez, Rodriguez, Sanchez, Perez, Ramirez,* and *Flores*. The Portuguese in the East have made only slight changes in their surnames.

French surnames have been subject to constant pressure on this side of the Atlantic because of their pronunciation, alien to English ears.

For example, *Revere* is from *Rivoire*, a change closer in appearance rather than in sound. Others are *Jarvis* for *Gervaise*; *Sewell* for *Soulé*; and *Gossett* for *Guizot*.

Southern Louisiana with its early French settlers has preserved intact many French surnames such as *Bouvier, Benoît,* and *Guidry* as well as such long ones as *Delahoussaye* and *Domengeaux.* Some later German settlers even translated their names into French, as *Weiss* became *Le Blanc,* and *Koenig, Roy.* In other cases the spelling was altered to conform to French pronunciation.

The Germans who came over before the Revolution, a conservative people, lived together in small towns and kept the dialect and spelling of their names. Later immigrants from Germany and Austria mixed more with others in the cities, and corruption of their names resulted. German sounds were spelled according to English ears. Thus *Stehli* became *Staley, Gebel* changed to *Gable, Bauman* became *Bowman, Mauer* altered to *Mowrer,* and *Heinz* acquired the spelling *Hines.* The umlaut was ignored. *J* became *y,* as *Young* for *Jung.* Z changed to *s,* and *k* and *c* were interchangeable, as when *Kurtz* became *Curts. Ch* changed into *gh* in such names as *Albright* from *Albrecht* and *Slaughter* from *Schlachter. Sch* was simplified to *s,* as *Slagle* for *Schlegel.* These are just samples of the many German-American spelling changes. Many others are easily recognized.

Many Czech names have given trouble to Americans who are neither able to pronounce them when meeting with them in print, or to write them after hearing them. Of foreign names, Czech names present more difficulty to English language speakers than any other group. Some of these Bohemian names are *Hořčička, Hruška, Otčenášek, Pospíšil, Růžička, Stoklasa, Tůma,* and *Cvrkál.* Czechs have resented the flippant way in which Americans treat their names. They do little themselves to alter their names; to American ears they are so queer and outlandish that the names are altered without the bearer being able to do anything about it. Names ending in *a* are often simplified by changing the *a* to a *y.* Bohemian communities have ostracized some of their compatriots who have dared to assume simpler names. They raised a storm of protest when an office-seeker in Nebraska announced his name change from *Lapáček to LaPache.* The commonest method of change with the Czechs is exact or approximate translation, or alteration to a real or fancied resemblance to an American name. Americans make no effort to spell Czech names correctly. And they refuse to bother with diacritical marks. *Dvořák* immediately becomes *Dvorak*. Dropping the diacritical marks tends to corrupt the pronunciation.

Swedes in America find that their neighbors have most trouble pronouncing the names beginning *Bj-*, *Hj-*, *Kj-*, *Lilj-*, and *Sjo-*. The *Hjelms* tend to drop the offending *j* although in Sweden it is the *H* that is silent; the *Bjorns* also drop the *j*. *Kj's* change to *Ch-*; the *Lilj's* become *Lily-*, and the *Sjo's* twist to *Sho* if the word is not translated. Other names cause some trouble to English tongues, but these are perhaps the worst. Some names like *Sjöstrand* and *Eklöf* are translated in America to *Seashore* and *Oakleaf* respectively and become native American—found only in the United States.

The "priest names" are favored by the Swedes in America and are seldom changed. These have classical terminations in *-us* and *-ander*, such as *Sibelius*, *Geselius*, *Helander*, and *Thelander*, and have substantial prestige value. *Johnson* is not a Swedish name at all but is merely the Swede's idea of the American equivalent of the common *Jansson*, *Jonsson*, and *Johansson*. Dropping the extra *s* is the first change adopted in the New World. Swedish *Johnsons*, *Andersons*, and *Petersons* are so numerous in some small towns in Nebraska that various unambiguous nicknames are coined to distinguish them.

Because of the paucity of well-established family names in Norway at the time of the Norwegian emigration to America, one of the first things a new arrival must have decided was the choice of a permanent family name from the several surnames used in the Old Country. The tendency was first to choose the patronymic, since it was relatively easy to spell and was easily understood in America because of the similar English names such as *Anderson* and *Johnson*. Then because of the number of people with the same name, many were changed during the 1870s to the original farm name or a shortened form more or less Americanized. Brothers did not feel obligated in many cases to agree on the same family name.

From the time the first Greek immigrants arrived in America, pressure was exerted on them to shorten and simplify their surnames. Most of them quickly transliterated their names from the Greek alphabet according to the phonemic pattern of the American language, and at the same time shortened it, as *Alex* for the patronymic *Alexopoulos*, and *Paul* for *Polkouras*. Others roughly translated their names. *Petrakis* (diminutive of Peter) became *Peterson*. *Ioannou* (son of

13

John) adopted the form *Johnson*. Mr. *Mpozines* became Mr. *Bozin*. Unpronounced letters like the *P* in *Psoras* were dropped to give the spelling *Soras*. *Pappas* (priest) has become a common Greek name in America, and some have even shortened it into *Papa*. The honorific prefix *Papa*, indicating descent from a priest, was joined to the given name of the priest in question, and as the Greek priests were the important spiritual leaders of their country during the prolonged Turkish occupation, these names were highly respected. Because of this others adopted the name *Pappas*. The patronymic suffix *-poulos* has made many American *Pouloses*. Sometimes letters are removed as when *Adamantides* becomes *Adams*. Many American Greek names can be recognized from the terminations *-as*, *-es*, *-is*, and *-os*.

Most of the Italians in America who alter their surnames merely drop the final vowel. Some change the terminal *i* to *y* or *e*. Names starting with the prepositions *da*, *de*, *di*, and *d'* or the articles *li*, *lo*, and *la* often have them merged with the rest of the name in America, as *Deluca*, *Loverde*, and *Dellaquila*. Spellings are sometimes changed to preserve the Italian pronunciation, as in the change from *c* to *ch*, as in *Cherry* from *Cerri* and *Checko* from *Cecco*. The Italians in America have made little or no attempt to hide the Italian character of their surnames.

In America many Finns shortened their names by clipping either a prefix or a suffix but keeping an unmistakable Finnish identity. Diacritical marks have been dropped from vowels and the pronunciation altered accordingly. Yet most Finns have held fast to their ancestral names probably because many are quite easy for Americans.

Although some Dutch families around New York kept their surnames, such as the *Schuylers*, *Stuyvesants*, *Ten Eycks*, and *Van Rensselaers*, many lesser families acquired names easier for the English.

Prejudice against the Irish in America caused many to drop the *O* and *Mac* from their names. During the last century eastern merchants advertising for help often added "No Irish need apply."

Americans have little trouble with Chinese and Japanese names. The principal change is putting the surname last instead of before the given names as is the custom in many Asiatic countries.

The Poles generally refused to abandon their native surnames, and as long as they continued to reside in neighborhoods where there were many of Polish or Slavic descent, they had little difficulty with them. With later generations there came a slow alteration in their

14

names, but sometimes a sharp slash was in order. Teodor Józef Konrad Naecz Korzeniowski, the novelist, became a British subject in 1886 under the name of Joseph Conrad.

With the Russians there was another problem in acquiring a name for use in America: the transliteration from the Cyrillic alphabet, when no uniform method of transliteration had ever been adopted by the authorities. The Slavic distinction between the feminine and masculine form of the surnames is eliminated with the disappearance of the feminine style.

Foreigners in America tend to alter their names in one of the following ways:

1. By translation, as *Kuiper* to *Cooper* and *Fontaine* to *Fountain*

2. By dropping the last part, as *Pappas* for *Pappadakis*, *Bozo* for *Bozoian*, and *Hampar* for *Hampartzoomian*

3. By cutting off the first part, leaving *Poulos* from *Constantinopoulos*, and *Strand* for *Sjöstrand*

4. By dropping both first and last parts, as *Pappapolychronopoulos* to *Chronos*

5. By respelling in accordance with pronunciation as *Kuntz* to *Coons*, *Blum* to *Bloom*, and *Jung* to *Young*

6. By partial translation, as *Steinweg* to *Steinway*, *Wannamacher* to *Wanamaker*

7. By adopting another name with a similar sound, as *Dejean* to *Deshong*, and *Guizot* to *Gossett*

8. By transliteration to the Latin alphabet

9. By taking an entirely different name, as *Mueller* to *Johnson*.

Among most minority groups in the United States the gradual use of American given names is slower among boys' names than among girls'. This is probably because girls' names are more often chosen by the mother who sees more movies and reads more romantic literature and is more influenced by them than her husband who plays a more decisive role with the boys' names. However, practically all foreign groups quickly change to the English form of Christian names selected for their children.

AMERICAN NAMES

Except for the corruption in spelling and pronunciation of foreign names and the few American Indian names, there are no truly Amer-

15

ican names. The Africans who first received names in America merely adopted the names of people they knew. In the early colonies the English traditions of naming were closely followed. In New England after 1640 the choice of Biblical names was the traditional practice, especially the Old Testament names. This continued until about the middle of the nineteenth century.

American name forms, customs, and practices, such as the use of the middle initial and the early use of Puritan names, have been noted elsewhere in this book. Attaching *Jr.* to a name is an Americanism. A curious Biblical name in early America, observed by Professor George R. Stewart, was *Ebenezer*, a place name. It might be noted that Americans did not adopt Indian names as given names. *Hiawatha* and *Pocahontas* may be used in commerce but they have never become familiar names for children.

There are, of course, minor variations in naming customs in different parts of the country such as in New England, the Midwest, the South, and the Spanish Southwest. However, these deviations seem to be gradually diminishing. In the South the practice of giving double forenames to girl babies and using both in ordinary conversation has been widespread. Names like *Betty Sue, Mary Jane, Dorothy Mae, Tommie Sue,* and *Edie Mae* were common. Sometimes two names or parts of two names were joined together, such as *Mollieann, Shirleen, Janell, Raylynn,* and *Jolayne.* In many cases originality was achieved by variant spellings.

See H. L. Mencken, *The American Language,* Fourth Ed., New York, 1936; *ibid.,* Supplement II, New York, 1948; *ibid.,* Fifth Ed., New York, 1963. Elsdon C. Smith, *Dictionary of American Family Names,* New York, 1956.

See also AMERICANIZATION OF NAMES

AMERICAN NAME SOCIETY *See* NAME ORGANIZATIONS

ANAGRAMS

An anagram is the dissolution of a name by transposition of its letters into a word or words applicable to the person designated without addition, subtraction, or change of any letter. From the ancient Greeks down to the present day anagrams have been a source of amusement for the intellectually inclined. In times past they have been widely employed for purposes of flattery, sometimes with minor cheating on the rules.

David A. Borgmann of Oak Park, Illinois, the country's leading anagram designer, shook up the name Lyndon Baines Johnson to "No ninny, he's on job, lads." For Barry Morris Goldwater he saw, "Grrr! I lost my 'A' wardrobe!" Some of his many other anagrams are: Disraeli—"Sir, I lead!"; Ralph Waldo Emerson—"Power shall adorn me!" and "Person whom all read"; William Shakespeare— "I ask me, has Will a peer?"

Lester Wood of Stillwater, Oklahoma, made twenty-six anagrams from his name. Among them were "So we're told," "Low red toes," "Ed wore lots," "To see world," "Drew to lose," and "We told Rose."

The plant "Thismia" was named for Thomas Smith, a defective anagram of his surname.

Lady Eleanor Davies, the wife of the poet Sir John Davies, with some success fancied herself a prophetess who had received the spirit of Daniel from an anagram she had formed of her name: Eleanor Davies—"Reveal O Daniel," even though the anagram had too much by an L and too little by an S. Since her prophecies were usually against the government, she was in trouble with the authorities, who tried to discourage her from what they regarded as troublemaking. Finally one of her interrogators brought her down with another anagram: Dame Eleanor Davies—"Never so mad a Ladie," with just an E left over. This put the court into a loud gale of laughter which so unnerved the Lady that she never ventured to prophesy again.

ANCIENT EGYPTIAN NAMES

Most of the Pharaohs, Ptolemies, and Roman emperors of ancient Egypt had five names. The first and oldest was as the representative of Horus, at first the great God of Heaven, then later imbued with various other attributes. This name indicated that he was the "son of the gods," particularly the son of Re (or Ra). The second name represented the symbol of the goddesses of the North and the South. The third name was the Golden Horus name, showing that the bearer was of the same substance as Horus or Ra. The fourth name was the *Suten Bat* name, representing the Pharaoh as king of Upper

17

and Lower Egypt. The fifth name, the Son of Ra name, was the private given name that was bestowed upon him at birth. Various titles were prefixed to the names. Modern authorities are not agreed on the transliteration of the ancient Egyptian names, so they are found spelled in many different ways.

The names of four kings of the Fifth Dynasty included the name of the principal Egyptian deity Re (or Ra), *Neferefra*, *Nieuserra*, *Neferirkara*, and *Sahura*. Fourth Dynasty kings, the early pyramid builders, are *Dedefre*, *Khefre*, and *Menkure*. *Thothmes*, the name of several Egyptian kings, starts with the name of the god, Thoth. Merneptah, the successor of Rameses II, contained Ptah. All the old Egyptian gods can be found in the names of men. Boys were often given the name of the reigning Pharaoh. Names were sometimes changed when a new king ascended the throne.

Nicknames were common among the subjects of the Pharaohs more than three thousand years ago. Translated, they are like the ones we find today. Authorities on Egypt have called attention to such names as, transliterated, *Big Head, Baldy, Red, Sweet, Lazy, Happy*, and *Gloomy*.

The Egyptians believed in an afterlife. A man was divided into eight parts. There was (1) the physical body, (2) the double or guardian spirit or ghost, (3) the soul, (4) the heart, (5) the celestial spirit of the man, (6) the embodiment of his vital power, (7) his shadow, and (8) his name. The name was one of the most important parts. If the name were blotted out, the man and all his afterlife was destroyed.

The Eighteenth Dynasty Pharaoh, Thothmes III, upon ascending the throne about 1493 B.C., expressed his hatred by ordering that the name of Hatshepsut, his father's wife and his mother-in-law who had reigned before him as queen in her own right, be expunged from history. He ordered her name and the years of her reign chipped off from every monument on which they were carved, and decreed that the start of his reign was to be reckoned from the date of his father's death. This action he felt absolutely destroyed her for all time.

In the sixth year of his reign (about 1373 B.C.) Amenhotep IV announced that henceforth Aten was the only god to be worshiped (in place of Amon), and changed his name from *Amenhotep* (Amon is content) to *Akhnaten* (he who serves Aten). Thereupon he ordered the name of Amon and other gods obliterated from all monuments. Squads of men were sent throughout Egypt, with instructions to hack the name of Amon, and even the word *amon* (hidden), from every monument and inscription in the land. Going further, he ordered that every name containing the hated god's name be erased, including his own former name of Amenhotep IV. Thus the name of his father, Amenhotep III, was also entirely obliterated, and since the hope of eternal life lay in the supernatural powers of the name, the father was thought to be utterly and completely destroyed. It was a son's duty in Egypt to keep the name of his father sacred, and, attempting to spare his father, he had his men chisel in *Neb-maat-re*, the coronation name, in place of Amenhotep wherever they could. This coronation name contains the name of *Maat*, the goddess of truth, and of *Re*.

When the famous King Tut, possibly the half brother of Akhnaten, was born he received the name of Tutankhaten (living image of Aten). His wife was Ankhesenpaaten. To symbolize the restoration of Amon their names were changed to Tutankhamen (living image of Amon) and Ankhesenamen. Upon the death of Tutankhamen he was succeeded by Ay, and then by Horemheb, who proceeded to erase the names and memory of Akhnaten and his wife, Nefertiti, and Aten wherever they appeared. He decreed it to be unlawful even to pronounce Akhnaten's name.

ANCIENT NAMES *See* ANCIENT EGYPTIAN NAMES; CLASSICAL NAMES; EARLY BABYLONIAN NAMES; OLD GERMANIC NAMES; ROMAN NAMES

ARABIC NAMES

Arabic names have changed little in the last two thousand years. Moslems and Christians have shared a common culture in the Arab countries. Adults are seldom called by their given names. Using the first name of a parent or elder is considered to be a slight. Prefixes like *Abu* (father of) and *Um* (mother of) are often attached to the name of the oldest son. If the oldest son is Musa, the father may be called *Abu-Musa*, and the mother, *Um-Musa*.

The Arabian names can be classified in the following patterns: religious, relating to nature, genealogical, descriptive, admirable qualities, and occupational.

19

For many centuries the names of religious leaders mentioned in the Bible and the Koran have been popular. The Moslem Arabs use many names which refer to the ninety-nine qualities of God treated in the Koran, such as *Abdullah, Abdul-Rahim, Abdul-Karim,* and *Abdul Iader.* The prefix *Abd* means "servant," so these names refer to the "servant of Allah." The name of Abdel Nasser, the president of Egypt and Syria, means "the servant of the victorious one." *Nasser* (victorious) is also one of the many names for God. Other names refer to the descendants of the Prophet Mohammed, such as *Hashim, Hussein,* and *Ali.* Names relating to the family of Mohammed are popular, such as *Fatima* and *Kadija.* Names mentioned in both the Old Testament and the Koran are found; *Dawud* (David), *Ibrahim* (Abraham), *Musa* (Moses), *Sulaiman* (Solomon), *Sara, Yacoub* (Jacob), and *Yusuf* (Joseph) are popular among Moslems. Christians in the Arabian countries prefer names like *Boulus* (Paul), *Butrus* (Peter), *Hanna* (John), *Eisa* (Jesus), and *Mariam* (Mary).

Names relating to nature are frequent, and many can be rendered in English, as *the light of the sun* and *the charm of the moon.* The names *Nour* for boys and *Noura* for girls mean "light," indicating a hope that the person will provide illumination by his or her presence. *Iamar* (moon) is a girl's name, and *Rabi* (breeze) is a boy's name. Other nature names are *Asfour* (bird), *Shunnar* (pleasant), *Saqr* (falcon), *Kharouf* (lamb), *Baghel* (ox), *Sarsour* (bug), and *Yasmeen* (jasmine).

Genealogical names appear in early Arab writings and in more recent literature. The word *Ibn,* or *Ben* (sometimes *Beni*), means "son of," and *Al,* or *El,* is merely the definite article. In recent times Mohammed Ben Bella and Ahmed Ben Yusuf have appeared in the news. In early Arab writings are found such names as *Muhammed Ibn Abdul Wahab, Omar Ibn Al-Khattab,* and *Ali Ibn Aby Taleb.* A name may be a long one, indicating the male ancestral line. The first name is the person's given name, the next is his father's name, then comes the grandfather's name, then the great-grandfather's name, etc. Often the words *Ibn* or *Ben* are omitted.

Like all nationalities the Arabs resort at times to descriptive names or nicknames. Some bear names such as *Taweel* (tall) and *Saghir* (short). A fat person might be *Mudawar,* meaning "circular" or "round." Admirable qualities, such as *Nabil* (noble), *Sharif* (honest), *Karim* (generous), *Sameh* (forgiver), *Hakeem* (wise), *Sadiq* (friend),

Wafiyy (loyal), *Zaki* (intelligent), and *Amineh* (faithful) are found. Many of these are feminized by the addition of *-eh*. There are many occupational names such as *Najjar* (carpenter), *Haddad* (smith), *Kateb* (writer), *Khayyat* (tailor), *Hakem* (ruler), *Samman* (purveyor of foods), *Farran* (baker), and *Khoury* (priest).

The complete name of an Arab may be made up of all or part of the following: a conventional or professional title, an individual name, a term like *Ibn, Bin,* or *Binte* (son or daughter of), the name of the father with possibly the names of some earlier ancestors, the term *Abu* or *Um* (father or mother of) followed by the name of the son, and an adjective denoting tribe, trade, or place.

Many Moroccan names are a combination of the bearer's father's, grandfather's, and great-grandfather's names, such as *Mohammed Ben Ali Ben Ahmed.* Under a decree promulgated in 1950 Moroccans are expected to adopt surnames using localities or occupations such as *Mohammed Samman* and *Ali Sahara.*

See also MOSLEM NAMES

ARMENIAN NAMES

Almost all Armenian surnames end in *-ian,* the genitive singular, as *Missirian, Khodjian, Kooyumjian,* and *Goodsoozian.* When the last sound of the stem ends in a vowel the *i* changes to a *y,* as in *Saroyan* and *Babayan.* The termination generally implies descent, as *Bedrosian* (descended from Peter), although other classes of names use it, as *Izmirlian* (from Izmir) and *Karayan* (the dark or black one).

The Christian names are as interesting as the family names. Some date back to remote antiquity, as *Arshavir* and *Yervant.* Others come from the Bible, as *Sahak* (Isaac), *Boghos* (Paul), and *Ghoukas* (Luke). Two found only among Armenians are *Haroutyoun* (resurrection) and *Garabed* (forerunner, referring to John the Baptist). Common names for men are *Krikor* (from St. Gregory, patron saint of Armenia), *Hovhannes* (John), *Hovsep* (Joseph), and *Hagop* (James). Girls are called *Vartouhi* (Rose), *Takouhi* (queen), *Miriam,* and *Shoushan* (lily).

In America few Armenians have altered their family names. A clannish group, they have regarded name change with disdain. The spelling of many names has been corrupted through transliteration because Armenia does not employ the Latin alphabet; and transliteration brings about difficulties in pronunciation. Shortened forms retain their foreign flavor so that device is not popular. But, like other nationalities, they are usually willing to select English forenames for their American-born children. Some girls' names easily slide into American names as when *Margarid* becomes *Marguerite* and *Shakeh* becomes *Kay*.

AUSTRALIAN ABORIGINAL NAMES

Each aboriginal has at least two given names, one—often derived from the spot where birth occurred—is for ordinary use in speaking to or of him. The second is the secret or sacred name given shortly after birth by the headman of the particular group after consultation with the older men. Some outstanding feature may give rise to this nickname, and it may not be uttered in the hearing of women or of uninitiated men or of strangers. When mentioned at all it is only in a whisper after taking the most elaborate precautions. Men are told their secret names only after maturity, being fully initiated, and after they have shown that they are capable of self-restraint. Women are never told their secret names.

In addition to these two names each man has a status term indicating the stage of initiation which he has reached. A woman has only three status terms, the first designating her life before the first menstruation, the second from then until she is fully grown and her breasts hang pendant, and the third for the rest of her life. Other names designate the subclass and the animal totem to which the individual belongs. Customs in respect to names vary somewhat among the different tribes, particularly as to who gives the names, and the regard to, and belief in, the power of the secret and sacred name.

The natives of the Adelaide district of Australia call their children, translated, *One, Two, Three*, etc.

See also PRIMITIVE NAMES

AUSTRIAN NAMES

Names in Austria are much like German names—as one would expect, since the two countries have a common language. Inspection of the Vienna *Addressbuch* discloses that the following are the most common surnames: *Bauer, Berger, Fischer, Mayer, Müller, Schneider, Schmid, Schmidt,* and *Schwartz*.

Popular Christian names are *Franz, Johann, Josef, Karl,* and *Rudolf* for boys, and *Anna, Leopoldine, Margarete,* and *Maria,* for girls. *See also* GERMAN NAMES

AWARD NAMES

Christian names have been applied to various awards and prizes. Probably the first and best known is the *Oscar,* applied to the gold-plated, bronze statuette awarded annually each year since 1931 by the Academy of Motion Picture Arts and Sciences for the best in various classifications relating to the production of cinematic works. Mrs. Margaret Herrick, executive secretary of the academy, exclaimed when she saw the statuette on her first day of employment, "It looks just like my Uncle Oscar." A reporter overheard the remark and dubbed the little fellow Oscar in his article the next morning. The name caught on and *Oscar* is now an Americanism for any symbol of excellence. Margaret O'Brien, child actress, was given an "Oscar-ette."

With the success of the Oscar, several other groups presented various satirical awards to which personal names were affixed. Professor Mamie J. Meredith, the eminent etymologist and lexicographer, collected many of them and described them in the December 1954 issue of *Names,* to which the author is indebted for most of this article. The Harvard *Lampoon* came up with the satirical *Roscoes* for the actor or actress who "helped Hollywood become what it is today." The first one was set out for Elizabeth Taylor for "so gallantly persisting in her career despite a total inability to act." Since 1946, the Mystery Writers of America, Inc., have alloted *Edgars* to "people who have contributed outstandingly to the field of crime entertainment." *Edgar* is derived from Edgar Allan Poe, the patron saint of the mystery writers. Following this the Western Writers of America, commencing in 1953, presented an *Ernie* (from Ernest Haycox) for excellence in Western stories.

The Academy of Radio and Television Arts and Sciences since 1949 have awarded a *Michael* for meritorious achievement in their entertainment field. *Tonys* are presented by the American Theatre Wing for notable contributions to the theater. *Gertrudes* are granted by the Million-Copy Club of Pocket Books to authors or publishers who in Pocket editions have sold more than a million copies. Car-

23

toonists of merit receive *Barneys* (from the comic strip, Barney Google and Snuffy Smith). *Mehitabel* is the name of an annual award for a fashion "careerist." *Apparel Annie* is another fashion award given by the Manufacturers and Wholesalers Association of San Francisco. Ever since 1942 the Coty American Fashion Critics award has been the *Winnie*. *Christopher* awards are made by the organization founded by Father James Keller, a Roman Catholic priest, to encourage people to combine the spreading of Christian values with their daily jobs. The American Schools and Colleges Association presents the *Horatio Alger* "to dramatize the ideal of individual self-reliance." *Brendas* are the awards granted by the Atlanta, Georgia, alumnae chapter of Theta Sigma Phi for distinction in journalism. *McCall's* magazine bestows the *Golden Mike* for outstanding public service. The Printing Industry of America, Inc., in 1955, commenced the practice of awarding *Bennys* (after Benjamin Franklin). *Annas* are given to amateur painters in oil and water color by *Artnews*. *Printer's Ink* presents *Joshuas* for outstanding advertising, named for Joshua Pusey who invented match books.

Awards by various other organizations have been given common Christian names, and the custom has become a regular American publicity feature. There are *Patsys*, the brain child of the Society for Prevention of Cruelty to Animals and the American Humane Association. German listeners in 1948 awarded a *Kilroy* to the Columbia Broadcasting System for its "Suspense" program. Other awards embodying names will appear in the future.

BABYLONIAN NAMES *See* EARLY BABYLONIAN NAMES

BELGIAN NAMES

Two chief languages are spoken in Belgium. Well over one-half the people speak Dutch (as in the Netherlands) in the North, while most of the rest stick to French, particularly the Walloon dialect of French. Naturally the surnames the people bear are thus primarily of Dutch and French origin.

Some of the most common surnames in the Brussels telephone directory are *Claes, De Coster, De Greef, De Ridder, De Smedt, De Smet, Dubois, Dumont, Dupont, Fontaine, François, Gérard, Goossens, Jacobs, Janssens, Lambert, Leclercq, Leroy, Martin, Mer-*

24

tens, Michel, Michiels, Pauwels, Peeters, Smets, Stevens, Timmermans, Wauters, and *Willems.* About one out of every twelve persons in Brussels has a name beginning with *Van* or *Van-.*

Many occupational names are preceded by *De* (the), as in *De Clerq* (the clerk), *De Decker* (the roofer), *De Meyer* (the bailiff, farm manager), *De Poorter* (the burgher), *De Potter* (the potter), and *De Preter* (the talker, chatterer). Various other nouns are preceded by *De,* as *De Keyser* (the emperor) and *De Pauw* (the peacock). Owing to the French influence many names beginning with *De* are written together without a capital, as in *Decoster* and *Degreef.* *De* and *Van* are generally written with capital *D* and *V* in South Netherlandic or Flemish family names, as *De Smet,* but usually with small *d* and *v* in North Netherlandic or Dutch family names, as *de Smet.*
See also DUTCH NAMES; FRENCH NAMES

BIBLIOGRAPHIES

The New York Public Library published in its *Bulletin* (July 1950 to and including November 1951), "Personal Names, an Annotated Bibliography," compiled and annotated by Elsdon C. Smith. This was reprinted (New York, 1952), in an edition now out of print. It was republished in 1965 by Gale Research Company of Detroit, Michigan.

A bibliography of personal names in English has been published annually in *Names,* the journal of the American Name Society. Jack Autrey Dabbs has compiled a list of works on name lore in Latin America which has appeared in *Names* (Vol. I, pp. 177–87; Vol. II, pp. 234–48; Vol. III, pp 168–75).

On place names the American Library Association published *Bibliography of Place Name Literature United States, Canada, Alaska and Newfoundland,* compiled by Richard B. Sealock and Pauline A. Seely (Chicago, 1948). Supplements have appeared in *Names* from time to time.

Since 1950 the International Centre of Onomastics, which has its office at the Instituut voor Naamkunde in Louvain, Belgium, has published *Onoma,* an annual biblographical and informative bulletin. Each year it contains comprehensive bibliographies of both personal and place names of almost every country.

BOYS' NAMES *See* FASHIONS IN BOYS' NAMES

BRAZILIAN NAMES

Brazilian names are derived from Portuguese names in the same way that early American names followed English customs. Surnames of Brazilians are confusing to Americans because it is often difficult to select the correct compound or actual surname when preceded by one or more forenames. Thus *Domingos Malaquias Aguiar Pires Ferreira* is a compound family name beginning with *Aguiar*. As even the Brazilians have trouble deciding which one is the surname, some reference books have begun to play safe by indexing only by the last name, even though it is part of a compound surname. In some cases where the parent's names are hyphenated the solution is easy. Many surnames have one or more of the various particles, *de, do, da, dos,* and *das,* but in addressing people these are not used. José da Costa would be referred to as Señor Costa, not Señor da Costa. However some Brazilians in the United States do use the particles and seem to like the custom. As in Portugal the most common family name is *Silva*. Other common names are *Santos, Pereira, Sousa, Ferreira, Carvalho, Teixeira, Gomes,* and *Pinto*.

Brazilians attach great importance to the Christian name, and it is used in all walks of life. Even today in many official lists the order is alphabetically by forename, and parents are known to bestow on children names beginning with A to enable them to lead in the list. Famous people are known by their first name rather than their surname.

The law also emphasizes the first name; no signature is legal without it. A surname can be changed but not a given name, although the spelling can be changed as long as the pronunciation is retained. The civil register clerks can refuse to register an infant given a name susceptible to ridicule, but invented names are not forbidden.

The most common male given name is *José,* then come such names as *Antônio, João, Manuel, Joaquim,* and *Jorge*. The most common names for girls are *Maria, Joana, Tereza, Ana,* and *Emilia*. *Dona* precedes women's Christian names, but *Dom* is never used for men in Brazil except for royalty and high church dignitaries.

Married women take the husband's surname along with their own. When *Maria Rebelo* marries *Jorge dos Santos* she becomes *Maria*

26

Rebelo dos Santos. Their son might be *Antônio Rebelo dos Santos* or *Antônio R. dos Santos.* The mother's maiden name when used comes first even when it is just represented by an initial; this Portuguese custom differs from the Spanish.

See also PORTUGUESE NAMES; SPANISH NAMES

BURMESE NAMES

The Burmese people have some of the shortest names of any group; they are musical and decidedly picturesque. All names are composed of words with meanings. Before a Burmese name there is a first element, or title, indicating age or status. For a young boy it is *Maung.* A young man has the prefix of *Ko,* meaning roughly, "master." When one becomes an older or important man it is *U.* This *U* is an honorific ranging somewhere in meaning between English *Mr.* and *Sir,* with possibly the note of respect often put in *Uncle.* *Ma* is the prefix for a young woman and *Daw* for an older woman or one of distinct accomplishment or high social status. An older man will address a much younger man as *Maung.* A landowner or a businessman would address a tenant farmer or laborer as *Maung.* The boundaries between these classes are somewhat hazy. Titles are confusing because *Maung* and *Ma* are also common personal names.

Superstition sometimes influences the choice of a name. When selecting a name for a baby the Burmese parents take into account the day of the week on which the child was born. One or more of a Burmese child's names is almost certain to indicate the day of his birth. Certain sounds or letters of the alphabet are ascribed to each day of the week. For example, Thursday's child would have one name beginning with *B, M,* or *P.* If one is dogged by bad luck or ill health, one will not hesitate to choose a new name. A simple insertion of an announcemnt in the paper of the change of name is sufficient.

U Nu, who became the Burmese Premier in 1947, was the first-born son of U San Htun and Daw Saw Khin. He was born on a Saturday, and the Burmese think that Saturday's child will be quarrelsome. To overcome this and propitiate the spirits he was given the name *Nu* meaning "gentle" or "soft." When Maung Nu attained the enhanced status of a university student he was known as Ko Nu. U Thant, the Secretary General of the United Nations, modestly signs his correspondence Maung Thant. It would be un-

27

thinkable for an *U* to call himself *U*. Thant has a brother U Khant; they are sons of U Pho Hnit and Daw Nan Thaung. Thant married Daw Thein Tin and their daughter is Aye Aye. The Burmese do not have family names as we in the Western world do. The son of U Sein Tun might be Maung Saw Tin, and his wife might be called Daw Mya Aye. One short name used as a prefix appears adequate to them. U Tun Tin was Minister of Health in 1960 while U Chit Thoung was Minister for Union Culture. Their Asian neighbors invariably support names of many syllables, also usually without family names, although in Malaya there is a campaign for the adoption of family names. Some individual Burmese given names are *Lay, Tun Pe, Kyin, Pe,* and *Ni Ni.*

CALLING NAMES *See* NAME-CALLING

CAPITALIZATION

Some people put two names together but retain the initial capital letter of the second name, as *BelGeddes* and *BenAmi.* Of course the use of *Fitz, Mac, O, Ten, Van,* and *Von* with capitals is common. Many names beginning with *Da, De, Di, Do, Du, La,* or *Le* are often observed connected with a name beginning with a capital letter. Some commence their names with a *D'*, as *D'Dio, D'Silva,* and *D'Hooge.* Some odd surnames involving internal capitals are: *A'Brook, AuBuchon, BeLieu, FlaHavhan, F'Meyer, GaNun, G'Schwind, I'Anson, KenMore, KleinSmid, LeWine, Lund-Quist, MiXail, ReQua, RiDant, RossKam, SaCoolidge, SeBoyar, 's Gravesande, SubbaRow, TePas, TenBroek, VirDen, VisKocil, V'Soske,* and *ZaBach.* Unusual capitalizations are *Van Der AA* and *ten Eicken.* Many of these arose from arbitrary meddling. On the other hand, there was the well-known poet-writer who abhorred capitals and delighted in writing his name *e. e. cummings.*

CATHOLIC NAMES

The Code of Canon Law of the Roman Catholic Church, Canon 761, provides: "Let parish priests take care that a Christian name be given to him who is baptized; if they cannot do this, let them add the name of some saint to the name chosen by the parents, and enter both in the register of baptisms." The Greek Orthodox Church also insists that its priests christen babies with the names of saints they recognize. The reason advanced is that the child may have a particular patron or guardian in heaven to watch over him as well as a model for his imitation and inspiration. As almost all our common Christian names have been borne by saints, Catholic parents are not unduly restricted. As early as the year 400, St. John Chrysostom urged parents to select names of saints for their children.

Many Catholics take the matter of Christian names very seriously. To some a given name is not a Christian name unless it is a name from the *Roman Martyrology* or the *Calendar of Saints* given to a baptized Catholic child. Any other name, even though bestowed on a baptized Catholic baby, is not to them a "Christian" name. They contend that one cannot have a "Christian" name until he has been christened or baptized. All other names are to them grotesque; the saints' names are wonderful and glorious. Some saints' names are even unpronounceable to American Catholics, such as Borhedbesheba, Guhsiatazades, Jafkeranaegzia, and Ptdlemachos. In some Catholic countries, such as France and Greece, one celebrates his name day, that is the feast day of the saint after whom one is named, rather than his own birthday.

A new name can be given at confirmation, a practice which was recognized by English law when Lord Coke declared that a man might validly buy land in his confirmation name. Henry II of France had two sons christened respectively Alexander and Hercules, names which yielded to Henry and Francis at their confirmation.

Many Catholics look with horror on nickname or pet forms and on diminutives, and insist that the name must be spelled exactly as listed in the official lists, taking no notice of the fact that in early times the saint himself probably spelled it in many different ways in the course of a lifetime, and that some saints are known by diminutive or pet forms, as St. *Rita*, the pet form of Margarita. One of the most popular saints is St. Francis of Assisi. As applied to this saint, Francis is only a nickname given because of his father's absence in France at the time of his birth about 1182. His real name was Giovanni. Some wish to honor all the saints and give their children the French name Touissant (*tous les saints*). Many variants and corruptions are used with little regard for logic or etymology, and are considered "legitimate"; others are frowned upon. Names

29

containing the names of pagan gods are freely permissible as long as they have been borne by saints recognized by the church, such as *Apollo, Apollinaris, Artemas, Diana, Dionysius, Hermes,* and *Mercurius.*

In 1961 the Sacred Congregation of Rites decided that St. Philomena had been venerated in error and directed that churches bearing this name adopt a new one. In the future babies are not to be named *Philomena,* or *Filomena* in Italian, a popular name for girls in southern Italy. The name was "desainted."

In entering the old orders and most of the religious institutes the novice receives a new name at clothing, thus immediately renouncing family ties and cutting herself off from her old contacts. Nuns often receive the names of male saints. Some orders always add *Mary* to the new name, for both men and women. Other orders add the name of a mystery such as *John-of-Jesus* or *John-of-the-Cross.* These religious are known only by their new names. The old family name is dropped entirely in many orders.

See Benjamin Francis Musser, *What is Your Name?* Manchester, N.H., 1937.

CEREMONY OF EXCHANGING NAMES

Today this is just an introduction between strangers. The exchange of names and the development of the more or less formal introduction was a slow process among many primitive peoples because of the rather widespread belief that one who knew another's name could exercise an evil power over him.

From early times the problem of precedence entered the ceremony. The ordinary person is presented to the king, president, governor, tribal chief, important member of the clergy, or other distinguished personage. Starting during the age of chivalry, among persons of approximately equal rank, the man was presented to the woman, which means that the woman's name was mentioned first.

See also ADDRESSING STRANGE LADIES

CHANGE OF NAME

A furious controversy arose in England in 1862 as to whether it was lawful to change one's surname without obtaining a royal license when William Jones of Clytha announced that his name was changed from Jones to Herbert. Letters flashed back and forth between important public officials. Articles were written and letters sent to the *Times* and the country newspapers. Books and pamphlets were heatedly published pro and con. The matter in several speeches was brought before the House of Commons. It was pointed out that the queen could give one a license to walk the streets but one had that power without the license. So any man might take any name he pleased, and the queen's license gave him no power in addition to his own will. Reply was made that others could not be forced to recognize and use the new name. Commons passed no statute on the subject. Men could change their name without first applying for the royal license. Joshua Bug announced in the *Times* of June 26, 1862, that henceforth he was to be called and known by the name of *Norfolk Howard*. Although this was accepted by many, others contended that there never was a *Joshua Bug*.

In the European countries names cannot be changed without official permission. By a law passed in 1858 it was made unlawful in France to assume any additional names. M. Hadot added his wife's name *Dorville* to his own, as d'Orville, and although he protested that it was done to distinguish him from others with the name of Hadot and not from any desire to pretend to noble birth by use of the particle, *de*, he was convicted and fined five hundred francs.

In ancient times many men adopted the names of famous characters to glorify themselves and gain acceptance for their deeds and writings. Several Greek poets wrote under the name of Homer, which has even caused some to assert that Homer never lived. As a result, it is accepted that some poems attributed to Homer were not written by the widely recognized poet.

A great number of men named Zoroaster (about sixth century B.C.) followed each other in regular succession. Zoroaster even came to have the meaning of philosopher. Other disciples of the great philosophers, even if they did not take the masters' names, attributed to them their opinions and their works. Almost every eminent personage of ancient times has been followed by another or others who took the name to secure fame for their works.

Persons who desire to drop out of sight permanently seldom change their names, as they feel that distance affords enough protection.

They find that changing names leads to difficulties when prospective employers demand to see social security cards. Those who trace missing persons have found that if the missing persons do change their names, they are likely to use their mother's maiden name, some local name near their home, or a name very similar to their real name.

Many convicts and indentured servants transported from England to America fled their bonds and found freedom under different names. It is impossible to estimate with any degree of accuracy the number who changed their names, but it may well have been large. Professor W. E. Mockler observed, "In the absence of any other data, the incidence of non-traditional surnames and of baptismal names as surnames appears to form the only tangible evidence on the subject."

Most people who are dissatisfied with their names just go along with them and do not go to the trouble of changing them. Those who are not dissatisfied have given the matter of change of name little or no thought. After one reaches adulthood, alteration of a name and forcing others to accept the change is a difficult process. Even a president of the United States can do little about his name. Lyndon B. Johnson might start a nuclear war with a brief word, but he cannot easily do anything about his name. One thing is clear: Surnames have been far from stable before the middle of the nineteenth century, although for a century before they had been slowly crystallizing into stability.

After the attack on Pearl Harbor, December 7, 1941, large numbers of persons petitioned to change their names. The desire of persons of foreign extraction to be recognized as good Americans was the principal reason given. In time of war or threat of war many people with names suggesting former allegiance to the enemy country rush to change them even though the family may have lived honorably in the country for many generations with the name.

There seems to be no rule for the changing of names nor any accounting for the tastes which dictate the change. Some Chinese who emigrated to Trinidad took Jewish names, hoping that by so doing they could demonstrate the same skill in commerce that their namesakes possessed. The following recorded changes are a sampling of instances in modern times which reflect the relationship and attitude of man to his singular possession, his name.

In Albuquerque, New Mexico, in 1959, George *Peter* Janetakos petitioned the court to change his name to George *Bill* Janetakos.

Zdislaw Sibilski filed his application in court in San Angelo, Texas, to have his name changed to *Chester* Zdislaw Sibilski. In Knoxville, Tennessee, *Miguel* Pszyk did not like his name; so he had it changed in 1954, in federal court, to *Michael* Pszyk. *Raymond* Frank Dziewiantkowski of Rhinelander, Wisconsin, petitioned to change his name to *Harry* Frank Dziewiantkowski.

In Hungary lived a simple civil servant, often teased by his friends. Once, getting him drunk, they persuaded him to sign a petition to his Imperial Majesty Francis Joseph I to change his name. In due time the emperor's certificate came through, giving gracious permission to the petitioner to call himself Mr. *Swashswishbrummer* in the future, and that name he carried the rest of his life.

Mrs. Blatz, wife of the brewery owner in Milwaukee, was working on the family tree when she noticed another Gustave Blatz in the telephone directory. So she said to Gust, "We are the *only* Blatz family in Milwaukee, and here is another Gust Blatz. You must call and see if he is related."

So Gust went to the address given and found it to be a little fruit store, and he asked for Mr. Gust Blatz. He was told, "Oh, Mr. Gust Blatz has gone to Greece on his honeymoon to visit relatives."

"To Greece!" exclaimed Gust Blatz. "Why my own name is Gust Blatz and we are all German. How can this be?"

"Oh," explained the manager, "his name wasn't Blatz at all. It was such a long name ending in -*popolous*, so he took the phone book, closed his eyes, opened the book, ran his finger down the page and it pointed to Gustave Blatz, so he said, 'That's what my name will be.'"

Sik Kwui Chin and Chui Ngor Chin, his wife, of Chicago, got a little excited when their children were born and named them *Tay Keing, Liavearn, Tay Yee,* and *Gan Jing.* Later Chin was chided for not selecting American names, and people warned him that the children would have trouble with the names. He therefore petitioned in Superior Court in 1953 when the oldest was only four, to have them named to *Anna Taykeing, Lillian Liavearn, Carol Tayyee,* and *Thomas Ganjing* respectively.

In several instances when top sergeants have arbitrarily changed the family names of new recruits in the army because their names were difficult, the soldier has applied to the court for his old name back after his discharge. A young man about to go into uniform in

Jersey City, New Jersey, went to court in 1955 to change his name to Borodin, on the ground that his real name was *Goldbrick* which would be mighty embarrassing in the army.

A man named *Frankenstein* became weary of people who called and asked to speak with the monster, and went to court in Milwaukee, Wisconsin, for a change of name. Mr. *Damm* rushed to court in Tennessee to get a new name when a souvenir postcard publisher came out with a family portrait designated as "The Whole Damm Family." Many men change their names just before marriage because their intended spouses do not relish their names.

One young businessman, asking the judge to change his name, said that it took all morning to leave a message that he had telephoned someone. He received permission of the court to change from *Chasalambos Triantafyllopoulos* to *Charles Tryon*. In Detroit, Philip Corton O'Neal petitioned the Probate Court to change his name to *Mohandus Takai Asaka*. George *Pravda* and his wife petitioned for change of name in Phoenix, Arizona, in 1958 to *Prav* because of the embarrassment arising from the fact that *Pravda*, meaning "truth," is an official newspaper of the Soviet Union and is used as an organ of Communist propaganda.

Edward *Looney* of New Haven, Connecticut, requested court permission to change his name to *Lowney*, explaining that he planned to became a psychiatrist. Richard *Rotten* changed his family name to *Wroughton*.

Mahran Gouzoukouchokian of Elizabeth, New Jersey, asked the court to change his name to Mahron *Levon* because too many people were saying "Gesundheit" when he told them his name. Some years ago Allan Haines *Lockheed*, the famous aircraft engineer, changed from *Loughead* because, it is said, people kept calling him *Loghead*. Otto *Hell* petitioned the court to change the vowel in his surname from *e* to *a* because neighbors delighted in addressing him by the initial of his first name along with his last name in full.

In New York in 1960 Wlodzimierz Roger *Leliwa*-Tyszkiewicz, a New York architect, obtained the court's permission to change to *Wlodzimierz Roger Tyszkiewicz* which he designated as "less complicated." In New Britain, Connecticut, Edward J. *Oleskiewicz* received court permission to change to Edward J. *Okay*. Paul E. *Unnewehr* petitioned the court in 1956 to change his name to *Wehr* because his four children were continually ribbed about their name in school. Efstatios *Christosodoulopoulos* of Leominster, Massachusetts, in 1950 changed his surname to *Christy* by order of the court. *Geza E. Szentgyoergyvoelgyi* came to this country from Vienna to practice as an architect but found it difficult to get work because of his name. He petitioned the court in Pittsburgh, Pennsylvania, to change to *Andrew G. Valley.*

A judge in San Francisco refused permission to Mr. Tharnmidsbe Lurgy Praghustspondgifcem to change his name. He wanted to change it to *Miswaldpornghuestficset Balstemdrigneshoiwintpluaslof Wradvaistplondqueskycrufemglish.* The gentleman was born Edward L. Hayes, but thought that name had no future for him. The first change did not bring quite the good fortune he anticipated so he wanted to try again for more future. When Lea Delene Anscott tried to change her name in a Los Angeles court, in 1960, to *Baby Doll*, the court rejected her petition as capricious. A New York judge, in 1965, refused to allow Howard Burton Zaimant to change to *Baron de Z'Aimant,* observing that "only a king can create a baron or a duke or a count." The court further objected on the grounds that "de" indicated nobility.

Karl *Erster* whose surname in German means "first," was first in a bicycle race in Vienna in 1951. Hans *Zehnter* was tenth in the same race. His surname is the German equivalent of tenth, and he quickly decided to change his name saying that he had been tenth in too many races.

Father Divine, head of an active Negro sect in the nineteen fifties, encouraged its members to adopt fanciful names. Philadelphia courts granted one man's wish to be named *Peaceful Heart* and a young lady's desire to be called *Sweete Love.*

Owen Patrick McNulty sang on radio with Jack Benny under the stage name of *Dennis Day,* and in 1944 legally changed it to Dennis Day in hopes that it would attract favorable treatment to his attempt to enlist in the Navy. In 1947 he asked permission of the Superior Court in Hollywood to change back to McNulty to please his family who were disappointed with his former change.

Eddie Cantor was born Isidore Itzkowitz, but was reared by his maternal grandmother, named Kantrowitz, since his parents died when he was quite young. When she registered him in school, she forgot and said, "Isidore Kantro—." The teacher broke in with "Kantor, that's enough," so he was Isidore Kantor. Upon moving to another school, he became Isadore Cantor. Ida Tobias, whom he later married, suggested Eddie as a first name, and so at the third school he became Eddie Cantor.

Googie Withers refused to change to a more dignified name when she became a dramatic actress, and about 1950 became one of the most important, leading dramatic actresses in England. If one has talent, success is assured, but it takes more talent to be successful if an undignified name must be overcome.

The ham actor changed his name to *Exit* in order to see his name in lights. There was the man who changed his surname to *Narrow*. He pointed to the fact that there were bridges all over the country commemorating his new name—an Englishman traveling in this country inquired who the famous Mr. Narrow was who had so many small bridges named after him. Then there was the traveling thief who wanted personalized towels so he changed his name to *Pullman*.

Ernest Brown of Jersey City was converted to the Moslem religion and in 1957 petitioned the court to change his name to *Nasir Ibnu-D-Din* saying that he wanted a name in accord with the tenets of his religion. Screen writer Frank Stanley Gilman Borden Chase Fowler, in Hollywood in 1955, received permission of the court to change to *Borden Chase* saying, "I was named after a flock of rich relatives but never inherited a thing."

The family of William Heirens, the youthful murderer serving a life term for the slaying of Suzanne Degnan and the slaughter of two women, petitioned the court in Chicago to change the family name in 1946. After Oscar Wilde was convicted and sent to jail for indecent behavior, his sons, Cyril and Vyvyan, were taken to Switzerland by their mother and the surname of all three was changed to *Holland* by royal warrant.

Laws providing for the registration of births and deaths; the proliferation of records necessary for the operation of various veterans' benefits provisions for those who fought in World Wars I and II and the Korean and Vietnam disturbances; the widespread acceptance of life insurance; automobile registration and annual licenses; the lifetime operation of the social security law; and the increase of bank and savings and loan accounts have all contributed to the stability of American family nomenclature. All of these things must be taken into account when a change of name is made. Their complexities often stop a man in his tracks when he today considers altering his cognomen.

Reasons for Name-Changing

The principal reasons given for changing names in America are:

1. Difficulties in spelling and pronunciation
2. Desire to break with the past
3. Anticipation of bias against nationality or religion
4. Need of soldiers to mislead the enemy in event of capture
5. The wish to have the same adopted name as another family member
6. Desire to avoid ridicule
7. Desire to avoid embarrassment or reprisals to the family living elsewhere
8. Request of employer or relative
9. To qualify for inheritance conditioned on change of name
10. Superstitious effort to change one's luck
11. To emphasize nationality or religion
12. Desire to legalize name used for years
13. Desire for name previously used, as resumption of maiden name after divorce
14. Because too many other people have the same name
15. Desire to give child surname of guardian or of mother's second husband
16. Because intended wife objects to name.

On the pros and cons of name changing see Louis Adamic, *What's Your Name?* New York, 1942.

See also ALIASES; LAW ON NAMES; MOVIE NAMES

CHINESE NAMES

For centuries the Chinese have had the most complete system of personal nomenclature found anywhere. All family names in China must be selected from the *Pe-Kia-Sin*, the families of a hundred houses, which alludes to the tradition that the Chinese were early divided into a hundred families or clans. This poem, which contains 408 single words and thirty double words, none of which are repeated, is attributed to the semilegendary Chinese Emperor, Yao, supposed to have reigned from 2357 to 2258 B.C. Some authorities assert, however, that family names came into use in China about two thousand years ago. No one could invent a name for himself, and no one could change his family name except in the event of adoption into another family.

A family may adopt a poem with about twenty or more words no two of which are alike. Then the first generation takes the first word of the poem as a genealogical name, the next generation the second word and so on. The premier of China, *Chou En-lai*, has *Chou* for his surname, *En* for his generation name and *Lai* for his given name. In ancient China, names were important and care was expended in their selection. An old saying is, "If names be not correct, language is not in accordance with the truth of things."

In a ceremony a month after a baby is born it is given a milk name, often consisting of two elements, such as *Heaven's Blessing* or *Jade Lotus*. One of the elements, especially for boys, has often been selected by a remote ancestor. There is an almost complete absence of religious names. A good name with a good meaning gives a Chinese social status. A baby is not named after a relative or an admirable character, but an original name is created for that particular child. As names are an indication of character or destiny, great care is exercised in the selection. The girls are given graceful, dainty names, such as, in English, *Precious Flower*, or *Shining Cloud*. All the names in one family must match. Thus the sisters of Precious Flower might be *Precious Dawn* and *Precious Peace*. Or they might be *Morning Flower* or *Spring Flower*. The milk names for girl babies are more elegant and flowery than for boys, which are usually quite plain, sometimes even repugnant. With their predisposition for males, parents have sought to deceive the devils of the air by tempting them to seize the girls and ignore the boys.

When the child goes to school a book or school name is selected by the father or teacher. The father usually does not use either the milk name or school name but will often address the child by its position in the household, as *Oldest One*. A bridegroom acquires a marriage name, and if he begins a business or professional career, another name is selected. If he enters government service of any kind, he takes an official name. Even intimate friends may take new names by which they address each other. A man of means may take a house or ancestral name, to which is added the word *tong*; in many cases it may represent a whole family. This name is often used in business.

Formerly there was bestowed on great men a posthumous title, but this practice died out with the establishment of the Republic. New names are not substitutes for earlier names but are added names, and all may be used throughout life. Girls are named the same way, but do not receive book or official names. When they marry they keep their maiden surname, although the husband's family name may by courtesy be prefixed to their own and a title equivalent to the English *Mrs.* may be used to indicate the marriage status.

During their lifetime the Chinese often take a fancy or ornamental name. Sometimes it is applied by others. As judgment and discrimination develop and sagacity increases, a Chinese man may take a liking to a certain word or phrase which has meaning to him and give himself another name which outlines his intellectual progress. A common Chinese saying is, "A shallow scholar always has too many names." A person may have several such fancy names. *Confucius* is the Latinized form of the Chinese *K'ungfutse* (Master K'ung), a fancy name applied to K'ung Ch'iu. Successful people are often addressed by their birthplace. These fancy names in addition to their earlier formal names provide a bewildering confusion of names for the foreign students of Chinese history and literature.

One Chinese scholar estimated that about 40 per cent of the world's Chinese are surnamed *Chang, Chao, Chen, Chu, Ho, Hsu, Hu, Li, Liu, Wang,* or *Wu.* There are about two hundred family names in common use and only a little over two thousand altogether, there being a few not listed in the *Pe-Kia-Sin.* More than half of them are derived from place names, and about a quarter are ancestral in origin. Under the law a man could not marry a woman with the same surname.

Most surnames have only one syllable. If a Chinese calls himself *Wang Ta-tao* or *Ta-tao Wang,* it is fairly safe to assume that the family name is *Wang.* If he signs *Wang Ta Tao,* there is confusion, as *Tao* is also a family name. There is no uniform practice of transliterating Chinese names. *Loo Che Min* may be writen *Loo-che-min,* or *Loo Che-min.* The surname is written first. In Little Rock, Arkansas, *Yee Yim Hong* asked the court in 1958 to "Americanize" his name to *Yim Hong Yee.* The surname may, however, have two characters and be *Kungyang* or *Kung Yang.* Inverted commas may separate the different parts to show aspiration. Children and young people whose names consist of two characters are frequently, in familiar discourse, addressed by the last one, there being prefixed the vowel sound of A or *Ah; Che-min* might be called *Amin.*

The Chinese feel that the publication in a newspaper of given names or full names of a public official is not compatible with the dignity of the official position. The phrase "a good name," referring to a good reputation, is used in China the same as it is in Europe and America. In 1777 a book was published setting out the ordinary names of the Emperor Kien-Lung and his ancestors in which the young were warned not to allude to them. Under the laws then in force the writer was charged with high treason and sentenced to death. *See also* AMERICANIZATION OF NAMES

CHRISTIAN NAME

This is the name which one is given when christened or baptized. It really refers to the "Christened name," that is, the name given at baptism, and thus means the same as "baptismal name" or "font name." In the early Christian church it was the practice to assume a new Christian name at baptism. The new name did not supplant the old one but was added to it. Christian name has become such a common term that it is sometimes used in referring to Jewish or other non-Christian forenames. The terms "first name" and "forename" are used when one desires to avoid "Christian." In Scotland and the United States "given name" is commonly heard, but the term is rare in England.

See also PATTERNS IN CHRISTIAN NAMES; TYPES OF CHRISTIAN NAMES

CHRISTIAN NAMES AS SURNAMES

While most Christian names have entered into surnames with the addition of a patronymical or diminutive suffix or affix, many given names are used as family names without any change whatever. This is especially the case with many German names. The most common of such English names are *Thomas* and *James*, but these really do not come under this section as their terminal *-s* conceals the patronymical *-s*. Christian names found in America as family names without change are, in order of frequency, *Henry, Lawrence, George, Harvey, Lucas, Humphrey, Francis, Frank, Simon, Herman, Paul, Albert,*

Bryan, Joseph, Patrick, Conrad, Charles, Michael, Herbert, August, Arthur, and *David.*

This type of surname is found as early as the eleventh century in England, possibly due to the dropping of the Latin *filius,* or, more likely, to merely scribal designations of the father. While these names arose in England independent of other countries, the French and German influence is important, especially in such names as *Frank, Herman, Albert, Conrad, Charles, Michel,* and *August.*

CHRISTIAN NAMES IN COMMON USE

According to a count made by the Social Security Administration in 1957 of the Christian names of those with the ten most common surnames, the following is a reasonable estimate of the most common Christian names, in order of popularity:

Male	*Female*
John	Mary
William	Dorothy
James	Helen
Robert	Margaret
Charles	Ruth
George	Betty
Willie	Elizabeth
Joseph	Anna
Frank	Mildred
Richard	Frances

These twenty Christian names account for about 30 per cent of the people in the United States. The list of the ten most frequently used given names will vary in different places and at different times. The fact that few English surnames are derived from them discloses that such names as *Arthur, Charles, George, James,* and *Joseph* were not particularly popular during medieval times.

See also FASHIONS IN BOYS' NAMES; FASHIONS IN GIRLS' NAMES

CLASS NAMES

Personal names, especially given names, are frequently used as class names denoting human beings generally. Almost all of the very common Christian names acquire their place in the English and other languages as class names, often in an unfavorable sense. *Jack*, meaning a man, a fellow, is the most used name. *Fritz* has the same signification in German. Coupled with other words such as *Jack in office* (petty official), *Jack of all trades*, *Jack-o-lantern*, *Jack Tar* (a sailor), it is very common. *John* is not used quite so much as *Jack*, but the connotations are similar. Other common names are: *Billy* (a fellow), *Hick* (ignorant countryman), *Mick* (an Irishman), *Tom of Bedlam*, *Tom fool*, *doubting Thomas*, *Tommygun*, *Simple Simon*, and *Holy Joe*. Feminine names are also used but are not quite so common as men's names. The pet forms of Mary, such as *Polly* (parrot), *Poll* (prostitute), *Moll* (hoodlum's girl), and *Molly* (a country wench) are used. *Dolly* is a female pet, and *Jenny* is a country girl. *Dumb Dora* is self explanatory. Use of these names often offends sensitive people bearing them. These meanings change from time to time and in different places.

See Josef Reinius, *On Transferred Appellations of Human Beings*, Göteborg, 1903. H. O. Ostberg, *Personal Names in Appellative Use in English*, Uppsala, 1905.

See also ACQUIRED MEANINGS; TOM, DICK, AND HARRY

CLASSICAL NAMES

The classical names of antiquity which we regard with so much awe are just the same down-to-earth names found among the peasantry (and aristocracy) of every country. To give a few Roman examples: there is *Aurelius* (golden), *Brutus* (brutal), *Calvus* (bald), *Capito* (big head), *Cicero* (vetch, or pea, grower), *Cincinnatus* (curly), *Claudius* (lame), *Cocles* (one eye), *Coesius* (cat's eyes), *Crassus* (fat), *Fabius* (bean grower), *Flaccus* (flap-eared), *Furius* (raving), *Lucius* (light), *Naso* (big nose), *Strabo* (squinting), and *Varus* (bow-legged).

The Roman senate, like the ancient Egyptian pharaohs, often adopted decrees abolishing the memory of emperors or members of the imperial families, and their names were erased from inscriptions. Some of the obliterated names are *Caligula*, *Nero*, *Domitian*, *Severus*, *Alexander*, *Maximus*, *Valerian*, *Messalina* (wife of Claudius), and *Julia Agrippina* (mother of Nero).

In ancient Greece each individual had but one given name: *Aristophanes*, *Andromache*, *Pericles*, *Sophocles*. There were no family names. To avoid ambiguity they sometimes added the name of the father in the genitive case and the name of the country, deme, or parish where the man lived, or the gens, or the name of the trade. *Demosthenes Demosthenous Paianieus* was Demosthenes the son of Demosthenes of the district of Paianieus. Or there might be *Cleon the Tanner*. In ordinary daily use the names were *Demosthenes* and *Cleon*. The eldest son was usually given the name of his paternal grandfather. The Greeks were highly conscious of the meaning of their names. *Nikephoros* (bearer of victory), *Demosthenes* (power of the people), *Polycrates* (to great power), and *Alexander* (protector of man) are some examples. Many names ending in -*ides* are patronyms, such as *Euripides* (descendant of Euripus) and *Atriedes* (son of Atreus). No nation has shown greater ingenuity and taste in the selection of names.

Some of the more common Greek name elements are: *agath* (good), as in *Agathyrus*; *andr* (man), as in *Andreas* and *Leander*; *arch* (chief), as in *Archelaos* and *Archimedes*; *arist* (best), as in *Aristarchus* and *Aristides*; *demos* (people), as in *Demosthenes*; *eu* (well), as in *Eugenes* and *Euphemia*; *ge* (earth), as in *Georgius*; *hier* (sacred), as in *Hieronymus*; *hippos* (horse), as in *Hippocrates* and *Hipparchos*; *laos* (people), as in Nicolaus; *mache* (fight, war), as in *Andromache* and *Telemachus*; *nico* (conquering) as in *Nicolaus* and *Nicander*; *nike* (victory) as in *Nicodemus*; *phil* (love), as in *Philippus* and *Philadelphus*; *poly* (much, many), as in *Polycrates* and *Polynices*; *soph* (wisdom), as in *Sophocles* and *Sophia*; *tim* (honor), as in *Timotheos*; and *theo* (god), as in *Theophilos* and *Theodoros*. *See also* GREEK NAMES; ROMAN NAMES

CLASSIFICATION OF DESCRIPTIVE SURNAMES

Nicknames, in all countries and at all times, which have evolved into family names seem to follow regular rules as to their origin or reference, and most might be classified in one of the following ten ways:

1. Referring to color of hair, skin, or complexion, such as *Brown*, *Fairfax* (fair hair), *Lloyd* (gray), *Reid* (red), and *Schwartz* (black)
2. Referring to body build or peculiarity, such as *Gaunt*, *Kennedy* (big head), *Kraus* (curly hair), *Littlejohn*, *Longfellow*, and *Short*
3. Referring to physical defects, such as *Calvin* (bald), *Cameron*

(crooked nose), *Crotty* (hunchbacked), and *Cruickshanks* (bow legs)

4. Referring to mental or moral characteristics, quirks, or peculiarities, such as *Curtis* (courteous), *Froelich* (merry or cheerful), *Goodfellow, Goodheart, Gutknecht* (good servant), *Jolly, Lovejoy, Meek, Proudfoot* (haughty step), *Toogood,* and *Truman* (true servant)

5. Referring to physical action, such as *Armstrong, Drinkwater, Foljambe* (awkward leg), *Lightfoot, Shakespeare,* and *Smiley*

6. Referring to real or fancied resemblance to animals, birds, fish, and insects, such as *Crab, Fox* (clever), *Mussolini* (gnat), *Oliphant* (elephantine), *Poe* (peacock, vanity), and *Vogel* (bird)

7. Referring to comparative age, as *Altman* (old servant), *Child, Oldfather, Senior,* and *Young*

8. Referring to habits of speech, such as *Bigot* (by God), *Godsafe* (God's half), *Goodspeed* (God speed you), *Pardew* (par Dieu), and *Sprowl* (slow voice)

9. Referring to occupations, such as *Bishop, Duke, King, Monk,* and *Pope*

10. Referring to articles of dress, such as *Burrell* (coarse woolen cloth), *Gildersleeve* (golden sleeve), *Greenleaf, Hatt,* and *Hood.* (Many apparently in this classification are derived mostly from occupations.)

Some of the names given as illustrations also have other derivations. Properly translated, these are the same nicknames often applied today.

COCKTAIL PARTY NAMESMANSHIP

When a person has forgotten the name of the man being introduced, the experts have decided that there are ten alternatives, all inadequate:

1. Evasion. Turn your back on the party being introduced, clearly pronounce the name of the other party and then mumble some words —even foreign words will suffice. The friend will generally be too timid to complain and if he does, you can drop him from your invitation list.

2. Avoidance. When about to say the name, break off and say, "Just how do you spell your name?" It will turn out to be Hill, Jones, or Brown.

3. Diversion. Suddenly look at the party whose name you can't remember, and quickly change the subject by remarking about his hair or nearsightedness.

4. Silence. Just stop talking until the parties shake hands and disclose their names to each other.

5. Desertion. Quickly leave the scene after saying, "I think you two should know each other. Shake hands."

6. Admission. Be quite blatant in admitting that you have a block about memory and go on and talk about it.

7. Omission. Just omit the name forgotten and talk about something else.

8. Distortion. Emit some gurgling sound so that the man being introduced will be forced to pronounce his name upon request from the other party.

9. Substitution. Call everybody Jack, Dearie, or Cousin to give the impression (false) of being humorous.

10. Prevarication. Just remark quickly, "I know you two have met."

See also REMEMBERING NAMES

CODE NAMES

Code names are words or phrases used to designate a person, place, object, operation, or plan of action. They include acronyms and nicknames. They have two principal uses: (1) to conceal the identity of a person, place, object, or course of action; and (2) as an easy, definite designation or identification of a person, place, object, or course of action.

The history of code names goes back to very early times. Although World War I produced many code names, it was in World War II that the practice became widespread. Today both military and scientific bodies seem to have a penchant for giving secret or nonsecret code names to new projects of all kinds. The Navy published a partial list in 1948 to aid historians in understanding war documents.

Among the most famous code names used in World War II are *Admiral Q* for President Franklin D. Roosevelt and *Duckpin* for General Dwight D. Eisenhower. *Overlord* was the secret code word for Allied plans for invading northwest Europe. The atomic bomb was developed under the title of *Manhattan Project*. Some unusual terms used as code names were *Queen Cobra, Jackaroo, Zuni, Rat Week, Red Cow, Alibaba, Aunt Polly, Bazooka, Pants,* and *Moonlight Sonata*. In World War II these names were selected without reference to any secret connection with the person, place, or action designated. Some Jews who settled in Israel after the war (where changing names was encouraged) chose as surnames the code name by which they were known in the underground organization during the period of the mandate.

See *Code Names Dictionary*, ed. Frederick G. Ruffner, Jr., and Robert C. Thomas, Detroit, 1963.

See also ACRONYMS

COLOR NAMES

Color names are popular in all Western countries. The more common of the family names indicating color are *Brown, White, Green, Read, Reid, Reed, Rede, Rod, Gray,* and *Black.* With the exception of *Green,* these generally have been held to refer to complexion or color of the hair. The early Hebrews used *Laban* (white) and *Zohar* (reddish white).

Definite evidence that color names refer to the color of hair rather than complexion is not easily found. Bede, speaking of the two missionary apostles of the old Saxons, explained:

> *And as they were both of one devotion, so they both had one name, for each of them was called Hewald, yet with this distinction, taken from the colour of their hair, that one was styled Black Hewald, and the other White Hewald.*

Occasionally one earns a color nickname through some unusual event. *Wulric the Black* was so named because he once blackened his face with charcoal as a disguise and penetrated enemy territory killing ten of the opposition before retreating.

While these names do undoubtedly apply at times to complexion, they refer much more often to the color of the original bearer's hair. Important evidence of this statement will be observed upon reference to the words meaning "red." Even today one with red or sandy hair is frequently nicknamed *Red.* One with a ruddy complexion might be called *Reid, Reed, Rede, Read,* or *Rod,* the early English spellings of red, but that would be unusual. Snow-white or red hair is much more of an outstanding characteristic than a dark, white, or ruddy complexion.

Berrey and van den Bark in their *The American Thesaurus of Slang* (1942) list twenty-eight nicknames referring to the hair. Except for Negro color distinctions, there are few slang terms for light or dark complexions as applied to men. This, it must be admitted, is some evidence that hair color invites attention more than complexion. What attracts men's eyes today is the same as what attracted them in the Middle Ages when surnames were being adopted.

All the color names may have as their origin the color of garments usually worn by the original bearer, but very few color names arise in this manner. It might be thought that *Green* is popular because of the frequent use of green clothing worn in medieval England. But almost all *Green* names are local, as proved by the fact that they are practically always found in early times in forms such as "atte grene" or "de la grene," that is, one who lived on or near the village green or grassy ground. In a few cases *Green* refers to the young, immature person. *Greenman* usually designates the dweller at the sign of the green man. *Greenleaf* does name one dressed in green leaves, that is, the wild man in public pageants, but this may also be a sign name.

The popular color names are very common because they have more than one origin. *Brown* might be thought to refer to complexion more than any other color name, it being the most common color name. A common derivation is as a descendant of *Brun*, a popular forename in medieval England, Scotland, France, and Germany. The personal name *Brun* means "brown" or "dark red."

Black may be derived from Old English *blaec* meaning black, or from Old English *blac* meaning white or pale, and there is no way to be sure as to any particular name. In most cases it means what it says—that is, black. One with a very dark or swarthy complexion among lighter-skinned persons may well acquire the name of *Black*. Because black hair was much more common among medieval peoples than red or white hair, one would expect it to be used as a surname much less than *White* or *Reid*, and inspection of a large group of family names will confirm the suspicion.

White, when it is not derived from the Old English personal name *Hwita*, designates the man with white hair. It might well be applied to one with very white skin such as an albino, but they were rare in medieval times compared to elderly men with snow-white hair. *White* is sometimes a variant of *wait* or *wayte* (watchman).

Other color names, in order of frequency, are *Pink, Blue, Lavender, Orange,* and *Purple*. None of these names refer to the physical appearance of the person. *Pink* designates one with some quality of a chaffinch, or dweller at the sign of the chaffinch. *Blue* is a rare name, referring to one dressed in blue, although it could designate one with a livid complexion. *Lavender* is an occupational name for one who washes, a washerman. *Orange* designates one who came from Orange, a town on the river Araise in France. *Purple* is a rare name, possibly a corruption of Italian *Porpora* or *Purpura* (red).

Common color cognomina among Roman soldiers were *Albus* and *Candidus* (white), *Niger* (black), and *Rufus* (red). These cognomens of soldiers coming from Rome, Africa, and the Near East undoubtedly designated hair color rather than complexion.

COMBINATION WITH SURNAME

Some names combine poorly with the family name due to the habit of elision. If the surname is Snow, Alice is not good. Say Alice Snow three times in quick succession, and you have *Alice No*. Combinations that invite snide remarks are not appropriate for lifetime use. Those named *Sharp* or *Piper* would do well to avoid the given names of Luke and Peter unless they desire to sentence their children to a life of stale witticisms. If the surname is *Rot* (German, red), the use of Thomas is inadvisable due to the pet form Tommy.

The citizen walked up to the post office window and asked, "Any mail for Mike Howe?" The clerk glared at him and shouted, "No, not for your cow or anybody else's cow."

In New York Jim Die, a Chinaman, was taken to Bellevue Hospital, and a policeman went to the relatives to advise them. "Jim Die's in Bellevue Hospital," the officer said. Whereupon the relatives hired an undertaker and made burial plans before another policeman asked why no one had visited the patient.

The late Syngman Rhee, president of the Republic of Korea, was an enigma, and one writer observed that *Mr. Rhee* was truly a mystery. The *Canup* family named their son *Shay*, from the mother's maiden name. *Walter Wall Rugg* is just a phrase for a system of floor covering. Harry is not a good name for Mrs. Legg's son.

He: "Do you know that you look like Helen Brown?"

She: "I can't help it, but I look worse in blue."

The girl called the coal yard and asked if an elderly man had ordered a load to be delivered today. "Why, yes," the coal man replied, "we have an order from a Mr. Canbee."

"That's fine," exclaimed the girl, "he's my father. I'm Gladys Canbee."

"Well, I feel happy, too," was the rejoinder.

A college professor was walking on the street in Iowa City, Iowa, when he was asked, "Where does Joan of Arc live?" He was about to say that he didn't know when he looked up and saw the sign of a well-known lawyer of Bohemian origin, JNO. NOVAK. So he just said, "There," and walked on.

Alden Ames is a lawyer in San Francisco. Not knowing his telephone number a client called Information and said, "Could I have Alden Ames on Clay Street, please?"

Information tartly replied, "I couldn't give you all the names on Clay Street or any *other* street."

Jack *Asadorian* of Fresno, California, changed his surname to Dorian in 1949 because he found that people were likely to pronounce his old name too fast. After reading *Gone with the Wind* one young lady decided to name her first girl *Scarlett*. Then she became engaged to Douglas Feaver and wisely changed her mind.

COMMON CHRISTIAN NAMES *See* CHRISTIAN NAMES IN COMMON USE

COMMON SURNAMES *See* SURNAMES IN COMMON USE

COMPOUND SURNAMES

Compound surnames are among the most interesting and colorful family names. They may consist of an adjective plus a noun, as *Blackstone, Goodchild, Littlefield, Newmark,* and *Westlake.* Or they may be a verb plus a noun, as *Drinkwater, Lovejoy, Scattergood, Shakespeare,* and *Wagstaff.* Others are a noun plus a noun; there are *Churchill, Cranshaw* (crane wood), *Moorman,* and *Ridgeway.* Still others consist of a preposition plus a noun, as *Bywater, Overstreet,* and *Underhill.* Many are translations of German names, especially those descriptive of occupations. They are found in all European countries, and are particularly common in France and Germany.

There are many compound occupational names, the most com-

49

mon of which are those terminating in -herd, -maker, -man, -monger, -smith, -ward, and -wright, such as Cowherd, Shepherd, Botelmaker, Shoemaker, Chapman, Watman, Fishmonger, Ironmonger, Arrowsmith, Goldsmith, Hayward, Woodward, Cheesewright, and Wainwright. The w is omitted in some -wright names. Other occupational names are Todhunter and Grosvenor.

Compounds with Christian names give us Micklejohn, Littlejohn, Goodwillie, and a few others. The French and the Germans have many names in this class, as Grandclemente, Grosjean, Grossjohann, Kleinhans, Petiteperrin, and Schwarzhans. The element Good- is found in many names, such as Gooddale, Goodbody, Goodsmith, and Goodland. From French influence we have the Bon- names, such as Bonhomme (good man), Bonifant (good infant), and Boniface (good fate). Some miscellaneous compound names are Doubleday, Fairweather, Loveday, Whitehead, and Younghusband. Names of this kind easily arose as nicknames as proved by the fact that many nicknames formed at the present time are like these compound surnames.

CRIMINALS' ALIASES See under ALIASES

CRIMINALS' NICKNAMES See under NICKNAMES

CZECH NAMES

Czech names are shorter than Polish names, to which they are related, and easier to pronounce, since they are not so lavishly sprinkled with consonants. The pronunciation of Czech names is somewhat staccato, and their spelling is phonetic. One who knows the sounds of Czech characters can always pronounce the name correctly if he knows how it is spelled, and if he hears it pronounced right, he can spell it correctly. The accent is invariably on the first syllable. Some common Czech endings are -ek, -ny, -ka, -ic, -ac, and -ak. The -ova is the feminine grammatical ending which is sometimes reduced to -a when the name ends in a vowel.

Some of the short family names are Cermak (robin), Kozel (goat), Kopecký (hill), Lev (lion), Mroz (walrus), Chval (flattery), Silný (strong), *Krasna* (beautiful), *Kral* (king), *Kafka* (bird), *Novák* (newcomer), *Dudek* (bagpiper), *Ryba* (fish), *Černý* (black), *Zelený* (green), *Bílý* (white) and *Hnědý* (brown). There are several names without vowels which are confusing to Americans, such as *Chrt*, *Krc*, *Srb*, *Srch*, and *Trc*.

There are the usual patronymical surnames, as *Toman* (from Thomas), *Pavlov* (from Paul), *Petrov* (from Peter), *Benes* (from Benedict), and *Ondrus* (from Andrew). Occupational names are: *Bednar* (cooper), *Holič* (barber), *Kovár* (smith), *Mlynář* (miller), *Pekař* (baker), *Řezník* (butcher), *Rybař* (fisher), *Švec* (shoemaker), *Tesař* (carpenter), and *Krejčí* (tailor). Surnames from nicknames are common. Some of the surnames from places are *Prazac* (from Prague), *Lomsky* (from Lomy), *Slansky* (from *slane*, salty), and *Vrba* (willow), *Zapotocky*, the name of a former president, designates one who lived beyond the brook. Diminutive forms are common, as *Čapek* (little stork), *Zelenka* (little green one), *Kocourek* (little tomcat), and *Juřík* (little George).

Many Czech names are encumbered with diacritical marks, as *Shořepa*, *Žižala*, *Švadleňák*, *Kolářík*, *Košař*, *Ještěrka*, *Pospíšil*, and *Růžička*, and are real tongue-twisters of the most tortuous kind to English tongues. To Americans, the seemingly uncouth names, when translated, are seen to be the simple names known everywhere. Most of these simple names also take diminutive endings which sometimes change the meanings in other ways than merely inferring smallness.

After a discussion of some of these difficult Czech names, two worthy but cunning Englishmen, meeting in an airline waiting room, made a bet with each other as to which one had the hardest name. The one who challenged the wager produced his card to show that his name was Stone, and demanded the money. "No," replied the other quietly, "for my name is Harder."

Many Czechs have German or partially Germanized names. Czechoslovakian law allows married couples to adopt either the bride's or the bridegroom's family name as their permanent legal name.

Most of the common Christian names are in use by the Czechs and are generally easily recognizable. For boys there are *Antonín*, *Barnabáš*, *Filip*, *František*, *Jan*, *Jakub*, *Jindřich*, *Josef*, *Jiří* (George), *Karel*, *Ludvík*, *Michal*, *Mikuláš* (Nicholas), *Ondřej* (Andrew), *Pavel* (Paul), *Petr*, *Silvestr*, *Štěpán*, *Tomáš*, *Valentin*, *Vasil*, *Vavřinec* (Lawrence), and *Vilém* (William). Some other Czech names for boys,

51

not common English Christian names, are *Bohdan* (God-given), *Bohumil* (beloved of God), *Bohumír* (peace of God), *Budislav* (future glory), *Jaroslav* (glory of spring), *Ladislav* (glorious government), *Miroslav* (glorious peace), *Radomil* (love of peace), and *Václav* (glorious wreath). It will be seen that many male names terminate in *-slav* (glory). The Slavs are the glorious ones.

Many masculine names may be made into girls' names by adding an *-a*. Some popular girls' names are *Anežka* (Agnes), *Bĕla* (white one), *Františka* (Frances), *Johanna*, *Karolina*, *Krasava* (beautiful one), *Ludmila* (love of people), *Ludovíka*, *Marie*, *Rusalka* (wood nymph), *Svetla* (light), and *Zofie* (Sophie).

See also AMERICANIZATION OF NAMES

DANISH NAMES

Near the turn of the century about 60 per cent of the population of Denmark outside of Copenhagen had family names ending in *-sen*. Such names as *Hansen, Petersen,* and *Andersen* were prevalent. Before the nineteenth century most people were content with only a given name. In 1828 the Danish government ordained that at baptism children should be given a family name as well as a Christian name. This did not work out very well, as the priests merely added *-sen* to the name of the child's father, or sometimes *-datter*. The son of Jörgen Petersen thus acquired the surname Jörgensen. Then by an act passed in the late 1860s these names were made permanent. In 1904, Danish legislation encouraged the adoption of family names other than the *-sen* names, and registration charges were reduced. In response, many people kept their *-sen* patronymics by hyphenating them with place or occupational names.

Married women are known by their husband's occupation. For example, Fru *Boghandler* Bolwig refers to Mrs. *Bookseller* Bolwig. If she is a bookseller in her own right, she is *Boghandler* Fru Bolwig.

Some prevailing Danish given names for men are: *Anders, Axel, Christian, Enok, Ejnar, Erik, Eskild, Frederik, Fritz, Georg, Hans, Harald, Holger, Henrik, Josef, Jakob, Jens, Jorgen, Karl, Klaus, Knud, Lars, Lauritz, Mikkel, Magnus, Niels, Olaf, Ole, Peder, Poul, Svend, Soren, Thor, Ulrik,* and *Vilhelm*. For girls there are *Astrid, Andrea, Bergitte, Dorothea, Else, Eleonore, Eva, Frederikke, Gjerta, Hedvig, Ingeborg, Jensine, Katrine, Kirsten, Kristine, Margrethe, Nielsine, Petrine, Sigrid, Sorine, Thora,* and *Thyra*.

DIMINUTIVES

In many countries diminutive endings added to Christian names, especially pet forms, are exceedingly common. The French, Italian, and Slavic peoples are particularly fond of the use of diminutives. The most used diminutive suffixes in England are *-el, -en, -et, -in, -on, -ot* (these come from the French), *-cock, -ie, -y,* and *-kin,* as found in such names as *Pannel, Dicken, Janet, Hutchin, Gibbon, Philpot, Hancock, Davie, Ricky,* and *Watkin.* The Flemings originated *-kin.* The French diminutives came earlier and were widely used. The English *-kin* and *-cock* were used mostly by the lower classes before the sixteenth century and survive now mostly in surnames. The English diminutive suffixes used today are *-ie* and *-y,* as in *Jimmie* and *Johnny,* originally more common in the north of England and in Scotland. The extended feminine diminutive forms of *-etta, -ette, -otta,* and *-otte* are observed in such names as *Henrietta, Babette, Carlotta,* and *Charlotte.*

Double French diminutives are not uncommon. Jack plus *-el* and *-in* produce *Jacklin;* Rob plus *-el* and *-ot* gives us *Roblett;* Bart plus *-el* and *-et* produce *Bartelet* or *Bartlet;* and Hamo plus *-el* and *-in* becomes *Hamelin* or *Hamlin;* these names become surnames.

There are three types of diminutives: (1) those expressing the simple idea of smallness, (2) those expressing a feeling of endearment, and (3) those expressing a sense of incompetency or contempt. As used in given names and surnames the connotation of endearment is the most usual.

See also NICKNAMES; PET NAMES

DISLIKE OF ONE'S NAME

That many children, indeed most of them at one time or another, dislike their names and ask to be called by one they have selected is known to everyone. Shakespeare knew the practice when he included the comparison, "as school-maids change their names by vain, though apt, affection" (*Measure for Measure,* I, iv, 46). Some parents have sought to remedy the situation by giving the child a choice. Mrs. Price named her daughter *Martha Sarah Sophia Grace Clementina Adelina Henriette Lynn* Price. That child had plenty from which to choose. Dr. Harry Raymond Pierce, of Mount Berry College, Mount Berry, Georgia, found that boys dislike such names as *Clarence,*

Oscar, Merton, Wellingham, and *Ezra,* and girls dislike such names as *Bertha, Frances, Isabell, Ophelia,* and *Maybel.* Another researcher observed that the most disliked names for boys are *Clarence* and *Percy,* and for girls, *Gladys* and *Matilda.* Many boys heartily dislike *Junior.* Other researchers would find other names to be the most hated. *Zarathustra* and *Ichabod* would certainly be in this class if they ever attained some frequency.

There are many reasons for dislike of one's name. The most important is memory, conscious or unconscious, of some disagreeable person, thing, or action brought to mind by the name. One little boy disliked his name, Thomas, because that was the name of the neighbor's cat. A reason for dissatisfaction with one's name is a wish that another name had been chosen—one that brings to mind a friend or other person especially liked and admired.

A poll taken by the *Woman's Home Companion* in the nineteen fifties found that one out of three women dislikes her name. The most popular or average popular names are more apt to be liked by their bearers than the uncommon names. Of the ten most common names listed in the poll, the least liked was *May.* The most liked was *Barbara.* Names disliked are feminine names used in popular or humorous literature or songs, such as *Mabel, Gertrude, Rose, Belle, Myrtle,* and *Ethel.*

A principal cause for disliking names is the nickname or pet form likely to be used by others. The most frequently given reason for dislike of name is the difficulty others have in pronouncing it, with difficulties in spelling next. Researchers found that men do not like names that are unusual while women complain if their names are too common. Unusual names have more effect on boys than on girls probably because of more difficulties during their early school life. More dislike their given names than their family names. Many who detest their names as children because of teasing and ridicule change their attitude to liking, as adults, because the names are distinctive. About half the people express positive satisfaction with their names. Many who dislike their first name attempt to remedy the matter by encouraging others to use a nickname. Others arbitrarily substitute another name. A few grit their teeth and go through life wincing each time their name is noticed.

Alben William Barkley, who became majority leader of the United States Senate in 1936 and vice president of the United States under

Harry S. Truman, was originally named Willie Alben Barkley. Although named *Willie* (not William) after two uncles, he hated the name and refused to use it. He contended that no one named Willie Alben could be elected assistant superintendent of a county poorhouse. In later years he confessed that he had often considered introducing a federal bill making it mandatory to postpone the naming of children until they were old enough to be consulted.

Many with unusual names have written concerning their troubles with them. Those with a sense of humor rose above their names. Sometimes the distaste for one's name decreases when one learns its meanings and interesting historical associations. Studies have shown that those who dislike their names are also likely to have a low regard for themselves while those who like their names generally exude self-confidence.

DIVINE NAMES

Gods were first called by some epithet thought to be descriptive of them, which later came to be a personal name. Many gods of savage tribes are known by epithets describing them rather than by a personal name, the meaning of which has been lost. When there is a great number of deities, their names come and go. Often when the meaning has been lost, the name has become too sacred to be pronounced and other descriptive epithets are substituted. Many epithets of gods mean "master," "father," "grandfather," or "creator," or refer to the place of habitation as "the one on high," or "the one above." Two divine names sometimes fuse into a single name. The Egyptian *Amon-Re* is an example.

The names of many gods came from the names of men, especially kings or rulers, who actually lived but were given divine status after their death. Romulus, the legendary founder of Rome, was worshiped as a god by the Romans under the name of *Quirinus*. Other gods acquired their names from the names of the places where they were worshiped.

Many names and epithets are applied to deities and their attributes. The reason often given is that no one name can describe the god. Acts of worship may consist merely of reciting the names of the god. The prayers of some of the Hindus are limited to a repetition or constant meditation on the mysterious name *Aum* or *Om*. The

55

Moslems venerate the ninety-nine names of Allah. The Adi-Buddha, or the first Buddha of the Chinese, has never been seen, but has innumerable names. In some instances different names are given in different countries for the same god. The Roman and Greek gods were the same. Each had a Roman and a Greek name under which each was worshiped. Sometimes this plurality of names for one god caused a multiplication of gods when in the course of time the god was worshiped in different places under different names. Names of gods in all civilizations are considered sacred in one way or another. Even the material on which they are written is often held to be mystic and sacred.

In Athens and elsewhere altars have been erected to unknown or nameless gods. Paul (Acts 17:23) observed an altar with the inscription, "To an unknown god." Spirits or demons are often too numerous to have a separate personal name for each and are called by some collective name or description.

See also THEOPHOROUS NAMES OF MEN

DUTCH NAMES

Many Dutch names are easily recognized from the words *van, van der, van den,* and *ver* (a contraction of van der) meaning "from" or "from the," and *ten* and *ter* meaning "at the," prefixed to words designating place of residence, as *Van Dyck* (from the dike), *Vanderpoel* (from the pool), *van der Bilt* and *Vandenberg* (from the hill), *van der Veer* (from the ferry), *Verbrugge* (from the bridge), *ten Eyck* (at the oak), *ter Heide* (at the heath). *Het* (the) is sometimes abbreviated *'t* as in *Visser't Hooft*, the surname of the former general secretary of the World Council of Churches. *Van* is also prefixed to names of villages, counties, and districts from which the bearer came, as *Van Aken* (from Aachen) and *van Cortlandt* (from the district of Cortlandt). The Dutch *van* does not hint at nobility as does the German *von*. If one lived on a farm, *op* or *on* might be prefixed to the farm name. Some of these place names have *-man* affixed to the place, as *Geldersman* (from Guelders).

Some other common Dutch surnames are *de Visser* (fisher), *Vogel* (bird), *de Haan* (cock), *de Vos* (fox), *de Vries* (the Frisian), *Woudman* (forester), *Wevers* (weaver), *Smedt, Smit,* or *Smid* (smith), and *Bleecker* (bleacher of cloth). The Dutch also used characteristic nicknames which became surnames. There is *de Vroome* (pious or wise man), *Stille* (silent person), *de Groot* (the big man), *de Lange* (the tall man), and *de Wit* (the white one). It must be remembered that Dutch *de* does not mean "of" or "from" as in French, but is the definite article "the."

The Dutch, like many others, long used patronymics which changed with each generation. The son of Jan *Barentzen* would be Pieter *Jansen*, and his son William *Pieterse*. The man himself might use the different patronymic forms. At various times he might sign as Pieter *Janse*, *Jansen*, *Janszen*, or *Janz*.

Although hereditary family names began as early as the thirteenth and fourteenth centuries elsewhere in the Low Countries, it was not until the middle of the seventeenth century that the people of the lower middle class in Holland had hereditary family names. Such family names are derived from bynames or nicknames which in one way or another described the individual. *Roosevelt*, as early as about 1500, was a farm or field called *het Rosevelt* (the reed field) in Tholen, Zeeland, and there, about 1638, lived a certain Pieter Jorisse *op het* Rosevelt whose son was called Joris Pieterse. Later the farm was sold to Maertin Cornelisse Geldersman who had a son Claes Martenszen van Rosenvelt who moved to the New World to found the famous Roosevelt family in America. Also where the mother's family was better known and had a surname, the children might carry on the mother's surname rather than the father's.

See also AMERICANIZATION OF NAMES

EARLY BABYLONIAN NAMES

By the time of the Hammurabi dynasty (about 1700 B.C.), the majority of the names found on the many clay tablets and ostraka that have been discovered give the impression of a more or less conventional system of name-giving, although a few new names were still being coined. The meaning of the names was still pretty well understood by the people. Because the scribes wrote the names according to the elements of which they were composed, they had to know the meanings, and this has enabled scholars to analyze and understand Babylonian names in a way that is not possible with any other ancient people. Two-element names predominated, although some had as many as three, four, five, and more elements and were complete prayers. The name *Asur-etil-same-u-irsiti-bullit-su* would be translated as "O Ashur, the lord of heaven and earth, give him life."

There are many names composed of a single element indicating an occupation, as *Atu* (overseer), *Isparu* (weaver), and *Nappahu* (smith). Others are the names of plants, animals, and inanimate objects. The meanings provide an outline of the social life and conditions of the day. Scholars are able in most cases to differentiate the names derived from the West Semitic, Akkadian, Sumerian, Hurrian, and other tongues all inscribed in cuneiform script. Sometimes the name is followed by the name of the father or mother preceded by *mar* (son) or *marat* (daughter), producing a surname (not a family name) similar to our more modern nomenclature. Children were never found bearing the names of their parents in early Babylonian writings.

The many names referring to deities and religious hopes and aspirations give proof of the advanced civilization of the people. Besides names containing the name of a god, such as *Marduk-abi* (Marduk is my father), *Naram-Sin* (beloved of Sin), *Hammurabi* (Amm is great), *Asurbaniapal* (Ashur is creating a son), and *Esarhaddon* (Ashur has given a brother), some names contain such elements as *abu* (father), *ummu* (mother), and *ahu* (brother) as substitutes for the name of the god. Many names contain *ilu,* a determinant indicating deity, such as *Sumu-la-ilu* and *Jaqar-ilu.* Babylon is from *Babili* (gate of god). Other names refer to the general attributes of deity such as infinity, immutability, and immensity, or to supposed activities such as creation, protection, justice, power, and goodness.

Many names, like our modern forms, are hypocoristic in form, as indicated by the affixes, such as *-ja, -an, -atum,* and combinations like *-jatum* and *-atija* in such names as *Sinija, Danja, Samanum, Adatum, Lamazatum, Rabatum, Adajatum,* and *Hunabatija.* This last name, for example, containing the double diminutive, might be translated as "dear little Hunabum." Like our names these hypocoristic suffixes are added to abbreviated forms. The termination *-sha* is often a feminine suffix indicating the omitted name of a goddess, as *Ikubisha* for Ikubi-Shamash.

After the Babylonian captivity of the Jews many names familiar in the Old Testament are found. The exact pronunciation of many Hebrew names, written only in the consonants of the Semitic script, can be better determined when found in the cuneiform literature where the vowels are included.

ENGLISH PRONUNCIATIONS

Almost everyone knows that in England Mary *Cholmondeley,* the novelist, and her family pronounce it "chumli." Many other names have lost part of their sounds. *Wrensfordsley* is pronounced "rensli" and *Wriothesley* comes out as "roxli"; *Gillingham* is "jillingam." Even a simple name like *Home* may be pronounced to rhyme with fume, and Lord Home does. Legend has it that four and a half centuries ago at the battle of Flodden Field, Lord Home at a critical point sought to rally his battered forces through the inspiration of his name, by shouting "Home, Home, Home," pronouncing it as spelled. Taking him at his word the troops immediately started for home. The next day the crestfallen lord decreed that henceforth his name be pronounced "hume."

The diarist Samuel Pepys pronounced his name "peeps," and the lineal descendants of his sister, Paulina, the only one of his family to leave children, so pronounce it to this day. The *Encyclopaedia Britannica* states that it has always been pronounced by the family as "peeps," and most people were so taught to pronounce it. The present head of the family, John Digby Thomas Pepys, the seventh Earl of Cottingham and the tenth Baron Pepys, contends that the other branches of the family all pronounce it "peppiss."

An English policeman one windy evening saw a young couple sitting on a bench in the park.

"Airy, isn't it?" he said pleasantly.

"No," replied the girl, "Charlie."

ETIQUETTE OF NAMES

John J. Smith, the son of John J. Smith, is John J. Smith, Jr., and his son, John J. Smith, is John J. Smith, III or 3rd. When the father dies Jr. is dropped, and some authorities assert that III must change to Jr. A boy named after an uncle is II or 2nd, never Jr. John J. Smith, the grandson of John J. Smith, is II or 2nd, sometimes Jr., so long as the grandfather is living. If William Smith, the brother of John J. Smith, Jr., also names his son after the grandfather, he becomes John J. Smith III or 3rd, the same as his cousin. The son of John J. Smith III or 3rd is John J. Smith IV or 4th. Some contend that the Roman numeral should be reserved for rulers and kings.

With girls the question is not so important. When Miss Mary

59

Smith is named after her mother, the mother is Mrs. John Smith, and there is little conflict of identity. If they are both in the same profession using their Christian names, the daughter is not Mary Smith Jr., which is the same as saying "my son," but is correctly Yr. or *the younger.*

When Miss Mary Ann Jones marries George Henry Coldbeer, her formal name becomes Mrs. George Henry Coldbeer and her informal name is Mary Ann Coldbeer or Mary Jones Coldbeer. Her new visiting card contains the full formal name, which should be used on all social occasions. On cards the use of initials is not good form. She signs her letters with her informal name—never Mrs. George Henry Coldbeer. On checks and legal documents the informal name is considered to be the real name. The wife does not use the husband's title. She is never Mrs. Dr. Coldbeer or Mrs. Judge Coldbeer.

A married woman should be addressed socially as Mrs. John Smith. If she uses her married name in business, she should also be addressed as Mrs. John Smith. However, if in business she is known as Mary Smith, referring to her as Mrs. Mary Smith may be unavoidable, but it is undesirable. So say Amy Vanderbilt, Emily Post, and other authorities, but some readers protest.

Widows are "Mrs. John Smith" and not "Mrs. Mary Smith." If they have a son with the same name as the father, they refer to themselves as Mrs. John Smith, Sr. If they are young and refuse to use Sr., the son may be obliged to retain *Jr.*

The etiquette authorities say that a divorced woman must become Mrs. Jones Brown when she has been divorced from Mr. Brown and her maiden name was Jones. But few divorcees pay much attention to this so-called rule. Emily Post would allow a divorced woman to prefix her mother's maiden name to her maiden name if the ex-husband's surname were distasteful.

One of the most exacting rules in good etiquette is the one which requires a woman, when speaking about her husband to strangers, to say "my husband," never "Mr. Jones," except in business or when speaking to employees. To those the wife knows well, only the forename of her husband should be used. Correspondingly, the husband refers to "my wife" when speaking to strangers, and says "Mrs. Jones" in business matters, or when speaking to employees. The Christian name of the wife may be used by the husband in speaking about her to close friends.

In signatures it is proper for both a single and a married woman to sign "Mary Jones." If it is desired to indicate that the signer is married, she can prefix "Mrs. William" in parentheses. Without this information one can assume that the proper title is "Miss." If a man or a woman has a forename that does not indicate sex, then "Mr." or "Miss" may be prefixed.

Emily Post always asserted that older persons who encourage boys and girls to call them by their first names are lacking in dignity. Practically all the arbiters of etiquette and good taste echo her sentiments constantly in their writings. But there is now a tendency to ignore this rule. To many older persons, first-name calling is the special privilege of intimate friendship. It is admitted, however, that greeting acquaintances by first name is the greatest vote-getting asset in political circles. Most of the authorities on good breeding insist that office workers refrain from calling each other by their first names unless they have been together a long time.

Unwritten rules in the past have provided that as between a man and a woman, the woman should be the first to use the Christian name, although it is permissible for the man to break the ice by asking, "May I call you Mary?" Nowadays such requests are considered superfluous. Between persons of the same sex the one substantially older should ordinarily take the lead. A general rule still is: When in doubt, don't!

On the telephone, a man may identify himself simply as "George Bennett." A woman would say "Mary Bennett" and, if necessary, add "Mrs. George Bennett." When calling someone on the telephone, unless the voice is recognized, always ask for Miss, Mrs., or Mr. So-and-So, and use the first name only after he or she answers.

EXCHANGING NAMES *See* CEREMONY OF EXCHANGING NAMES

FANCY NAMES

These are those odd, peculiar, unusual variants bestowed on helpless babies by parents in a highly imaginative effort to display refined taste and elegance and to confer a uniquely individual and beautiful name. People began to develop pretty names for girls even in the Middle Ages. *Dulcibella* is an early formation. Shakespeare invented *Dowsabel* for a fat woman (*Comedy of Errors*, IV, i, 110).

Professor Thomas Pyles believes that the center of this style of nomenclature is in Oklahoma, although it is found in every state in the union. His research shows that many of the bearers of these names in Oklahoma are highly sophisticated scions of wealth and social position, which is not so true elsewhere. One reason advanced for the many odd, bizarre, and whimsical names conferred on helpless infants in the South is that the many Baptists and other relogous groups there do not believe in infant baptism, and thus there is no name-giving ceremony at which a clergyman can protest or influence the parents.

Some of these names collected by Professor Pyles are: *Aprienne, Bevelene, Cleron, Cloa, D'Ann, De Owen, Dorweta, Euris, Flay, Glathu, Ish, Ivo Amazon, Jedolyn, Jiola, Jur, J'Val, L'Deane, Lueverine, Moita, Naul, Olla, Predirta, Quilla, Sanjean Twyla, Tyty, Uana, Veroqua, Wilburta,* and *Zazzelle.* He carefully avoided misprints.

The South and rural Midwest have been dubbed the "Fancy Names Belt," because of the tendency there to invent new and gilt-edged, florid names for children too young and inexperienced to defend themselves properly. A few examples are: *Lovie Flowers, Precious Hart, Little Bit White, Lemon Green,* and *Handsome Mann.* Some of the eccentric names of recent years are *Blooma, Chlorine, Dewdrop, Dinette, Faucette, Larceny, Lotawanna, Mecca, Twitty,* and *Zippa.* This southern proclivity for unusual names started before the turn of the century and has been growing ever since.

See also SPELLING VARIATIONS

FASHIONS IN BOYS' NAMES

Fashions in names are extremely difficult to pinpoint because of variances in different places and different times. Local heroes and eminent personages give rise to certain names which continue for a longer or shorter period. Here the matter can be accurately set out only in its broad outline.

In England before the Norman invasion in 1066 men's names were the old Saxon names. These are illustrated by the names of the kings: *Egbert, Ethelwulf, Ethelbald, Ethelbert, Ethelred, Alfred, Edward, Athelstan, Edmund, Edred, Edwy,* and *Edgar.* Other common names were *Ælfric, Leofwine, Randwulf,* and *Thurstan.* After William the Conqueror began to control England, the Norman names came in and almost completely ousted the Old Saxon names, although such names as *Edward, Edgar, Edwin,* and *Edmund* later reappeared. About 1185

62

the fifteen most popular men's names were, in order of popularity, *William, Robert, Richard, Ralph, Hugo, Walter, Roger, John, Geoffrey, Gilbert, Thomas, Henry, Adam, Simon,* and *Alan,* the names of conquerors and heroes. In everyday life these were all known by common pet forms. These names have continued in favor to the present day. By the end of the thirteenth century *John* had jumped to first place, reflecting the increasing influence of the church.

Over the centuries many names became popular because of the reigning monarchs. In England, for example, *Charles* became common only after the execution of Charles I, and *George* came in with the Hanoverian dynasty. That *Charles* and *George* were not popular at any time during the twelfth to fourteenth centuries is evidenced by the paucity of English surnames derived from them. The stream of fashion can be traced to royalty, elected heads of state, and, nowadays, entertainers, particularly those connected with the movies and television.

The names of the favorite male saints became popular in the Middle Ages, such as *John, James, Peter, Martin,* and *Anthony.* The names of the patron saints of the different countries began to be widely used in very early times. *Andrew* became a favorite in Scotland, *Patrick* in Ireland, and *David* in Wales. Following the murder of Archbishop Thomas à Becket in Canterbury in 1170, *Thomas* was chosen by many.

After Martin Luther broke with the Catholic Church in 1517 the Protestants attempted to replace the saints' names with other names from the Bible, particularly the Old Testament characters. The Genevan Bible came along in 1560, the first truly popular version available to all men. Such names as *Abraham, Caleb, Ebenezer, Gideon, Isaac, Jacob, Joshua, Josiah,* and *Moses* were common. Others chosen were *Aholiab, Ezekiel, Ichabod, Obadiah,* and *Zebulun.* Indeed, the name of every prophet from Isaiah to Malachi was usurped for the nomenclature of the sons of those dissatisfied with the Catholic Church. These names from the Bible became the popular names in the American colonies. In the seventeenth century this shift to Biblical names was quite sharp in the New World. Many of the Puritans in both England and America, not content with the Old Testament names, seized upon abstract virtues and phrases from the Bible.

Before the end of the nineteenth century the revolt against the Catholic Church had run its course, and the common saints' names and the Norman and Germanic names slowly returned to favor. Also many of the old Anglo-Saxon names, such as *Alfred, Arthur, Edgar,*

Edwin, Harold, and *Oswald,* came back into more popular use. The union between England and Scotland gave greater vogue to such Scottish names as *Bruce, Donald, Douglas, Duncan, Kenneth, Malcolm,* and *Wallace.*

In America, by the nineteenth century the names of famous statesmen and writers were influencing the choice of names. Many were given the forenames of *Washington, Franklin, Hamilton, Jefferson, Madison, Monroe, Jackson, Harrison,* and *Lincoln.* Some became well known: *Washington Irving, Franklin Pierce, Hamilton Fish, Franklin Delano Roosevelt.* Frequently, babies were given the full name of famous statesmen as their given names.

In recent years *Allan, Brian, Bruce, Colin, David, Donald, Gary, Gregory, Keith, Kevin, Lynn, Mark, Michael, Peter, Robert, Roger,* and *Steven* have increased in popularity. Since *John* surpassed *William* in the Middle Ages it has retained its rank, but in the present century there appears considerable evidence that it is slipping.

Distinctly foreign Christian names are becoming rare in the United States. Names like *Giuseppe, Giovanni, Hans,* and *Pedro* are less frequently observed. Names from the Old Testament are gradually disappearing. Few *Isaacs, Abrahams,* and *Ebenezers* are born. The tendency seems to be toward what is often called "American" first names, the common *Robert, John, Henry,* etc. The odd, unusual, bizarre spellings are reserved mostly for girls.

Mockery by the mass media such as television or radio can tend to drive a name out of circulation. After Jerry Lewis started to use *Melvin* as the name of a fool, the number of parents selecting this name for their sons dropped sharply. Lewis recently apologized to Melvins over television after receiving hundreds of complaints by outraged bearers of that Christian name.

See also Puritan Names

FASHIONS IN GIRLS' NAMES

Notwithstanding the swirl of fashions in girls' names over the years, the tendency is to return to the old tried and true names. The headmaster of a school in Shropshire, England, searched a local parish register to find the most popular girls' names in 1583 and in 1783. In the first list the names in order of popularity were *Jane, Elizabeth, Margaret, Ann,* and *Mary.* In 1783 they were *Mary, Ann, Elizabeth,*

Sarah, and *Margaret*. Compare these names with J. W. Leaver's London *Times* list in 1959: *Jane, Mary, Ann, Elizabeth*, and *Sarah*. His 1962 list was the same. In 1965 the five leaders were *Jane, Mary, Elizabeth, Sarah*, and *Ann*. Fashion does not seem to affect girls' names in Britain so much as in the United States.

The four great virgin saints in the Middle Ages, *Agnes, Barbara, Catherine*, and *Margaret*, account for the popularity of these names.

After the English Reformation and the publication of the Genevan Bible in 1560, many turned to the names in the Old Testament. "And in all the land were no women found so fair as the daughters of Job" (Job 42:15), and their names, *Jemima, Kezia*, and *Kerenhappuch* were selected by many parents although the last was too cumbersome to please many. Other popular names for girls were *Abigail, Beulah, Deborah, Dorcas, Esther, Eunice, Rebecca, Rachel, Sharon*, and *Tabitha*. The Puritans produced *Desire, Obedience, Patience, Prudence, Submit, Temperance, Virtue*, and other similar names.

Approvals and disapprovals of names rise and fall over the years. When Victoria came to the throne of England in the early part of the nineteenth century her name was considered grotesquely un-English and some expressed the hope that she would have the good sense to change it. She had the good sense to keep it. When she selected Prince Albert as her consort, the English sneered at his, as they thought, uncouth German name. But it quickly became one of the commonest English names.

Novelists have been instrumental in bringing about acceptance of many Christian names. *Estelle* was established by Dickens in *Great Expectations* in 1860; *Diana* was revived by Scott in *Rob Roy*, 1817; and *Ethel* by Thackeray in *The Newcomes*, 1853. Shakespeare brought out *Jessica* in *The Merchant of Venice* in 1595 and was responsible for such names as *Bianca, Beatrice, Olivia, Rosalind*, and *Sylvia*.

The royal house in England influences the names of babies much more than does the family of our president. In England, the royal house includes not only the queen, her husband and children, but various relatives. Also our presidents are usually older men, and few babies are born in the White House. The first Queen Elizabeth started the popularity of that name as well as the name *Virginia*. No one in America exerted more influence on the names of girl babies than the appealing child movie actress, Shirley Temple, who was born in 1929 and started in movies at the age of five.

In the last hundred years the practice of using pet or shortened forms or variants of girls' names has increased. Elizabeth has furnished *Eliza, Liza, Elsie, Lizzie, Liz, Beth, Betsy, Betty, Bet,* and *Bess* and many others; Mary produced *May, Molly,* and *Polly;* Margaret gives rise to *Margie, Margot,* and *Rita.* Dorothy launches *Doll, Dolly, Dot, Dottie,* and *Dodie.* In the gay nineties, *Rose, Daisy,* and *Blossom* as well as the jewel names of *Jewel, Opal, Pearl, Ruby,* and *Sapphire* were well received.

Coming down to the twentieth century, the names that have attracted attention because of their more freqeunt use are 1900–1909: *Agnes, Ethel, Maude, Olive,* and *Rose;* 1910–20: *Alice, Annie, Dorothy, Ellen, Esther, Helen, Ida, Melissa, Rose,* and *Sarah;* 1921–30: *Anne, Barbara, Betty, Gloria, Irene, Jean, Judith, Lucille, Patricia, Ruth,* and *Teresa;* 1931–40: *Anne, Barbara, Beverly, Brenda, Carol, Gloria, Helen, Joan, Judith, Linda, Nancy, Patricia, Sandra,* and *Susan;* 1941–50: *Ann* or *Anne, Barbara, Carol, Cheryl, Diane, Gail, Kathleen, Linda, Jean, Joan, Judith, Nancy, Patricia, Sharon, Sheila* and *Susan;* 1951–60: *Barbara, Betty, Carol, Deborah, Debra, Denise, Diane, Karen, Laura, Linda, Marilyn, Patricia, Sandra,* and *Susan;* 1961 on: *Caroline, Cheryl, Christine, Debbie, Debra, Denise, Jackie, Jacqueline, Karen, Linda, Lisa, Lori,* and *Susan. Mary* and *Elizabeth* are not quite so popular as they once were. Many recent aspiring Hollywood starlets have selected *Linda, Lynn, Lisa,* and *Lori* as first names. The currently popular names are the most attractive and appealing to parents at the present day. Ten years from now there will be a change.

See also FANCY NAMES

FICTIONAL NAMES

This is a novelist's headache; for real people may bob up with the name selected and sue for libel, especially if the name used is for an unsavory character. It is true that they generally do not get anywhere in court unless they can show that the author knew of them and intended to libel them, but no author wants to stand the expense and annoyance of a long lawsuit. If the name is used in an advertisement, courts are more likely to find in favor of the aggrieved man. New York has a statute specifically forbidding the use of the name of any living person without his permission.

Groucho Marx doubted whether there were any fictional names after

Mr. Brindlebug appeared to protest the use of his name. A real Ichabod Crane appeared to chide Washington Irving for using his name. In a long article by Arthur Train, the author of the Tutt stories in the *Saturday Evening Post*, he pointed out that an author must use names that sound real—the fact that the name is a real one used by several people is not enough. He concluded that the perfect name for a writer's use should not be so common as to be undistinguished, nor so distinguished as to be highfalutin, nor so peculiar as to be laughable where mirth is not intended, nor so bizarre as to be a source of annoyance to the bearer. The perfect name does not exist, most authors think.

One writer said that he used a Shanghai English directory of 1912 for some of his inspirations. Another used Christian names from the list of West Point cadets and surnames from the Annapolis roll. Others use the name of friends after getting releases from them. Preston Sturges, the Hollywood writer and director, was forced to invent names like *Kochenlocker, Ratskwatski, Glumpf, McNannym, Shottish,* and *Casalsis* in order to avoid offending people. Charles Chaplin chose the name Henri Verdoux for the wife murderer in his picture *Monsieur Verdoux* after ascertaining that the name did not appear in the Paris telephone directory. Nevertheless, a real Henri Verdoux showed up and sued United Artists and the distributors of the movie in France.

A major broadcasting network ruled that all names for characters in original scripts must be taken from a geographical atlas. Thereupon Parke Cummings pointed out that because of the number of towns named after people almost any combination of names of living persons could be selected. For example, from Elizabeth (N.J.) and Taylor (Pa.) could come Elizabeth Taylor.

FINNISH NAMES

Most Finnish surnames are patronymics and terminate in *-nen* (son) which makes them easy to recognize, such as *Heikkinen* (Henrickson). This suffix is added to many names which are not true patronymics. Perhaps the most common family name is *Mäki* (hill) which is also found preceded by various modifiers as *Kirkkomäki* (church hill), and *Hietamäki* (sand hill). Other common names are *Järvi* (lake), *Joki* (river), *Kivi* (stone), *Ruusu* (rose), *Talo* (house), *Mustanen* (black), *Valkoinen* (white), and *Seppänen* (smith).

The Finns have their own forms of the common given names. There is *Antti* for Andrew, *Heikki* for Henry, *Jani, Johan, Jussi,* and *Jukka* for John, *Joosep* for Joseph, *Kaarlo* for Carl, *Oskari* for Oscar, *Paaveli* and *Paavo* for Paul, *Taavetti* for David, *Tuomas* for Thomas, *Rikhard* for Richard, *Viljo* for William, and *Yrjö* for George. For girls there is *Dorotea* for Dorothy, *Helli* for Helen, *Katrina* for Katharine, *Kerttu* for Gertrude, *Liisa* for Elizabeth, *Maiju* for Mary, and *Mirjam* for Miriam. There are many other given names for which there are no English Christian name equivalents such as *Inkeri, Jaakkina, Kyllikki, Mielikki, Pärttyli,* and *Vellamo.*

See also AMERICANIZATION OF NAMES

FORTUNATE NAMES

An eccentric Frenchman willed his estate to his six nephews and six nieces on condition that the men marry women named Antonie, and the women marry only men named Anton, and name the first-born Anton or Antonie, and on the further condition that the marriage of each nephew be celebrated on one of St. Anthony's days, on pain of forfeiture of one-half of the legacy.

If you are short on cash and want to attend Harvard, it is important that your surname be Murphy. William Stanislaus Murphy left his entire estate to Harvard University as a scholarship fund for impecunious Murphys. John Nicholson of London, by his will dated April 28, 1717, left the residue of his estate for the use of poor persons in England who were Protestant and were named Nicholson.

When Elias Warner Leavenworth died in 1887 he bequeathed a sum to Yale for a scholarship of $900 a year to any student who met the admission requirements of the university and whose last name was Leavenworth. Since World War II, Yale has been searching for Leavenworths, a relatively rare surname. Hamilton College in Clinton, New York, also has a Leavenworth Scholarship and has had only two Leavenworths at the college in the last twenty years.

Dr. John Beans Carrell, of Hatboro, Pennsylvania, died in 1950 at the age of ninety-nine, leaving a will bequeathing $100 to every child delivered by him who was named after him. Some were difficult to locate. Early in his practice a Negro family named a baby after him. There were fourteen children in that family and they grew into adults and every single one of them named one of their children after the good doctor, and they received their legacies.

Fiorino Soldi, a young Italian partisan fighter, had been the butt of jokes because *soldi* meant "money." Toward the end of World War II, in northern Italy, he was captured by a retreating detachment of SS troops. They were about to execute him when their leader asked what the captive's name was.

"Fiorino Soldi," was the reply.

"Soldi," exclaimed the German lieutenant. "My mother was a Soldi too—from Italy," and he issued orders for the execution to be postponed. Later he let the man escape, "because you are a Soldi."

FOUNDLING NAMES

As late as 1934 the Spanish Ministry of Justice decreed that foundlings be given two names common in the locality of their birth, instead of the surname of *Exposita* (exposed), the custom formerly. *Esposito* is a common Italian name with the same connotation. There is a whole group of surnames in Italy which is recognized by the knowing ones as foundling names, and thus illegitimate, referring to a carefully wrapped up bundle left at the church door. Some of them are *Dei Benedetti, De Benedictis, Dei Angelli, De Angelis, Dei Santi, De Santis, della Chiesa,* and *della Croce.* Many times the name assigned to a foundling is subject to the momentary whim of the director of the asylum. Finally, in 1936, the Italian Parliament legislated against such ridiculous, cruel, and shameful names.

St. Augustine called his natural son *Adeodatus,* a name used in some localities for illegitimates. In many nations people have not hesitated to bestow surnames clearly indicating illegitimacy on poor helpless babies. With girls who marry these names tend to disappear, but boys do not have this remedial aid. Adoption allows a change of name for some fortunate ones.

English people did not hesitate to give a foundling the surname of *Bastard,* although this has now disappeared from our modern directories. *Bastard* was not always regarded as a stigma. In important state documents William the Conqueror was sometimes listed as William the Bastard. Children left in the Temple in London were often given the surname of Temple.

FRENCH NAMES

The French system of names is very much like the English except for the difference in the language. An important difference is the

69

French practice of omitting the final consonant in pronunciation; this often involves a change in the spelling. The preposition *de* in a name was in law considered to be a mark of honor and nobility, and permission to use it was expressly conferred as a great honor. As England was settled by many from the French provinces shortly before and during the development of English family names, and by Huguenot refugees mostly after 1685, it is not surprising to find that English nomenclature has been strongly influenced by the French. During the surname period a large part of the English population was bilingual.

The French are not so sensitive about their names as the English. For example, *Bastard* is not an uncommon French surname, and there are quite a few to be found in modern French directories.

Because of the many diminutive, double diminutive, and other suffixes, the relative number of surnames is larger in France than in England, and the French people are not plagued by so many common family names. These diminutive suffixes are added to both patronymics and occupational surnames. The French keep the preposition and the definite article more than the English; for example, they have *Salle* (room), *LaSalle*, and *Delasalle*; and *Croix* (cross), *Lacroix*, and *Delacroix*.

Whereas the English produce pet forms of Christian names, usually by dropping the last part, as *Ben* for Benjamin, *Tom* for Thomas, and *Nick* for Nicholas, the French tend to decapitate the name to produce a pet form, as *Jamin* for Benjamin, *Mas* for Thomas, and *Colas* for Nicolas. Then by adding many suffixes numerous names are produced which are often difficult to trace. For example, *Mas* from Thomas may become *Massillon* and a new decapitation can produce *Sillon*. For baptismal names, the French have relied on those from the Bible more than the English and Americans.

In 1957 the French Justice Ministry decreed that, according to a law dating back to the French Revolution (1803), French babies must have common French names—names of people known in ancient history, and they must be spelled in a French way, not in a foreign manner. At the present time an official list of names is issued (revised from time to time) which is not consistent in its rules. In the more liberal instructions published in 1966 by the Ministry of Justice the number of permissible first names was vastly increased to include names of mythological figures, optional spellings, names current in foreign languages, and pet forms of various names. The public registrar

70

refuses to record births unless the proper name is selected.

Jean for boys and *Marie* for girls are the overwhelmingly popular favorites in France. Other common names for boys are *Claude, Alain, Daniel, André, Bernard, Patrick, René, Roland,* and *Pierre;* and for girls, *Christiane, Michèle, Danielle, Martine, Brigitte, Astride, Simone, Anne,* and *Francine.* For boys, *Charles, Jacques,* and *Marie* are common as middle names, and girls often receive *Françoise, Marguerite, Denise, Elisabeth,* and *Madeleine.*

An examination of the *Paris Annuaire Officiel des Abonnés au Téléphone* discloses that *Martin* is by far the most common family name. Other popular surnames are: *Bernard, Bertrand, Dubois, Dupont, Durand, Girard, Lambert, Laurent, Lefèbvre, Legrand, Leroy, Lévy, Michel, Morel, Petit, Richard, Robert, Rousseau, Simon,* and *Thomas.* The directory does not list given names but only an initial together with the address. In some cases it is *Mme.* with or without an initial, together with the surname.

See also AMERICANIZATION OF NAMES

FRISIAN NAMES

Most Frisian family names are patronyms. They became fixed only in the sixteenth century, although some family names did not become permanent until the eighteenth and nineteenth centuries. In North Friesland many names reflect the Danish influence and end in -*sen,* as in *Boysen* (boy) and *Brodersen* (brother). Further south they tend to terminate in the genitive *s,* as *Douwes* (dove) and *Sieuwerts* (Siegfried). Other family names are short forms of Christian names, as *Bek, Col, Nan,* and *Wit.*

Dr. Geart B. Droege, the leading authority on Frisian names, has listed the more common terminations of family names, all of them ending in -*a.* The ending -*inga,* as in *Heidinga, Kruizinga,* and *Hajunga* designates clansmen and their serfs and servants. Patronymics ending in -*a,* -*ma,* and -*sma,* as *Roorda, Fokkema, Hallema, Kalma, Folkertsma, Fridsma,* and *Tolsma* are common. Terminations in -*na,* -*ena,* and -*sma* indicate the genitive case, as in *Agena* and *Popena.* Suffixes such as -*a,* -*ma,* -*sma,* -*na,* and -*sna* are usually attached to the Christian name of an ancestor and have the sense of "son." The suffix -*stra,* as in *Boonstra* (from Boon), *Dijkstra* (dike) *Feenstra* (bog), and *Poelstra* (pool) designates place or location, and indicates the man who came

71

from that place or who lived in or near a natural topographical feature. The termination -*sma*, as in *Bykersma* (beekeeper), indicates the occupational name.

FUGITIVES' NAMES *See under* ALIASES

GEORGE SPELVIN *See under* NICKNAMES

GERMAN NAMES

Like the French names, all the popular German surnames are familiar in the United States. Most of the German surnames correspond both in form and meaning with English surnames. For example, there are many German place and occupational names terminating in -*er* and -*mann*, the practice being even more pronounced in German names than in English names. Due to the national habit of description and differentiation there are many more long occupational surnames among the Germans than the English. All the common nicknames are found among the Germans: *Lange* (long), *Weiss* (white), *Klein* (small), *Adler* (eagle), *Hahn* (cock), *Fuchs* (fox).

Some of the common German locality terminations are -*au* (wet meadow land), -*bach* (brook), -*baum* (tree), -*berg* (mountain), -*brück* (bridge), -*burg* (castle), -*dorf* (village), -*hain* (hedge), -*heim* (home), -*hof* (enclosure or manor), -*horst* (wood), -*itz* and -*ow* (both of Slavic origin, the former being a diminutive, the latter signifying possession), -*reut* (clearing), -*stadt* (city), -*stein* (stone), -*thal* (dale, valley), and -*wald* (wood). The majority of German surnames are derived from places. The preposition *von* (of) has been retained by many German families and adopted by others because of the prestige arising from its use by families of the nobility taking their names after their estates. Other aristocratic names start with the prepositions *auf*- or *zu*-. The *Meier* in Germany was a most important man, the administrator of a large estate, an official of the king, bishop, or monastery. The *Schulz* was the highest judicial and administrative officer of a village or town. The *Lehmanns* and *Baumanns* were tenants but were personally free.

At an early period the Germans began to shorten many of their Teutonic names. The *kurzform* names are such common pet forms as *Fritz* (for Friedrich), *Heinz* and *Hinz* (for Heinrich), and *Kunz* (for Konrad). *Hinz und Kunz* is the German equivalent of Tom, Dick, and Harry. Edwin C. Roedder states that a minute study of the derivations of *Nikolaus*, the most popular saint of the Middle Ages, has turned up no less than 440 German family names traceable to this saint. Other very common names during the period of the rise of family names are *Johannes, Heinrich, Peter*, and *Jacob*.

During the ascendancy of Hitler the Nazis established strict censorship over both family and given names. If more than one given name were bestowed, the father was obliged to designate which one would be used, and if in later life a different one were selected, official permission was required. Nicknames were generally banned as first names except for some commonly used abbreviated forms, such as *Klaus* for Nikolaus, *Goetz* for Gottfried, and *Hans* for Johannes. All Jews were then required to have "Jewish-sounding" first names and surnames.

Some of the most popular Christian names for boys in Germany are *Wilhelm, Peter, Paul, Friedrich, Johannes (Hans), Karl, Max, Erich, Otto, Franz, Georg, Ernst, Richard*, and *Kurt*. Many girls are named *Margarete (Gretchen), Martha, Frida, Anna, Elsa, Maria, Hedwig, Charlotte, Erna*, and *Wilhelmina*.

Germanic names, comparatively, have been little influenced by foreign names—their Teutonic nomenclature entered into the names of other countries.

Sexauer is an ordinary German name referring to one who came from Sexau, in Germany. Looking for a Mr. Sexauer, a man in Washington called at the Senate Interstate and Foreign Commerce Committee. Helping him, a girl employee called the Banking and Currency Committee by telephone to check, and inquired politely, "Do you have a Sexauer over there?"

"Listen," the girl switchboard operator snapped, "We don't even have a ten-minute coffee break anymore."

See also AMERICANIZATION OF NAMES; DUTCH NAMES; JEWISH FORENAMES

GERMANIC NAMES *See* OLD GERMANIC NAMES

GIRLS' NAMES *See* FASHIONS IN GIRLS' NAMES

GREEK NAMES

In present-day Greece personal names are somewhat more complicated than in classical times, but scarcely less colorful. Every Greek has one Christian name only (very rarely two) and a family name.

Many, both men and single women, have as a middle name a patrony-mic, their father's name in the possessive case, which is helpful in distinguishing among cousins, who are often named after the paternal grandfather. A married woman changes her middle name to her husband's name. The family name of a woman is the genitive case form of the father's or husband's surname. The triple name of a male is, for example, *Dhimitrios Ioannou Yeorghakas* (Demetrius, [son of] John Yeorghakas), while that of the female is *Dhimitra Ioannou Yeorghaka* (Demetra [daughter or wife of] John Yeorghakas).

Modern Greek family names are derived from the usual four classes of surnames. They are (1) occupational, as (transliterated) Farmer, Shepherd, Hunter, Priest, Craftsman, or Miller; (2) patronymic, with suffixes meaning "son," as *-poulos*, and *-idhis, -adhis* and *-akis* (the last three confined to Crete), *-akos* and *-eas* (Mani), *-atos* (Kephallenia), *-elis* (Lesbos), *-udhis* (north), *-oghlu* (Asia Minor), also the genitive form *-ou*; (3) descriptive, as (transliterated) Blond, Black, Red, Gray-haired, Big Head, Thin, Fat, Short, Limping, Cross-eyed, or Deaf; and (4) from place or ethnic names, as *Kritikos* (Cretan), *Moraitis* (Peloponnesian), and *Arvanitis* (Albanian).

Greek family names tend to be long polysyllabic descriptions. Some of the common family names are *Anaghnostopoulos* (the acolyte's son), *Angelopoulos* (Angelo's son), *Arvanitis* (the Albanian), *Arvanitakis, Arvanitopoulos,* and *Arvanitidhis* (son of the Albanian), *Argyiros* (from Argyrios), *Dhimitrakopoulos* (Dhimitrakis' son), *Dhimitriadhis* and *Dhimitriou* (Demetrius' son), *Kaloyeropoulos* (Monk's son), *Konstandopoulos* (Constantine's son), *Mylonas* (miller), *Mylonopoulos* (the miller's son), *Nikolaidhis* (Nicholas's son), *Panayotopoulos* (Panayotis's son), *Panopoulos* (Panos's son), *Papadhopoulos* (priest's son), *Papaioannou* (Priest John's son), *Papanikolaou* (Priest Nicholas's son), *Papayeoryiou* (Priest George's son), *Petropoulos* (Peter's son), *Sakellariou* (son of the Sakellarios, a Byzantine ecclesiastical title), *Spanos* (beardless), *Spaneas, Spanidhis,* and *Spanopoulos* (son of the beardless one), *Vasilopoulos* (Basil's son), *Vlahos* (shepherd), *Vlahakis* and *Vlahopoulos* (son of the shepherd), *Yannakopoulos* (Johnnie's son), *Yeorghakopoulos* (Georgie's son), and *Yeoryiadhis* (George's son).

Priests of the Greek Orthodox Church may marry and rear families. Because of the regard and affection of the people for the priests, who were the spiritual leaders during the lengthy Turkish occupation, their children generally accepted as their surname the priest's Christian name preceded by *Papa*, the Greek word for priest. The best compliment that could be paid to a person was a reminder that one knew that the father or uncle was a priest. The name of the controversial prime minister, Papandreou, means "Priest Andrew." Names beginning *Papa-* are the most numerous in Greece.

The popular given names among the Greek people, with some of their diminutive and other forms, are *Dhimitrios, Dhimitris, Dhimitrakis, Mitsos, Mitros,* and *Mimis* (Demetrius), *Ilias* (Elias), *Ioannis, Yannis,* and *Yannakis* (John), *Konstandinos, Kostas,* and *Dinos,* (Constantine), *Nikolaos, Nikos,* and *Nikolos* (Nicholas), *Panayotis, Panos,* and *Takis* (Panaghiotis), *Vasileios, Vasilis,* and *Vasos* (Basil), *Yeorgios, Yorghos, and Yorghakis* (George) for boys.

For girls they are *Dhimitra* (Demetra), *Eleni, Elenitsa,* and *Nitsa* (Helen), *Ioanna* and *Yannoula* (Joan), *Konstandina* and *Dina* (Constance), *Maria* and *Meri* (Mary), *Nikoleta, Nikolia,* and *Niki* (Nicholette), *Sofia* and *Sofi* (Sophia), *Vasiliki* and *Vaso* (Basileia), and *Yeoryia* (Georgia).

See *also* AMERICANIZATION OF NAMES; CLASSICAL NAMES

HAWAIIAN NAMES

Given names are not endlessly repeated in Hawaii as they are in the European countries. Parents do not pick the name from a list. They have an unlimited choice and can choose from any occurrence happening at the time of the birth, either to the family or to others. Or they may make up a name from any event in their experience. In the past, kings conferred names as a favor or mark of distinction. No indication of sex is made in the names conferred. Such a name as, in English, "the Breath of Fragrance" could be applied equally to a boy or girl. Consequently in writing, the name is followed by *k* for *kane* (man) or *w* for *wahine* (woman). This corresponds to our Mr., Mrs., and Miss. A woman does not take her husband's name on marriage; so there is nothing to indicate marital status.

One frequently notices long names in Hawaii. An incident in the experience of the parents might be set out rather fully, which would produce a long name others would think cumbersome. The Hawaiian language, composed as it is of only the five vowels and seven consonants, usually written with vowels and consonants alternating, makes for an easy recognition of Hawaiian personal names.

See *also* LONG NAMES

HELPFUL NAMES *See* INFLUENCE OF NAMES; PSYCHOLOGY OF NAMES

HEREDITY OF SURNAMES

When surnames first came into being they were applied only to one person and not to the whole family. At first the use of surnames was more a matter of fashion than a settled rule or established practice. The hereditary quality of surnames originated in the obvious convenience of designating a child by its father's name and is entirely the creature of custom. The sons would be described in various ways. One might follow his father's occupation and thus have the same surname. But it would not become a family name until the son became known by the same name although he did not follow the occupation indicated by the name. The son might have inherited the land or come from the same place and thus be known by the same territorial name, but until he became known by the name of the land without inheriting the land, or without having previously resided in that place, the name could not be regarded as an hereditary family name.

It is, of course, impossible to give the year or even the exact century when fixed family names were generally adopted in a country. In most countries the process took two or three hundred years to become universal, and in some areas was completed much earlier than in others. In virtually all countries surnames or hereditary family names were first taken up by the nobility and wealthy landowners, followed by the merchants and common people.

Modern hereditary family names in the Western world originated first in Italy among the Venetian patricians about the tenth or eleventh centuries. From there through returning Crusaders they spread to France, the British Isles, and then to Germany—nations that were growing and ripe for the institution of a system that would more easily distinguish one man from another. Individual man was slowly becoming more prominent and important. Closely following France and England was the spread of family names in Spain, although there were a few earlier instances. In the fifteenth and sixteenth centuries fixed family names arose in Poland and Russia. The Scandinavian countries did not develop universal hereditary surnames until the beginning of the nineteenth century. Few family names were in use in Turkey until the practice was forced by the government in 1933.

Surnames, or bynames, were known in England even before the Norman Conquest, but none of them was an hereditary family name. Although the use of surnames was stimulated by the influx of foreigners into England after the Conquest, hereditary surnames did not become the universal custom until centuries later. The names of some followers of William the Conqueror apparently descended to their sons. No definite time can be fixed for the complete development of hereditary family names. It happened very slowly in a checkered pattern over a period of several hundred years. Stable family names existed alongside of more or less temporary individual bynames or descriptive terms. The first ones were borne by barons and important landowners who derived their names from their fiefs or manors. The practice was quickly followed by the merchant class, then by the skilled craftsmen, and last by the country people. The earliest, clear, written evidence of an hereditary family name among the common people in England, found by Dr. Gustav Fransson, is from the Assize Rolls of 1275. However, Professor Eilert Ekwall believes that hereditary family names appeared in London among the patrician classes as early as the middle of the twelfth century and were frequent by the end of the thirteenth century; but some of the early instances given by him may be questionable. The custom of hereditary family names was not widespread in England until the latter part of the fourteenth century, and even then many were known by surnames which were clearly not family names.

Surnames became hereditary because the lower classes sought to imitate the nobility whose names more easily became settled because their lands were hereditary. The place where a family lived was usually the same throughout several generations, and this factor substantially contributed to the fixing of family names. Local surnames and surnames from place names became established first. Those derived from nicknames became hereditary very early. Professor Fransson has asserted that occupational surnames became fixed fairly late and that patronymical surnames became hereditary still later.

If surnames were being formed today in thickly populated regions of the Western world, the occupational names would be different. There would be many names referring to automobiles, airplanes, railroads, farm machinery, and automotive parts. Radio and television would enter into many names. There would be few names of animals and not many names referring to landscape features. With the quick changes in our present age Mr. Townsend (end of the town) would find a whole new subdivision erected beyond his house before his neighbors could become familiar with Townsend as a surname. Small hills might even be obliterated by today's power shovel before the house is built.

The doctor, seeing his patient out of bed for the first time after having a baby, and noting that she was thumbing through the telephone directory, asked what she was looking for.

"I'm looking for a nice name for my baby."

"You don't have to use the telephone book," said the physician, "the hospital supplies you with a little book listing all the first names."

"You don't understand," she answered, "the baby already has a first name."

See also CHRISTIAN NAMES AS SURNAMES; COMPOUND SURNAMES; FOUNDLING NAMES; ORIGIN OF A SURNAME; SURNAMES IN COMMON USE

HINDU NAMES

In India from very ancient times children were given two or three names, one of which was a secret name. The early literature of India provides elaborate regulations for the names of male and female infants, which vary from time to time and place to place, and were not always followed in actual practice. Some of the rules provide that a boy must be given names containing an even number of syllables, usually two or four, and girls must be given names containing an odd number of syllables, generally three. There were various requirements of letters in the names and their terminations.

According to Hindu practice and belief, the individual or personal name should be drawn from the names of God, who is both nameless and multinamed. As everything is a manifestation of God the name of everything is a name of God. Thus all names have some connotation or reference to God or an attribute or manifestation of God. Constantly pronouncing the name of a god is believed to be a good work toward salvation. Some of the names of deities often used are *Rama, Krishna, Guba, Siva, Sita, Lakshmi, Valli,* and *Parvati.* A long individual name can sometimes be split into two words at the election of or choice of the bearer. When a person comes of age his name is often changed.

As ancestry is traced to one or another of a few hundred prehistoric Vedic ancestors, the Rishis, each family name is usually the name of a Rishi, such as *Bhardwaja, Kauntinya, Kausika, Srivastsa, Viswamitra,* and *Vyasa.* These names were formerly used only on intimate occasions such as prayer, family ceremonies, and marriage.

In business transactions the family names are not used. When necessary for identification the name of the father or a place name might be added. In other cases a word indicating caste, occupation, official rank, title, academic distinction, or religious status might be added, and some of these became family names. In some parts of India there is a trend to three-worded names, the individual or fore-name, the father's name, and a family name, and, following the custom of the Western world, the names are placed in that order. The family name is easily and often changed or dropped and a double-worded individual name only is retained. The generous use of honorifics tends to confuse the Westerner.

In many parts of India it is common practice to mention the caste or calling along with the personal name, and this helps to distinguish people with the same name. Some names, however, are favorites within a caste. Children are not named after the parents, a custom considered to be a sin, except in a few places in south India.

The superstitious custom of bestowing opprobrious names on children born after the death of a child is found throughout India, and is common to all classes. Such names as *Anpuchhâ* (unspeakable), *Bathâ* (fool), *Bhikhrâ* (beggar), *Gonaurâ* (dung hill), and *Kirwâ* (worm) are given to boys. Girls are sometimes named (*Chilrî* (louse), *Langdî* (lame), and (*Likhiâ* (nit). This practice, it is thought, is helpful in fooling the demons into believing that such children are not worth their notice.

In western India the Maratha-speaking races had only one name. Most of the names end in a vowel, such as *Tima, Mana,* and *Putla,* to which was generally added some sort of title. If Tima was born in a low caste, he would be *Timya* and probably remain so during life. If in a higher caste, he would have the termination *-ji,* and be *Timaji.* If a soldier or a gentleman, even though poor, gets along in the world, the courtesy title of *-rao* might be added and the man would be *Timajirao.* There are other additions of respect, such as *-nak* and *-ba,* similar to *-ji,* and various titles which may precede or follow the name. Some are known by a sobriquet or familiar name in conversation and ordinary correspondence. In serious writing the sobriquet may be set off by the word *urf*, the equivalent of our word *alias*. In high-caste men the name chosen is likely to be one of the thousand variations of the gods, *Siva* or *Vishnu*, such as *Sivaji*, *Sambhaji*, or *Vitoba*. Females are usually named after a goddess.

To the individual name might be added the name of the father, preceded, in some cases, by *bin* or *walad* meaning "son of." Some castes put the father's name first. Some add a surname often designating a tribe or clan. A few families have adopted English surnames. There are so many different tribes and castes and sectional and religious differences and local customs in India affecting names and titles that it is impossible to outline any comprehensive analysis of the matter in a short space.

In the Punjab names are derived from common words, almost any word, and there are many terminations that can be added to root words to form names that can safely designate separate individuals. There is thus a vast storehouse of names in use. For example, *Nath* (lord) can become *Nathâ*, *Nathî*, *Nathû*, *Natho*, *Nathân*, *Nathan*, *Nathî Râm*, *Nathû Mall*, *Nathâ Singh*, and *Nathû Rai*, all names for men. *Lâl*, *Râm*, *Mall*, *Singh*, and *Rai* (meaning cherished, god, warrior, lion, and prince respectively) are just five of about sixty common complementary forms, originally with a religious and caste connotation, which may be added to other words to produce separate masculine names. Various other terminations and complementary additions can be attached to *Nath* to form many feminine names. There are about ten common complementary forms that can be added to feminine names, with such meanings as goddess, knowledge, princess, and preserved. *Lâl* is very common in the Punjab, while among the Sikhs in India, *Singh* is most frequently observed.

Enough has been included to hint at the complex nature of the names of people in India, and any ordinary classification in a short sketch is inadequate. However, most Hindu names and the earlier Sanskrit names fall within one of the following descriptive groups:

1. Containing names of gods or with religious connotations
2. Relating in some way to nature, including animal names
3. Reflecting abstract qualities or virtues
4. Derived from words designating common objects
5. Referring to parts of the body
6. Dictated by superstition

7. Influenced by custom or group pattern

8. Occupational terms

Illustrating the difficulties of Hindu names is the instance where *Time* magazine in its issue of February 16, 1962, printed a letter from Bombay, with four apparent signatures appended, which was less than complimentary to the diplomat, Krishna Menon. In its issue a week later it printed a letter from Vinod C. Shah of Columbia University, which pointed out that the four "signatures" were not names at all but obscenities in Hindi, so vulgar that they were not to be found in dictionaries.

HUNGARIAN NAMES

With the Hungarians the surname comes first, followed by the Christian name. When Hungarians go to other Western countries they generally reverse their names in order to fall in line with the customs elsewhere. Thus Bartók Béla was the correct form in Hungary, but this famous composer became Bela Bartok in other countries.

The family names of most of the descendants of the nobility are recognizable by their many orthographical peculiarities. They have been careful to retain obsolete spellings, such as *cz* instead of *c*, as in *Czapkay* (one from Cayska); *th* in place of *t*, as in *Horváth* and *Tóth*; *eö* in place of *ö* and *gh* instead of *g*, as in *Eördeögh* (devil); *oo* in place of *ó*, as in *Soos* (salt merchant); *ss* instead of *zs*, *ew* instead of *ő*, *ff* instead of *f*, as in *Dessewffy* (son of Dezrő).

The final *y* in place of *i* is particularly common among the descendants of Hungarian noblemen. Most of their names call attention to the old ancestral estates. The suffix *-i* has the connotation of "residing at" or "being from." Thus one observes such spellings in the noble families as *Imrédy* (from Imréd), *Béldy* (from Béld), *Horthy* (from Hort), *Kúthy* (from Kút), and *Ághy* (from Ág). From inspection of many Hungarian names it is apparent that many of the bourgeoisie have aped the nobility by altering the spelling of their surnames. Certain surnames from place names that terminate in *-y* do not substitute *y* for *i*, such as *Szilágyi* (from Szilágy), *Pályi* (from Pály), *Csányi* (from Csány), and *Mutyi* (from Muty). Some exceptions are names of noble families who preferred not to use distinguishing features, as *Teleki* (from Telek), *Büki* (from Bük), and *Zabai* (from Zaba).

Some names from occupations are *Bíró* (judge), *Kocsis* (carter), *Kerekes* (wheeler), *Szűcs* (furrier), *Takács* (weaver) and *Fazekas* (potter). Surnames from nicknames are: *Fekete* (black hair), *Király* (king), *Sánta* (limping), *Fodor* (curly hair), and *Balog* (lefty).

Very common Hungarian surnames, as evidenced by the listings in the Budapest telephone book, are *Hegyi* (from the mountain), *Horváth* (from Croatia), *Kiss* (little), *Kovács* (smith), *Molnár* (miller), *Nagy* (big), *Németh* (from Germany), *Papp* (priest), *Sándor* (Alexander), *Szabó* (tailor), *Tóth* (small), and *Varga* (shoemaker).

Popular Christian names for boys are *Attila, András, Arpád, Béla, Ferenc, Gábor, Gergely, Géza, György, Imre, István, János, József, Kálmán, Károly, Lajos, László, Mátyás, Mihály, Miklós, Pál, Péter, Sándor, Tibor,* and *Zoltán.* For girls, popular names are *Ágnes, Anna, Erzsébet, Eszter, Eva, Ilona, Judit, Júlia, Katalin, Magda, Margit, Mária, Márta, Vera,* and *Zsuzsánna.* Men's names terminating in *-ne,* such as *Imréné* Szabó and *Istvánné* Molnár refer to Mrs. Emery Taylor, and Mrs. Stephen Miller.

HUSBANDS' PET NAMES *See under* PET NAMES

ICELANDIC NAMES

People in Iceland do not have family names as we know them. They have a Christian, or given, name followed by the name of their father in the genitive case to which is affixed *-son* or *-dottir,* and this system is sanctioned by law. Suppose *Magnus Jonsson* has a son *Stefán* and a daughter *Olafia.* They would be known as *Stefán Magnússon* and *Olafia Magnúsdottir.* Stefán's children might be *Axel Stefansson* and *Rosa Stefansdottir.* When a woman marries, she does not change her name except by use of the title *Fru* instead of *Froken.* A few foreign names are being imported into Iceland, which account for the exceptions to the above custom. In tracing genealogies the system is of considerable help.

Icelandic telephone directories list people in alphabetical order by their Christian or given name. Under each Christian name one will find listed the patronymic in alphabetical order, as *Björnson, Ketilsson, Kristjánsdóttir,* or *Petursdottir.* These are followed by the occupation in some cases and by the address.

Some of the most common names for boys are: *Árni, Björn, Einar, Guthjón, Guthrun, Gunnar, Jon, Jonas, Kristinn, Magnus, Ólafur, Óskar, Páll, Petur,* and *Stefán.* For girls there are: *Anna, Guthbjörg, Helga, Jonina, Katrin, Kristin, Margrét, María, Olafia,* and *Stefania.*

IDENTICAL NAMES

Winston Churchill, the illustrious British statesman and writer, often found that he was mistaken for the famous American writer, novelist Winston Churchill. The publication in 1899 of *Richard Carvel* had made the American Churchill fabulously popular. During visits by one Churchill to the country of the other mail was often mixed up. The British Winston Churchill wrote to the American, suggesting that one of them should change his name. The American agreed and pointed out that since he was three years older, it was up to the British writer to make the change. Until the American laid down his pen in 1917, he was the better known. The future Prime Minister agreed and thereafter added a middle initial—S, for Spencer.

Jerry Lewis the author led a pleasant life in Beverly Hills until Jerry Lewis the comedian moved into a house two blocks away. The author then moved to Pacific Palisades and settled down peaceably until the comedian also moved to Pacific Palisades. Paul Douglas, the United States Senator from Illinois, found that there was some confusion with Paul Douglas, the Broadway and Hollywood actor. Two famous French writers with the same name are Alexandre Dumas *père* and Alexandre Dumas *fils.*

In ancient times there have been many men with the same name, and in numerous cases it has been difficult to distinguish between them. Demetrius of Magnesia, who lived in the first century before Christ, compiled a *Dictionary of Men of the Same Name,* now lost, but extensively quoted by Diogenes Laertius. Several other ancient writers made collections of homonyms, recognizing the need for careful distinctions. Even in the New Testament there is a confusing number of men named James. In Christian history the Marys are not always easily identified. In every civilized country, in every age, there have been many men who have achieved some distinction with names like others.

Autograph collectors have trouble with the genuine signatures of other people with the same names. There were probably as many as twenty-five more or less prominent men named *John Adams* living in Massachusetts at the same time as the second president of the United States. The president's signature is well known, and it is not too hard to distinguish it from the others. But with many other famous persons with not uncommon names, such as Charles Dickens, Horace Walpole, Nathan Hale, and Alexander Hamilton, it is not always easy to differentiate between the genuine signatures of others with the same name and that of the famous man.

The boy asked for a job delivering milk and upon being asked his name by the manager, replied "Thomas Jefferson."

"Well," said the manager, "that's a pretty well-known name."

"It ought to be," said the boy, "I've delivered newspapers in this town for more than three years."

INDIAN NAMES *See* AMERICAN INDIAN NAMES; HINDU NAMES

INFLUENCE OF NAMES

Psychologists have discovered that if one is happy with his name, he is happy with himself. The average person is more interested in his own name than in all the other names on earth. If it is remembered, a subtle compliment has been paid him. If it is forgotten or misspelled, he has been slighted. The late Percy Hammond, drama critic, purposely misspelled a person's name when he wished to annoy him. To every man the most important sound is his own name. Prisoners in a penitentiary keenly feel the loss of their names and their replacement by a number. If a man is not important enough to have people interested in knowing his name, he feels most obscure.

The influence of names is felt in many subtle ways. Mrs. L. E. Fant's name, after her marriage, was not overlooked among her friends, and many presented her with toy elephants of every kind and description. Then she succumbed to the fascination of collecting and filled her house with the pachyderms. Howard T. Webb buys neckties with a prominent spider web in their design. A man who acquired in boyhood the nickname of *Piggy* tried to prove that he didn't mind the epithet by collecting all sorts of porcine objects—porcelain pigs, piggy banks, and pig paperweights of every kind. E. Herbert Stone wrote *The Stones of Stonehenge*. The name Grandma Moses, adopted by the painter of primitives, contributed greatly to her position and popularity.

A single letter can be a tragedy. Freddie Ribbens fought for England in the Boer War. The recruiting sergeant had listed him as Ribbons and Freddie had hesitated to call attention to the error. When it was about time for him to be pensioned his birth certificate read *Ribbens* and his army discharge read *Ribbons*. A friend told him, jokingly, that the government would never pay a pension to a man who had served under a phony name, and he committed suicide, leaving a note that explained the fatal *o*.

The insidious influence of names has been well illustrated among the Ashantis in West Africa. There each child is given the name corresponding with the day of the week on which it is born. The natives believe that each day-name has its particular character traits. For example, a boy born on a Monday is named *Kwadwo*, and is thought to be quiet and peaceful; one born on Wednesday, on the other hand, is called *Kwaku* and is believed to be quick-tempered, warlike and aggressive—a trouble-maker. The influence of the name and belief is disclosed by court statistics which show that twice as many Wednesday boys are brought in for wrongdoing as those bearing Monday names.

Ralph Capone, a nephew of Al Capone, the infamous gangster, graduated from college with an engineering degree. As no engineering firm would employ him because of his name, he changed it to Gabriel and opened a plant in South Chicago to manufacture prefabricated homes, married and became the father of a boy and a girl. With the success of his business it looked as if he were set for life. Then he met a former schoolmate who spread the word of his former name around. When a rumor started that he was operating a gambling joint on the side, customers withdrew their business and his plant had to close even though the police investigated and discovered the report to be untrue. Ralph changed his name again and opened a used car lot until his name caught up with him again. The car lot failed; his wife lost confidence in him and divorced him, obtaining custody of the two children. Other ventures under different names failed. Finally a job as a bartender was successful because there the customers did not seem to mind. It was not the job for which his education fitted him. But constant harassment was his lot whenever a murder was committed. Never much of a toper, he began to drink heavily. At the age of thirty-three he was found dead. On a table was a half-emptied whisky bottle and an empty medicine vial together with an unfinished note to a girl friend. Here was a man utterly destroyed by his name.

When Major Vidkun Quisling's surname became a word for a traitor, it was noted that aurally it managed to suggest something slippery and tortuous. And visually it began with a Q, a slightly disreputable letter suggestive of the queer, quitting, questionable, quirkish, querulous, quaking, quavering, quivering, quagmires, of quicksands, quibbles, and quarrels, of queasiness, quackery, and qualms, a thoroughly contemptible name.

Robert Young, the radio, television, and screen star, once wrote of the gallant taxi service he and his wife received from a Manhattan taxi driver in the theatrical district. The driver after making sure that they were most comfortable said, "You know, it was bound to happen. I've hauled so many celebrities that I knew I'd get you one of these days." Young looked up at the city permit which read, "Driver: Robert Young."

John Adamson's father died when he was twelve, and his mother had a difficult time in raising the children. A representative of a benevolent order took John to a clothing store for a new outfit. The clerk, seeing that it was a charity case, brought out a cheap, shoddy suit. Whereupon the man who had accompanied the timid, embarrassed boy spoke up indignantly. "Don't you recognize this boy?" he shouted. "This is John Adamson. Bring out your best suit." Forever after, John Adamson said, he tried to live up to the way the man spoke his name that day.

C. C. C. Tatum, the highly successful real estate operator, considered that his three-initial name had been an important factor in his success. On a sign it was an "eye-catcher" and easily remembered. Mr. Maurie J. November said that in the long run his name had been an asset. C. Wilbert Wiggle claimed that he had made a lot of friends through his name.

Coronet magazine in 1959 mentioned a traffic accident in a midwestern city where the driver of one car was Mr. Crash and the operator of the other, Miss Collision. Mr. Crash considered his name to be a source of trouble. Trying to take care, he would still get into a crash. Miss Collision thought her name just got her involved in you-know-what. Some years ago in Chicago a man named Grabney Gleason was being ridiculed in a bar for grabbing another man's drink. The fight ended with Gleason and another man dead and a third seriously injured.

Professor Ulysses S. Grant of UCLA, a grandson of the former president, said, on the Groucho Marx television show, that he was bored with his name because of the comments about it, and especially on being asked if he was buried in Grant's tomb, a reference to Groucho's easy question.

Help or Hindrance Names

That a name can be a definite help or hindrance in one's career can be gleaned from many other articles in this book. Those persons with queer names who have not thought about them do not regard them as unusual, and fail to recognize that they may be a hindrance in their business and social activities. They are the ones who should study carefully the use and effect of personal names upon people. No adequate, full-scale research has ever been made to determine what names are most helpful in our business and social lives.

Some of the attributes that go to make a personal name helpful are:

1. Ease in remembering
2. Ease in spelling
3. Ease in pronouncing
4. Musical or harmonious quality of the sound
5. Distinguished appearance, but not ridiculous or bizarre
6. Tendency to evoke agreeable words or thoughts
7. Pleasant relationship in one way or another with business or social activities
8. Designating the proper nationality

Naturally the opposite of any of the above would be likely to hinder one in the affairs of life.

A study I made of the two hundred most popular family names borne by men listed in *Who's Who in America* compared with the unusual or other names in that work disclosed the fact that one with an unusual family name had a slightly better chance to attain eminence than one with a common surname.

Howard *Snorf* (originally Schnorf) did not consider his surname either a help or a hindrance in his trade (candy salesman) or social life. He grew up with it, but his wife Mabel, to whom it was a new name, could see its disadvantages. A merchant who advertises along the road in Northern Indiana seems to have no compunction against publicizing his name as *Schoof*. Does he attract business or merely arouse remarks from motorists concerning the name? To the ears of English-speaking peoples these names have a peculiar sound. Five people with the not uncommon surname of *Hamburger* (one whose ancestors came from Hamburg, Germany) were queried by the Chicago *Tribune*'s "Inquiring Camera Girl" about what it's like to be a "hamburger." All seemed to like their name and found it an asset even though they had been teased in school.

See also CHANGE OF NAME; NAMES WITH DEROGATORY MEANING; PSYCHOLOGY OF NAMES; USE OF FIRST NAMES

INITIALS

In some business or social contacts the initials of the Christian names alone are used. The president of a company may be known throughout the company by such initials. Men of considerable status or reputation are sometimes so known. In some cases this practice has a slightly pompous connotation by implying that everyone must know who is meant.

Some famous people have been commonly known by initials, especially in England. A.J.B. was Arthur James Balfour, O.B. stood for Oscar Browning, and R.L.S. designated Robert Louis Stevenson. Artists and some writers have signed their works by their initials only. E. V. Durling, the newspaper columnist, wrote that he was always interested in men who used initials to conceal their real names. Never liking Edgar, he had his first cards printed "E. Vincent Durling."

Many people are confused as to what the initials are when the name is *Robert St. Clair, William O'Rourke, Ronald MacDavid,* or *James Fitzgerald*. The correct initials are *R.St.C., W.O'R., R.McD.* (or *MacD*), and *J.F.*

People who cannot write their names are advised to make an X in lieu thereof. There was the bank depositor who insisted on signing his checks XX. Not wishing to lose the account the bank accepted the situation. A few years later a check came through signed XXX. Being doubtful the cashier called the depositor. "My wife and I have been doing pretty well," explained the depositor. "We have been attending church regularly and have been invited out socially. So we thought that we should start to use my middle initial."

Mr. Vernon Edward Day of Irvin Falls, Idaho, scooted to fame when V-E Day became the subject of discussion in the newspapers. Then on V-E Day Mr. V. E. Day became the overwhelming favorite of the jokesters.

See also NICKNAMES

INITIALS FORMING A WORD

Sometimes parents neglect to note that the initials of the name form a word which will be brought to the attention of the child a zillion times during his lifetime. If the word is a favorable one, it may be a source of pleasure. If it is of bad import, it will be a constant source of petty annoyance. Words like FUN, JOY, PEP, PET, and VIM are happy words. ASS, CAT, COW, DOG, FAT, HOG, NUT, PIG, RAT, SAP, and SIN are irritating words. Others such as AND, BOY, DAD, HAM, OFF, OIL, SEW, SON are possibly neutral. In many parts of England and among Negroes a name is considered to be lucky if its initials form a word. Winthrop Rockefeller, son of John D. Rockefeller, Jr., was originally Winthrop Aldrich until it was pointed out to his peaceloving mother that the initials spelled WAR, whereupon the middle name was quickly dropped. Roy E. Davis, formerly connected with Rand McNally & Company, and a member of the 1936 American Olympic Committee engaged in considerable correspondence which he dictated. He searched tirelessly until he found a secretary whose initials were H.O.T.

In the Riley family a boy was given the forenames of *Samuel O'Brien.* When he grew up and ran for elective office his opponents referred to him as S.O.B. Riley, which may be why he remained a small-time politician instead of becoming a statesman.

INITIALS WHICH COMBINE WITH THE SURNAME

Mr. *S. HOVING* was a hauling and moving contractor in Chicago in 1958. Robert *C. LEE* worked in Chicago. Frank *D. PRESS* could ill afford to be an optimist. *DR. I. N. KING* claimed to be a teetotaler. The sign, *J. E. WELLER, JEWELLER,* was said to be repetitious. *F. E. MALE* was a male druggist in San Francisco. *B. A. HAND-SHAKER* is a farmer in central Iowa. Additional names of this nature are not difficult to find in any large telephone directory.

INSULT AND SLIGHT

One of the most insidious ways to insult a person is to distort, misspell, or mispronounce his name and convey to him in some subtle way that the mistake was intentional. Apparent deliberate failure to remember another's name creates resentment. Shakespeare was aware of this when he made Philip Faulconbridge exclaim, "And if his name be George, I'll call him Peter; For new-made honour doth forget men's names" (*King John*, I, i, 186). Luther deliberately wrote the name of one of his numerous enemies, Dr. Eck, as one word, *Dreck* (filth). Disagreeable name-punning is most effective.

Freud observed that aristocrats very frequently distorted the names of the physicians they consulted, from which he concluded that they unconsciously slight them, in spite of the politeness with which they were wont to greet them.

Gypsy Rose Lee was told that she was placed second to Ann Sheridan in a campus popularity contest and was asked what she thought of Sheridan. "I think he was a swell general," she cheerfully replied.

The strong feeling for names may upset a whole country. When the children of United States Ambassador to India John Kenneth Galbraith named their cat *Ahmedabad*, which they innocently shortened to Ahmed, one of the forms of the name of the Prophet, the protests over the imagined insult from the Moslem world were loud and sustained. The cat was quickly renamed *Gujarat*, the district in which the cat was given to the children, but the sensitive Moslems were not mollified.

INTERNATIONAL CONGRESS OF ONOMASTIC SCIENCES *See* NAME ORGANIZATIONS

IRANIAN NAMES

Family names were introduced by law in Persia in 1926, and everyone was forced to select and register in the city of his residence a family name, to be retained by his children and grandchildren. The family name of the royal family is *Pahlavi*. Married women were required to use the surname of their husbands. Nicknames were declared to be no part of the legal name. The many varied compound names and titles of a Persian man were thus simplified into a forename and a family name; middle names were not required or used. Because the area or district from which came the first bearer of the new name was often added to the family name, compound family names resulted, as *Sharīfi Nūrī*. These area adjectives usually terminate in *-ī*. The forename could be compound, that is, composed of more than one element or names, joined together with a hyphen, as *Hasan-'Alī* and *Mohammed-Taqī*.

Some typical Iranian names are *Bozorg Alavī*, *Ahmad Emami*, *Mahmud Mehran*, and *Fathallah Jalali*. Titles of respectful address are sometimes added as a prefix to the surname, as *Amīraştānī*, *Mīrfakhrā'ī*, and *Banīhāshemī*. The principal titles of address, corresponding to our Mr., Mrs., Sir, His Majesty, etc., are *Amīr*, *Banī*, *Key*, *Mīr*, *Pūr*, and *Shah*, and these are often separate from the name, as is American custom. Some typical forenames are *'Abdoltah*, *Ebrāhīm*, *Behrūz*, *Hamīd*, and *Sa'īd*. The Persian language, usually written in Arabic script, with its questions of transliteration, produces difficult onomastic problems for English readers.

IRISH NAMES

An old saying tells us, "By *Mac* and *O* you'll always know true Irishmen they say; but if they lack both *O* and *Mac*, no Irishmen are they." The *O* in Irish names such as *O'Brien* stands for the early word *ua* meaning "grandson" or "descended from," and not an abbreviation for *of*. The apostrophe was not originally a part of the name. In Gaelic for a woman the prefix would be *ni*, as in *niBrien*, that is, "daughter of Brian." *Mac* means "son." These words are sometimes prefixed to nicknames, as MacDowell (son of the black stranger). *Mac* is often abbreviated to *Mc* and *M'*. Over the years many dropped the *O* and the *Mac* because of persecution by the English. During the present century many resumed these prefixes due in great measure to the activities of the Gaelic League.

Besides these patronymical prefixes, some Irish acquired names beginning with the words *giolla* and *maol* both meaning "follower" or "servant," as *Mac Giolla Croist*, now often reduced to Gilchrist, (son of the servant of Christ) and *O'Maoilmhichil*, modern Mulvaney (descendant of the follower of Meana). These words are usually attached to saints' names, as *Mac Giolla Phóil*, now often Gilfoyle (son of the follower of St. Paul) and *O'Maoileoin*, now usually spelled Malone (descendant of the follower of St. John).

There are some occupational names with the *Mac* prefix as *Mac-*

Gowan (smith), *McCurdy* (navigator), and *McCraith* (weaver). A few nicknames have become hereditary family names in Ireland, such as *Bane* (white), *Duff* (black), *Lawder* (strong) *Roe* (red) and *McEvoy* (yellow-haired). Very few place names have become family names, and there is considerable doubt about those few that appear to be from Irish names of places.

Hereditary surnames came into use in Ireland as early as the tenth century when, it is said, King Brian decreed their use, although some have been noted before his time. However, the system grew up gradually as the population increased, and the custom was widespread, although not universal, by the twelfth century. Pedigrees were carefully kept in Ireland in the early Middle Ages because territorial rights were determined by relationship, but not necessarily by primogeniture as in England. Thus most Irish family names are patronymics, indicating descent from the male parent or an earlier ancestor.

Formerly there were not so many different Irish names as we find today. The originals were pronounced differently in the various dialects and accents and consequently were Anglicized with diverse spellings to produce many names. The Gaelic name *Ua Laighin* (a spear) thus became *Lane, Laney, Layne, Lean, Leane, Leyne, Lien, Loyne, Lyan, Lyen, Lyne,* and *Lyon,* twelve different forms, all of which could be varied by including the *O'* prefix.

Sir Robert Mathesson, assistant registrar general for Ireland, in 1890, complained of the great variation in names in Ireland, having found that many Irish use two entirely different names with about the same meaning, interchangeably, and that members of the same family would sometimes use different names with similar meanings. The use of two languages, English and Irish, caused some alterations, and illiteracy brought about many others. Others varied in spelling and form at the pleasure of the bearer.

The Anglo-Norman invaders brought in the names with the prefix *Fitz*, as well as many simple given names without any prefix. Some names in Ireland are strictly English. All Irishmen dwelling within the Pale, which comprised the counties of Dublin, Meath, Louth, and Kildare in the fifteenth century, were ordered by the Statute of 5 Edward IV (1465) to take an English surname under pain of forfeiture of his goods yearly. Although some translated their surnames into English or adopted English names, this was not done to any great extent in spite of the threatened forfeitures. Yet this and the influx of people from England and other countries over the years has produced a great many non-Irish names in the island.

In general the surnames we regard as Irish names are really Anglicized forms of Gaelic names. *Kelly* is from *Ceallaigh* (with either *Mac* or O); *Sullivan* is from *O'Súileabháin*; *Kennedy* was originally *O'Cinnéide*; *Murphy* comes from *O'Murchadha* and *MacMurchadha*; *Ryan* was originally *O'Maoilriain*. The ten most common Irish surnames are: *Murphy, Kelly, Sullivan, Walsh, Smith, O'Brien, Byrne, Ryan, Connor,* and *O'Neill.*

For Christian names the Irish seem now to prefer the common saints' names much more than other English-speaking peoples. Persons named *John, Patrick, Michael, William, Thomas,* and *James,* in about that order, are found in greater numbers, in proportion to the population, than in England. Some of the old Gaelic names, particularly those borne by early Irish saints, are common, such as *Brendan, Colman, Fergus, Finbar, Kevin,* and *Kiernan* for men. *Brigid* and *Ita* are often chosen as feminine names. In recent years many have substituted the Gaelic forms for the English forms, as *Sean* for John and *Liam* for William. *Maire* (Mary) is by far the most common of girls' names.

See also AMERICANIZATION OF NAMES

ISRAELI NAMES

Israel is the only country in the world, except the United States, which offers newcomers the right to choose a new name. It in fact encourages a change to a Hebrew name. An application to the Minister of the Interior and the payment of fifteen cents will bring a certificate of change. If the applicant is in the army, even the small fee is eliminated. David Ben-Gurion, former premier, has been the most outspoken proponent of name-changing, and most of Israel's officials have complied. Golda *Meyerson* became Golda *Meir* when she was appointed foreign minister of Israel.

No law restricts the choice. A regulation provides that the new resident must keep his old name on his identification cards for two years after assuming his new name. As the Jew arrives he starts a new life and wishes to erase all connections with the past. The new name cannot be changed for seven years. When Israel became a sovereign state in 1948, the Hebrew language became the state language. Even while the Arab-Israeli fighting was still going on, a pamphlet was circulated among the soldiers suggesting a change to Hebrew names.

The original surname of Moshe *Sharet*, the first foreign minister, was the Russianized *Shertok*. Taking the first three Hebrew consonants of that name for his Hebraic name he had *Sharet* meaning "servant." David *Green* from Poland became David *Ben-Gurion* of Palestine; Isaac *Shimshelevitz* changed to Isaac *Ben Zvi*, later elected president of Israel. Eliezer *Perlman*, the great lexicographer, became *Ben Yehudah*.

Some have taken the names of Biblical heroes or even villages. Many retained the same initial letter, as when *Berlin* became *Bar Ilan* and *Meisler* became *Mazar*; others kept one element: *Orenstein* became *Oren*, *Osovsky* became *Asaf*, *Biber* changed to *Rabib*. The most popular method of change, however, is translation of the former name or part of it into Hebrew. *Birnbaum* becomes *Agosi* (pear); *Fischer* becomes *Dayag*; *Wexler* becomes *Chalfan* (money-changer); *Jung* translates to *Elem* (young); *Silver* becomes *Kaspi*; *Steiner* is changed to *Avny* (stony). However, some non-Hebrew names are changed to other non-Hebrew names.

ITALIAN NAMES

Italian family names all end in a vowel. An outstanding feature of Italian family names is the number that evolved from descriptive nicknames, many of them crude, almost obscene, descriptions. Unlike in other countries, where the cruder nicknames were quickly dropped, the Italians placidly accepted them. One with curly hair would become *Rizzo*; a clipped head could be called *Caruso*.

Due to the paucity of surnames in a given area, even after hereditary surnames were the universal rule in Italy, most families, especially those in rural areas, were known by a nickname which was often transmitted from one generation to another. It frequently happened that this nickname became the only surname and the original hereditary name was dropped.

This has produced many animal, bird, fish, and insect names. If a man strutted like a rooster, he might acquire *Gallo* (rooster) as a name. Other common animal names are *Bovo* (ox), *Cagni* (dog), *Capra* (goat), *Cavallo* (horse), *Grifone* (vulture), *Gallina* (hen), *Gatto* (cat), *Gazza* (magpie), *Lizzi* (mackerel), *Lucciola* (firefly), *Lupo* and *Lupino* (wolf), *Orsi* and *Orselli* (bear), *Pecora* (sheep), *Pescio* (fish), *Porco* (pig), *Tortorello* (dove), *Trotta* (trout), *Vespi* (wasp), and *Zanzara* (mosquito). Some territorial and the numerous occupational names complete the category of Italian family appellations.

Italian family names such as *Minimi, Mininni,* and *Minunni* when written in longhand often present serious problems of which strokes to dot as *i*'s. Unless the bearer is most careful in his handwriting he cannot expect others to distinguish the different minims.

Pet names are very common. They are Christian names or parts of Christian names to which is attached one of the many diminutive suffixes. Some of the more common which can terminate also in either *a* or *i*, are: *-arello, -arino, -cello, -cillo, -cino, -ello, -erello, -etto, -icino, -iello, -illo, -ino, -itto, -occio, -olo, -ollo, -otto, -ozzo, -uccio, -ullo, -ulo, -usso,* and *-uzzo,* although there are many more variations of like import. As examples, the following are from *Giacomo* (James) and a few of its numerous hypocoristic forms: *Vucciarello, Giaccarini, Botticelli, Mocello, Pettoello, Comoletto, Iacoviello, Mucillo, Mucino, Giacolla, Giacomolo, Menotti, Copozza,, Iacovuccio, Vullo, Giacomusso,* and *Giacomuzzo.* Double diminutives are popular, as in *Vozzarella, Cavazzoni, Petrucello,* and *Marcuccillo.* The Italians also have two augmentative suffixes, *-one* and *-cione* as in *Giacopone* and *Ugoccione.*

Numerous compound names arose in Italy as family names. Some are composed of adjectives and nouns, as *Bonadonna* (good woman) and *Malfante* (bad child). Some have a number plus a noun, as *Quattrocchi* (four eyes), *Cinquemani* (five hands), and *Mezzofanti* (half soldier). Others have adjectives with forenames, as *Giangrasso* (fat John) and *Ciccotosto* (stubborn Frank). Some are font names combined with a noun, as *Notarangelo* (Notary Angelo) and *Papandrea* (Priest Andrea).

Like other Europeans, Italians bestow the names of rulers and kings on their children. This hero-worship stimulates the popularity of such names as *Amadeo, Vittorio, Emanuele, Umberto, Orlando, Elena, Margherita, Yolanda,* and *Mafalda.* Fictional characters have contributed names like *Beatrice* (Dante's *Vita Nuova* and *Divina Commedia*) and *Aida* (from the Verdi opera of that name). Some of the more common Christian names for boys are: *Alfredo, Angelo, Antonio, Carlo, Enrico, Domenico, Francesco, Giorgio, Giovanni, Guilio, Giuseppe, Gugliemo, Lorenzo, Luigi, Marco, Mario, Pietro, Vincenzo,* and *Vittorio.* For girls they are *Amelia, Angela, Bianca,*

95

Caterina, Elena, Francesca, Giulietta, Ida, Lucia, Louisa, Margherita, Maria, Rosa, and *Teresa.*

See Joseph G. Fucilla, *Our Italian Surnames,* Evanston, Ill., 1949.
See also AMERICANIZATION OF NAMES

JAPANESE NAMES

Until the restoration, in 1868, family names or surnames were borne only by the court nobles, the military class, and such members of the lower ranks of society as were granted the privilege by the ruling monarch. The possession of a family name entitled a man to wear a sword, the mark of a warrior and a gentleman. These surnames consisted of about fourteen hundred different characters used as initials together with about a hundred as finals, these latter being mostly of topographical import. There were also a dozen or so popular clan names borne by hereditary right or by special privilege. These followed the surname and were often followed by another name in signatures by the upper classes, consisting usually of a single character, with a complimentary meaning.

In Japan the surname is written first, followed by the given name. For the most part family names were taken from nature. One of the commonest surnames is *Ito* (only wisteria). Other common family names are *Sato* (wisteria prop), *Saito* (equal wisteria), *Nakagawa* (middle river), *Suzuki* (bell tree), *Togo* (east country), and *Yoshida* (happy field). Some other very common Japanese surnames are: *Abe, Inoue, Katō, Nakamura, Ono, Takahashi, Tanaka, Watanabe,* and *Yamamoto.* Craftsmen and other ordinary people were often known by their occupation. Some, chiefly swordsmiths and makers of sword furniture, received special names as a mark of imperial favor.

Boys of all classes receive a short and simple name in a ceremony on the sixth day after birth. At about the age of fifteen, in another ceremony another name would be adopted by which a boy would thereafter be known by those outside of his family. Many of these have reference to order of birth. Some are derived from certain official titles or attempts to reproduce them. Particular prefixes and suffixes, mostly of a complimentary significance added to the ordinary name, provide variations and often aid in recognition.

The Japanese usually do not bestow pretty names on their girls for aesthetic reasons. Most are not named after flowers, graceful shrubs, or beautiful objects. The intent of Japanese parents is to select a name ex-

96

pressing a virtue or moral or mental qualities, perhaps indicative of a desire for the child's careful training. Many names to which we would ascribe beauty would convey a different meaning to them. *Umé* (plum-blossom) is a name referring to wifely devotion and virtue. *Matsu* (pine) is not given because of the beauty of the tree, but because its evergreen foliage is the emblem of vigorous age. The majority of Japanese female names are abstract nouns, as *Jun* (obedience), *Kichi* (luck), and *Yoshi* (good).

Most names in use by others are preceded by the honorific *O*, except by the upper classes, and followed by the title *San* (an abbreviation of *Sama*), as *O-Matsu San*, although there are various exceptions to the general rule. *San* after a girl's name means "Miss" or "Mrs."; after a man's name it has the value of our "Mr." Any girl can add *ko* to her name, a term originally an honorific, but now almost an essential part of the name without honorific connotation. The husband may call his wife by her given name, but it is not proper for her to reciprocate; she may, however, call him *Anata*, a term used between spouses, or *Otoochan* (father).

The Nipponese artists, painters, writers, and entertainers adopt pseudonyms or sobriquets for use in their professional life. Sometimes these are quoted in company with their ordinary names. Buddhist priests and nuns, like the Catholics, drop their family names. Then there are semireligious (Buddhistic) names, usually posthumous, designating one who has entered the church. Many of these professional names may be recognized by their terminations, which refer in some manner to the occupation.

When a Japanese emperor dies, the name by which he was known dies with him, and thereafter he is known by the name of his reign which he had previously selected. When Hirohito dies he will be known in history as *Sowa*.

See also AMERICANIZATION OF NAMES

JEWISH FORENAMES

When Jews lived together in the ghetto, all that was needed was a Hebrew name. Those who had dealings with the outside world adopted a secular name. Now all Jews who give some attention to their religion are required to have both a Hebrew name (*shem hakodesh—* holy name), and a secular name in addition to their family name. This custom of linking a Jewish with a non-Jewish name started during the Greek period; in the twelfth century the rabbis decreed that every Jewish boy must be given a purely Jewish name at his circumcision. The Hebrew name is used only in the synagogue; and there are some Jews who are surprised to learn that they have a Hebrew name. Sometimes the synagogue name and the vernacular name are identical.

The two names are expected to be related in some way, such as similarity of sound or meaning. However, there is no religious rule or regulation governing the matter; it is merely a matter of custom. From early times many Hebrew names were simply translated into the language of the country of residence. Some parents seem to be satisfied if the two names begin with the same letter. At the present time very often the English name is selected first and then the Hebrew name is appended. The most popular of Hebrew names is *Moshe*. Some of the other more common Hebrew names, according to Rabbi Alfred J. Kolatch, are: *Avrawhawm, Chanaw, Dawvid, Estayr, Layaw, Miryawm, Rawchayl, Rivkaw, Sawraw, Shmuayl, Yaakov, and Yitzchawk.*

The baby, if a boy, is named on the eighth day after birth in the ritual of circumcision. Naming a Jewish girl is a ritual that takes place in a synagogue service attended by the father or a close member of the family as soon as possible after the girl is born, although in Reform temples the service is delayed until the mother and father attend together on a Friday night or Sabbath morning. In theory it is the father's duty to name the infant..

Certain forenames have been used so much by Jewish families that they are generally considered to be Jewish names. Names like *Harry, Isidore, Jacques, Julius, Ludwig, Maurice, Moritz, Morris, Moses, Regina, Rosa,* and *Sigbert* in Europe seem to be reserved to Jews. In more recent years names like *Sidney* and *Stanley* have been taken over by Jews.

Hitlerian Germany, in 1938, decreed that Jews having non-Jewish names must take the additional name of *Israel* if male and *Sarah* if female. The official Gazette listed 185 male names and 91 female names which were to be considered Jewish and whose bearers would not be required to take the names *Israel* or *Sarah* to identify them as Jews.

Many Jews select names that are not Jewish but definitely Christian in origin or concept, such as *Andrew, Anthony, Patricia, Paul, Stephen,* and *Thomas.* Some even name their daughters *Natalie* (birthday of

Christ) or *Dolores* (sorrows of Mary, mother of our Lord); boys are sometimes named *Noel* (Christmas).

Among Jewish families, naming children after ancestors is very common today; in Old Testament times the practice was almost unknown. Naming after the father or grandfather became prevalent during the first century of the Christian era. Among the Sephardic Jews (French, Italian, Spanish, and Portuguese), the custom of naming after relatives was deeply rooted, and is common today. The Ashkenazic Jews (German, Austrian, Polish, and Russian) are more superstitious and are loath to name the child after a living relative. They believe that naming after a living person would rob him of a full life and tend to upset the spirit of the dead.

There was the Italian mother and Jewish father who named their daughter Carmen Cohen, the surname being Ginsberg. The mother used only the first name and the father always called her by her middle name; thus the child never knew whether she was Carmen or Cohen.

See Alfred J. Kolatch, *These Are the Names*, New York, 1948; Nathan Gottlieb, *A Jewish Child Is Born*, New York, 1960.
See also ISRAELI NAMES; JEWISH SURNAMES; MAGIC NAMES; SUPERSTITION

JEWISH SUPERSTITION

The superstitious Ashkenazic Jews in Talmudic and later times feared to name a child after an older living person because they thought that when the angel of death went to look for the older person whose time had come, he might be confused and take the young child of the same name. They avoided naming children after a living father or grandfather or, indeed, after any living person. They not only feared for the death of the child but they thought that the angel charged to mete punishment upon the older person might be careless and inflict it upon a child of the same name. A parent or grandparent might also be severely injured by the use of his name by the child, since the older person's soul, believed identical with the name, might leave the older person and dwell in the younger body, thus causing the death of the older person. For this reason it was also considered dangerous to name a child after one who had departed this life, as the soul could not dwell both on the earth and in heaven. The soul might leave heaven, which would be disastrous for the deceased person. Superstition can overcome superstition, and some who believed in the complete identity of the name with the soul were eager to name a child after a departed relative to preserve the soul of the departed and bring it down to earth again. Some wanted to be born again, and it was considered proper to give the child the name of a departed relative in order to bring his soul into the child.

People hesitated to enter the house of an ill person with the same name; the angel of death might come at that time and by mistake take the well man. Changing the name of a sick man could save his life by hoodwinking the angel charged with bringing the disease to a fatal conclusion. The new name would be one which suggested long life, as *Hayim* (life), *Alter* (old man), or *Zeide* (grandfather). Changing the name of a sick person became a universal custom among the Jews. The angels of destruction were assumed to be stupid and easily confounded. (Washing off the old name and taking a new one by a sick man was also a custom among some American Indian tribes.) Two families with the same name would refuse to live in the same house. A widow would refuse to marry a man with the same name as her deceased husband. Among Palestinian Jews in Talmudic times, a husband and wife often exchanged names at night. He would address her by his name and she would call him by her name. This was considered an effective way to fool the demons.

In 1957, Maurice Schwab was rushed to a Chicago hospital with a critical heart attack. A member of his family recalled the ancient Hebrew custom of changing the name of an ill person. In a brief ceremony he was given the name *Hayim* and reports were that he convalesced nicely.

JEWISH SURNAMES

Many Arabic-speaking Jews carried the custom of surnames with them to Spain and Portugal, and they were among the first Jews in Europe to adopt family names. Portuguese Jews clung to their names without change, some of them being among the oldest and most respected names in Portugal. Most of the family names of Sephardic Jews are derived from place of origin, such as *Cardozo, Spinoza* (Espinoza), *Toledano, Villanova, Porto,* and *Montefiore.*

Among the Ashkenazim surnames were quite rare before the eighteenth century. Forced to live in special sections or ghettos, their need for surnames was not so great as for Christians, and also lack of iden-

100

tification was an aid in evading burdensome taxes and military conscription. In medieval German cities houses were identified by a sign, and some Jews were named after the house in which they lived. A sign bearing the picture of a *Loeb* (lion), a *Gans* (goose), or a *Strauss* (ostrich or bouquet) would give a surname to the Jew residing there. One of the best known is *Rothschild* (red shield).

Other names denote personal characteristics, as *Klein* (small), *Jaffe* (beautiful), and *Schwartz* (black). Names designating occupations are *Arzt* (doctor), *Shechter* (ritual slaughterer), *Wechsler* (money-changer), and *Sofer* (letter-writer). Most German-Jewish names, however, are derived from place names, as *Auerbach, Bachrach, Bernstein, Epstein, Florsheim, Ginsberg, Goldberg, Weil,* and *Wiener*. The surname used was generally the last city in which the bearer had resided. If an individual from Pressburg went to Vienna, he would become *Pressburger*. If he then moved to Berlin, he would be known as *Wiener*. Some place names were adopted as surnames merely because the bearer had traveled to that town or country. In patronymics the German *-sohn* and the Slavic *-vitch* are sometimes used, as *Abramsohn* and *Abramovitch* (son of Abram). The suffix *-kin* to denote descent is common, as in *Baskin, Barkin, Rivkin,* and *Sorkin.*

The Ashkenazim have many surnames derived from Biblical names, the most important of which are *Aaron, Abraham, Alexander, Asher, Baruch, Benjamin, David, Eleazar, Elias, Emanuel, Gabriel, Isaac, Israel, Jacob, Joseph, Judah, Levi, Manasseh, Menahem, Moses, Samuel, Simon, Solomon,* and *Zachariah.* Many others took names from the Bible in other ways. Those descended from the priestly caste became *Cohen, Kahn,* and *Katz;* those of Levitic descent became *Levy, Levi, Levin,* and *Levinsky. Cohen* and *Levy* are not German-Jewish names but belong to the worldwide stock of Jewish appellatives.

A curious custom arose during the Middle Ages among Jewish leaders of combining the abbreviation of a title with the initials of their name to form a single personal name by which they became widely known. Some of these are *Rashi* for Rabbi Solomon ben Isaac, *Rambam* for Rabbi Moses ben Maimon, *Ran* for Rabbi Nissim, *Besht* for Ba'al Shem-Tov, *Shak* for Shabbethai ha-Kohen, and *Hida* for Hayyim Joseph David Azulai. Other abbreviations commemorate a special event, as *Sak* from Sera K'doshim Spiro (descendants of the martyrs of Speyer).

Austria in 1785 required Jews to register family names. The gov-

ernment officials in charge of the registration enthusiastically went
to work. For a good name derived from flowers, gems, or elements of
nature, such as *Sonnenschein* (sunshine), *Rosenthal* (rose valley),
Goldblatt (gold leaf), *Edelstein* (noble stone), and *Blumberg* (flower
mountain), the highest charge was made; for ordinary names such
as *Stahl* and *Eisen* the exaction was less. Jews who could not afford
to pay were sometimes saddled with odd, whimsical, or ridiculous
names such as *Kanalgeruch* (canal smell), *Armenfreund* (friend of
the poor), *Ochsenschwanz* (oxtail), and *Schmalz* (grease), and the
like. One merchant was said to have paid half his fortune to have a
w inserted in *Schweisshund* so that he would be Herr *Bloodhound*
instead of Herr *Dog Excrement*. In 1787 the decree was extended to
all the Austrian provinces except Hungary, and the Jews were then
restricted mostly to Biblical names.

In Russia decrees in 1804 and 1835 prevented Jews from altering
their names but, until a statute was enacted in 1844, they were not
compelled to adopt surnames. The Kingdom of Westphalia in 1808
compelled Jews to adopt family names within three months. In the
same year Napoleon decreed that Jews must adopt fixed names, but
forbade them to select names based on place names or the names of
famous families. In 1812 the Prussians required Jews to take surnames
to be approved by the authorities, and by 1845 this requirement was
extended to all parts of the Prussian kingdom. The German authorities usually assigned geographical names, a place or country name,
to Jews. Some were artificial, patterned after place names although the
place did not exist. In some cases a suffix, such as *-heim* or *-stein*, was
added to places and used as surnames.

As early as 1821 in Poland the Jews were legally obligated to adopt
surnames, but at first the law was not strictly enforced. As late as 1942
Jews were forbidden to change their family names in France, and in
the same year were forbidden to bear Norwegian-sounding names in
Norway.

Jews have changed or adapted their names to fit the culture in every
country; yet they always seem to retain a distinctive Jewish flavor.
These characteristic Jewish names have played an important role in
maintaining the Jewish religious group.

Many Jewish refugees, coming to America, changed their names.
Most of them took a new surname with the same initial letter as their
former name. German-Jewish names had the greater prestige and were

adopted by many immigrants from countries east of Germany.

Harry Golden, the Jewish philosopher, points out that there is a way to insure perfect safety when one registers at a hotel or motel with a woman not one's wife. He advises, "Always use a Jewish name, which puts you above all suspicion and also thwarts any private detective scouring the area. No one makes up a Jewish name, or so people imagine."

See also ISRAELI NAMES; JEWISH FORENAMES

JOHN

The most common forename in the Western World is *John* (gracious gift of Yahveh) from the Hebrew *Yohanan*. It reached the Anglo-Saxon tongue as *Johannes,* and settled into John. It owes its popularity to the fact that it was borne by two men closely identified with Christ, John the Apostle and John the Baptist. Since then it has been borne by saints and by sinners, by priests and by thieves, by kings and by peasants. There are many Saint Johns. Twenty-three popes have borne the name, plus one antipope. Each one of the twelve men and the alternate was named *John* in a jury impaneled in St. Louis in August 1965.

In the various European languages the original Hebrew name became modulated through the laws of phonetics into many forms, and is found in every Western language in more than a hundred forms. Some of the best known are:

Armenian:	Hovhannes	Greek:	Ioannes
Basque:	Iban	Hungarian:	Janos
Bavarian:	Johan	Irish:	Sean, Shane
Belgian:	Jan, Jehan	Italian:	Giovanni
Bulgarian:	Ivan	Lapp:	Jofan, Joba
Croatian:	Ivan	Latin:	Johannes
Czech:	Jan	Lithuanian:	Jonas
Danish:	Hans, Jan	Norwegian:	Johan, Jens
Dutch:	Jan	Persian:	Jehan
Estonian:	Johan	Polish:	Jan, Iwan
Finnish:	Hannes	Portuguese:	João
French:	Jean	Rumanian:	Ioan
Gaelic:	Jan	Russian:	Ivan
German:	Johannes, Hans	Scotch:	Ian

103

Serbian:	Ivan	Turkish:	Ohannes
Slovak:	Jan	Ukrainian:	Ivan
Spanish:	Juan, Joao	Welsh:	Evan
Swedish:	Jonam, Jens	Yiddish:	Yochanan

John was not a popular name before the Norman Conquest in England. Indeed it was very rare, an adopted name borne only by a few religious. Until the middle of the fourteenth century *William* was the favorite name. The overwhelming popularity of *John* over the years is evidenced by two very common British surnames, *Johnson* and *Jones*, both of which mean "the son of John." Some of the other surnames meaning "the son of John," "descendant of John," or "son of a diminutive or pet form of John," are: *Bevans, Evans, Evensen, Hankinson, Hansen, Hanson, Ianson, Ibañez, Ivanov, Ivanovitch, Iwanowicz, Jackson, Jahnsen, Janczyk, Jankowski, Janoff, Janosfi, Janowicz, Janowiez, Janowitz, Janse, Jansen, Janson, Jantzen, Janzen, Jasinski, Jaxon, Jeneson, Jenkins, Jenkinson, Jenks, Jennings, Jennison, Jenzen, Jeske, Jessen, Johanson, Johns, Jonas, Jonikas, Jonsen, Jonson, Junkinson, MacShane, Yanke, Yankovitz, Yohanan,* and *Yonan.*

Perhaps the earliest famous John was Jonathan, son of Saul, and David's friend, who lived more than a thousand years before Christ. John was the name of one king of Bohemia, one of Denmark, eight of the Byzantine Empire, one of England, two of France, one of Saxony, three of Poland, six of Portugal, two of Aragon, two of Castile, three of Sweden, besides many dukes, archdukes, electors, counts, and other miscellaneous nobility. Most of them are not credited with happy or fortunate reigns.

In later times John has been the forename of five American presidents, Adams, (father and son), Tyler, Coolidge, and Kennedy. Other famous Johns are Brown, Bunyan, Burroughs, Cabot, Constable, Drinkwater, Dryden, Eliot, Evelyn, Galsworthy, Hancock, Harvard, Hopkins, Howard, Huss, Jay, Keats, Knox, Lyly, Marshall, Mill, Milton, Morgan, Payne, Pershing, Pope, Rockefeller, Ruskin, Sargent, Smith, Sousa, Wesley, Whittier, and Wycliffe. Some have to exhibit their middle names in order to be easily recognized.

There has been much controversy as to whether *Jack* derives from the French *Jacques* (for Jacob-James) or *John*. It was finally clearly settled by Mr. E. B. Nicholson in his *The Pedigree of "Jack" and of Various Allied Names*, London, 1892, who proved that after John acquired the diminutive forms of Jonkin and Jankin they were short-ened back to Jocky and Jacky (in the same way that monkin and dunkin became monkey and donkey) and then further shortened into Jock and Jack. *Jock* has been more popular in the north of England and especially in Scotland, while *Jack* has been most current in the south of England.

Jack was a popular boy in nursery rhymes. There were *Jack Sprat, Jack and Jill, Jack Horner, Jack the Giant Killer,* and others. In the Western languages there are hundreds of diminutive and pet forms of John.

At a dinner for the Reverend David H. Pottie, of Evanston, Illinois, the toastmaster spoke of the recent construction that the minister had inspired, and suggested that one part should commemorate his fine work by being named the Pottie Room. This reminded the next speaker of the very wealthy and discriminating congregation that wanted every detail in its new church to be impeccably correct even in such niceties as the proper ecclesiastical inscriptions. The church was blessed with three lavatories which thus naturally became known as I John, II John, and III John.

See Hallie Erminie Rives and Gabrielle Elliot Forbush, *The John Book,* New York, 1947.

KEYS TO ANCIENT LANGUAGES

Names, both personal and place names, often loom large as an aid in deciphering ancient and forgotten languages. For many centuries the tongues of ancient Egypt were silent until the great French Egyptologist, Jean François Champollion, suspected that the hieroglyphics might be phonetic and discovered the names Ptolemy and Cleopatra. The name of Ptolmis was known in its Greek form, and when three of the sounds of Ptolmis, *l, o,* and *p,* were found in their correct positions in what was thought might be *Cleopatra,* the first gleam of understanding appeared. Then Champollion found sounds he could identify from Ptolemy and Cleopatra as al-se-tr. The only Greek name with this arrangement of letters was Alksentrs (Alexander). Next Rameses and Thotmosis were identified.

Another example is the deciphering of cuneiform, which was first broken almost entirely by the recognition of the proper names of kings and provinces. Three royal names, Darius, Xerxes, and Hystaspes, provided the opening wedges when they were found to fit in the phrase, "Darius, great king, king of kings . . . son of Hystaspes/Xerxes, great king, king of kings . . . son of King Darius." Personal names are almost the only source of knowledge of the Amorite language

LAST NAMES ALPHABETICALLY

The telephone company found, in 1935, that the *Zzyns, Zzyxes,* and all the other names with double and triple z's were invented names in order to be listed last in the book, and they routed them from the directory. But it was not long before they were back in. The telephone companies keep on cleaning house from time to time.

In the Chicago 1964–65 telephone book the last name was *Zyzzy Zzyzzyxy,* the second one being the surname. If that name doesn't make the telephone company dizzy, nothing will. Mr. *Zzyzzyxy* did not appear in the 1965–66 directory. Archimedes I. *Zzzyandottie* managed to be the last individual in the Manhattan, New York, book. Mr. *Zzyzbohm* concludes the San Francisco directory. Some others who have ended their local directories are: *Zylicz* (New Orleans), *Zytt* (Cincinnati), *Zyvoloski* (Minneapolis), *Zywiec* (St Paul), *Zywusko* (Washington), *Zzyzz* (Los Angeles), and *Zyzniewski* (Cleveland and Milwaukee). But in some cities business firms with carefully concocted names have ousted individuals, such as the *Zzzy Zzy Ztamp Ztudios* Co. of Brooklyn and *Zzzzz Wake Up Service* of Los Angeles.

In Detroit a group of happy bachelors occupying an apartment had, for several years, their common telephone number inserted with the artificial name of *Zeke Zzzpt.* They planned to advise their girl friends to call them. "Just look in the phone book, the last name," they would tell the admiring young ladies. In the 1954 directory *Zeke Zzzpt* was ousted from last place by two men using the name *Zolf Zzzpt.* In 1957 the London telephone directory ended with V. K. *Zzzu,* displacing Lewis *Zzymbla* who had reigned in that spot for years. On the social security list the last name is *Zyzys.* The last name in the Library of Congress catalog is Jgo Wan *Zzays.* In the Union Catalog of the Library of Congress the last writer is D. A. *Zzuni.*

Dr. Trevor Weston, a London researcher, noted that those with surnames starting with a letter toward the end of the alphabet always were called upon last during both their school and adult career, a repeated unfairness which probably affected their emotional life. He said that ulcers, heart attacks, and mental troubles seemed to be more frequent among these unfortunate people. Maybe the good doctor with a "W" surname was biased.

LATIN AMERICAN NAMES *See* BRAZILIAN NAMES; MEXICAN NAMES; SOUTH AMERICAN NAMES

LAW ON NAMES

In law, a man's legal name is the name, that is the word, or combination of words, or initials, by which he is generally known and called in the community. It consists of a Christian, or given name, or names, and of a surname or family name which generally is derived from the common name of his parents. Anciently, the given name was regarded as the more important of the two, but in modern times the surname has become the principal name.

The Christian, or given, name is the one selected by parents after birth or at baptism. In early times the common law of England recognized only one Christian name and one family name. A middle name or initial was held to be immaterial and could be disregarded, but now there is a tendency to give more attention to a middle name or initial to avoid absurd or unjust results and for aid in identification, especially when the first name is represented only by an initial. The prefixes, *Mr.*, *Mrs.*, and *Dr.* and the suffixes, *Sr.*, *Jr.*, and *2nd*, or words of similar import are not generally part of the legal name. However, a woman may be known by her husband's name preceded by "Mrs."

In general, in the United States, with the possible exception of Pennsylvania, a person may, in the absence of fraud, infringement of trade-marks or trade names, or unfair competition, adopt or assume any name he chooses, and be known by such name without obtaining any court or judicial authority; and contracts, obligations, and transactions entered into under the assumed or fictitious name are valid and binding. Some jurisdictions have, however, by statute, imposed restrictions on the use of such fictitious names in specified circumstances such as in registering at a hotel, obtaining employment, and practicing medicine or law. Various state statutes require one doing business under an assumed name to file a prescribed affidavit, or certificate, or to register the name. These statutes are intended for the protection of those engaged in commercial transactions. They do not apply if the name used fairly discloses the true name of the individual even though not setting out the name in full. Contracts made by persons who are in violation of these statutes are ordinarily not for that reason invalid. Some statutes forbid the maintenance of a suit until there has been compliance therewith.

In most states there are statutes which prescribe a method by which a person may change his name or cause it to be changed, usually by filing a certificate or by application to, and order of, a court of record. Usually these statutes do not abrogate the common-law right to change of name without court application. Whether the petition for change of name is granted is a matter of judicial discretion, not of right. Unless there appears to be some substantial reason for denial, the application is usually granted. If one wanted to change his name for the purpose of dodging creditors or to change it to Woolworth for the purpose of opening a variety story, the courts would refuse permission. The courts have generally held that a request for a change of name will not be denied merely because the name desired is one borne by a respected member of the community, or because of the opposition of persons bearing the name chosen. Each case depends on its own particular facts; and the judges, unless there is a showing of actual fraud or actual invasion of the rights of another, will, often after rebuking the petitioner, grant the change. The value of a name change through court petition is that a definite, permanent record of the change and date of change is thereby made.

Applications to change the name of an infant will generally be granted if it is clearly in the best interests of the child. Change of name of the children of divorced parents will ordinarily not be allowed if it might contribute to the estrangement of the child from its father who has evinced a desire to preserve the parental relationship.

The law does not regard the spelling of a name so much as it does the sound. Two names that sound alike are regarded as the same, and a variance in their spelling is immaterial unless it is such that it misleads a person to his prejudice. This is the rule of *idem sonans*. Even a slight difference in pronunciaton is not important. For example, *Alford* and *Afford* have been held to *idem sonans;* so have *Bernard* and *Bernhard; Bulkley* and *Buckley; Cora* and *Carrie; Gowens* and *Goins; Kochannek* and *Kochawnek; McDough* and *McDole; and Zoder* and *Zoda.* Each case must depend on its particular facts, however, and with increased universal education courts are now less inclined to find two different names to be *idem sonans.*

Some courts have held that upon marriage a woman's surname changes to that of her husband. A wife is not, however, compelled to use her husband's name, and many women in business continue to use their maiden name (*See* Lucy Stone League *under* NAME ORGANIZATIONS).

Some years ago in Massachusetts, Reverberant Brown, being childless, told Joe and Jane Smith that he would give their baby $25,000 at age twenty-one if they would christen the boy Reverberant. They did, but when the boy became of age, Brown refused to pay. In a suit the court forced Brown to pay, saying the child had lost "the opportunity of receiving a more advantageous name," and was compelled "to bear whatever detriment may flow from the name imposed upon him."

"What's the judge's name?"

"His name is irrelevant."

"That's an odd name for a judge."

LITHUANIAN NAMES

Whereas in most countries men acquired surnames from the names of villages and inhabited places, in Lithuania about one-half of the inhabited places have been named after the original settlers. Family names came into use after 1400. In the latter part of the fourteenth century the Grand Duchy of Lithuania adopted Roman Catholicism as the state religion. The people were baptized in groups and given Christian names. Their former names then were used as family names and became hereditary.

Lithuanian surnames have three legally established forms, one masculine, many ending in *-as, -is,* and *-us* such as *Klìmas,* and two feminine. The family names of married women end in *-ienė,* such as *Klimíenė,* while girls and unmarried women have names terminating in one of several diminutive suffixes, such as *-aitė, -ytė, -utė,* and *-ūtė,* as in *Klimáitė.* The wife of Mr. *Stašinskas* would be Mrs. *Stašinskíenė,* and their daughter would be Miss *Stašinskáitė* before her marriage. In America the masculine form only is used, but in Lithuania it would be unthinkable to record family names incorrectly.

Alfred Senn, former president of the American Name Society and

109

leading authority on matters Lithuanian, notes that patronymics make up more than one-half of the Lithuanian surnames, some of which are of White Russian or Polish origin. The Lithuanian patronymical suffixes are *-átis*, *-ẽnas*, *-ónis*, *-ũnas*, and *-ùlis*. Some common surnames arise from nicknames, as *Vãbalas* (bug), *Smetonà* (sour cream), *Blỹnas* (pancake), *Pùskunigis* (half-priest), *Vilkas* (wolf), *Lãpinas* (fox), *Mýlimas* (beloved), *Barzdà* (beard), and *Ýlakis* (awl-eyed). Occupational names are *Dailìdė* (carpenter), *Stikliõrius* (glassmaker), and *Pùplesis* (bean picker). Several occupational and locational surnames have patronymical endings, as *Kalváitis* (son of the smith) and *Gudáitis* (son of a White Russian). There are many Russian, Polish, German, and other foreign family names in Lithuania.

The Lithuanians today have only one given name, usually selected from an approved list of saints' names. Common Christian names are *Antãnas*, *Juõzapas*, *Juõzas*, *Jõnas*, *Kazìmieras*, *Kazỹs*, *Póvilas*, *Pẽtras*, *Prãnas*, and *Tamõšius*, for men. For girls, *Marjonà*, *Marijà*, *Nijõle*, *Onà*, *Bronislavà*, *and Brõnė* are popular. Diminutive forms are frequently found. Many old Lithuanian names are made up from two stems with no relation between them. A child might be given a name made up of one stem from the name of the father and the other from the mother's name.

LOCALES OF ENGLISH NAMES

English surnames vary somewhat in different parts of England due to a great diversity in dialect. For example, a man with red hair could be so nicknamed everywhere. In the central and southern parts of England, it would be spelled *Read*, while in the southwest and north *Reed* would be preferred; *Reid* would be the spelling in Scotland. The descendants of little Hugh would be *Hutchins* in the main part of England, *Hutchings* in the southwest, *Hutchinson* in the north, and *Hutchison* in Scotland. *Harrisons* would be found in the north of England and *Harrises* in the south.

Tucker, *Fuller*, and *Walker* are all names for the artisan who cleaned and thickened cloth, each in his own area. The *Tuckers* worked in the southwest of England; the *Fullers* are confined to the eastern and southeastern coast counties; and the *Walkers* occupy the rest of the country, particularly in the north and west. A similar but more vague pattern is disclosed by the weavers. They are called *Webb*, the most

110

common form of the name, in the south half of the country; the *Webbers* are found in Devonshire and in Somerset; the *Weavers* are in Somerset, Worcestershire, and Gloucestershire; in the north of England they are called *Websters*. *Dyers* are confined to the three southwestern counties and Suffolk, but in many other places they are called *Listers*. *Reeves* is found in the southern part of England and *Graves* in the north; both were minor officials appointed by the lord of the manor to supervise the work of the villeins.

See Henry Brougham Guppy, *Homes of Family Names in Great Britain*, London, 1890.

LONG NAMES

The longest ordinary English surname is said to be *Featherstone-haugh* from the original form of Featherstone in Northumberland. In fiction *Aldiborontiphoscophornio* is the sesquipedalian cognomen of a pompous character in Henry Carey's *Chrononhotonthologos*, a burlesque acted in 1734 in London.

The newspapers never tire of calling attention to the long middle names bestowed upon many Hawaiians. Gwendolyn *Kuuleikailialo-haopiilaniwailaukekoaulumahiehiekealaoonoaonaopiikea* Kekino has a birth certificate to prove her name. Her family calls her *Piikea*. Albert K. Kahalekula, of Wailuku, Hawaii, was a private in the army in 1957. His middle name: *Kahekilikuiikalewaokamehameha.*

George *Pappavlahodimitrakopoulous*, a restaurant owner in Lansing, Michigan, according to reports in 1961, announced the offer of a free meal to any patron who could pronounce his name correctly. Lambros A. *Pappatoriantafillospoulous* of Chicopee, Massachusetts, was inducted into the armed forces in 1953. He was called Pappas or Mr. Alphabet.

A native policeman in Fiji, British Polynesia, has the name, Marika *Tuimudremudrenicagitokalaunatobakonatewaenagaunakalakivolaikoya-kinakotamanaenaiivolanikawabualenavalenivolavolaniyasanamaisomo-somo*, 130 letters in all. The name is said to tell that, with the aid of a northerly wind, Marika's father sailed from Natewa, on Vanua Levu, to the provincial office at Somosomo, Taveuni, to register the birth of the child. A long family name in Ljubljana, Yugoslavia, is *Papandoval-orokomonduronikolpakopulovski.*

The longest family name in the social security lists by 1938 was *Xenogianokopoulos*. The longest name in the Bible is the symbolic

111

name of the second son of Isaiah, *Maher-shalal-hash-baz* (the spoil speeds, the prey hastes).

In 1945 James J. *Pappatheodorokoummountourgeotopoulos* operated a restaurant in Chicago. Some newspaper accounts added a few letters, but the above spelling is as it occurs on his calling card.

In 1931 a Little Rock, Arkansas, trucker working for the Missouri Pacific answered to *Hansollensbockenoffenhassengraphensteiner* Holloway. Probably the railroad listed him as "H. Holloway." Cesaron *Tripletsezsilvermanson* boasts the longest name in Seattle.

A Fiji Island cricket player has 56 letters in his name: *Talebulamaineiilikenamainavaleniveivakabulaimakulalakeba*. An American G.I. from Hawaii married a German girl; and the registrar, contrary to law, omitted reading the name of the groom. It was *Kahokunsniokekahohiakoakuupuuwai*.

In 1956 at Fort Dix, New Jersey, the WAC with the longest name was Pfc. Marvalene *Kelehuakauikawekiu* Apiki, of Napoopoo, Hawaii. Her middle name translates to "flower of the fire goddess." Another Hawaiian girl was named Kalani *Kaumehamehakahikikalanynakawahinekuhao*. An observer observed that if she would move to that town in Wales called Llanfairpwllgwyngyllgogerychwyrndrobwllandysiliogogogoch, very few men would try to start a correspondence with her.

A clerk in an accounting department in Honolulu signs his name in full: *Floyd Kuikealakauaokalani Kealiiwailanamalie Kamaunuihalakaipo Hoopii*. Maybe no one told him of the English practice of resorting to initials. A man in New Orleans comes when called *Maillillikageyeaaegyaye Edeyoueayearayilo Anlillyilayio*.

Hubert Blaine *Wolfeschlegelsteinhausenbergerdorff*, Sr., a Philadelphian of German descent, appears from time to time in the newspapers because of his long name. If pressed, he will claim that his full name is: *Adolph Blaine Charles David Earl Frederick Gerald Hubert Irvin John Kenneth Lloyd Martin Nero Oliver Paul Quincy Randolph Sherman Thomas Uncas Victor William Xerxes Yancy Zeus Wolfeschlegelsteinhausenbergerdorffvoralternwarengewissenhaftschaferswessenschafswarenwohlgefutternundsorgfalugkeitbeschutzenvorangreifendurchihrraubgierigfeinds, Senior*, although in correspondence with the author in 1956 about his name only the form first above written was mentioned. This must be the longest name in the United States and will likely remain so until the next seeker after publicity adopts a longer one.

After an undue celebration Seaman Paul *Panagiotopoulos* of St.

Paul, Minnesota, spent the night in the police station. Before being released the next morning he was asked his name. "Paul Panagiotopoulos," he repdied.

"Why don't you shorten it?" the police lieutenant suggested.

"I did," said the sailor. "It used to be Paul Apostolopanagiotopoulos."

See also HAWAIIAN NAMES

LUCY STONE LEAGUE *See* NAME ORGANIZATIONS

MAGIC NAMES

Potent magical names could be produced in various ways from texts in the Bible, such as taking the first or final letter of a phrase or a verse. Thus the famous magical name *Agla* has been assumed to be derived from the first letters of the words (in Hebrew), *Ataw Gebor Leolam Adonai*, "Thou art mighty forever, O Lord." Germans who employed it thought it to be the initial letters of "Allmächtiger Gott, lösch'aus!" (Redeem, Almighty God). Many names believed to have magic powers have been created by figuring numerical values of Hebrew letters and combining them in various ways.

Some reputed magical names are just meaningless words. Examples of magic names are included in the following conjuration from the so-called *The Sixth and Seventh Books of Moses*, a collection of conjurations, seals, symbols, citations, tables of spirits, extracts, signs, revelations, meaningless hieroglyphics, and miscellaneous magical advice assembled by Johann Scheible and translated from the German:

I, N.N., a servant of God, desire, call upon the OCH, and conjure thee through water, † fire, air and earth, and everything that lives and moves therein, and by the most holy names of God, Agios, Tehirios Perailitus, Alpha et Omega, Beginning and End, God and Man-Sabaoth, Adanai, Agla, Tetragrammaton, Emanuel, Abua, Ceus, Elioa, Torna, Deus Salvator, Aramma, Messias, Clerob, Michael, Abreil, Achleof, Gachenas et Peraim, Eei Patris et Peraim Eei filii, et Peraim Dei spiritus Teti, and the words by which Solomon and Manasses, Cripinus and Agrippa conjured the spirits, and by whatever else thou mayest be conquered, that you will yield obedience to me, N.N. this instant, in the beautiful, mild, human form of a youth, and bring what I desire.

The form and ritual of ceremonial magic is the same in Egyptian, Jewish, Christian, and Mohammedan circles. Only sometimes the magical names vary. The Egyptians call on the names of their gods. The

Jews use the names of God and angels; the Christians add the name of Christ or of some saints; the Mohammedans insert the name of Mohammed. Each borrows from the others. Oftentimes the names are corrupted out of all resemblance to the original by ignorant copyists. *See also* SUPERSTITION

MARY

Mary is found as a very common name in all the European languages. In many it even has a connotation of girl or woman. In reverence to the Virgin many boys have been given the name of *Marie* or *Maria* as a middle name, sometimes even as a first or principal name, in Spain, Italy, France, and Germany. In Brittany, there is a widespread custom of putting boys under the special protection of the Holy Virgin Mother by giving them the middle name of *Marie*.

Outside of the English-speaking countries the most common feminine form of the name is *Maria*, and in this form it is common in Bulgaria, Germany, Greece, Holland, Hungary, Italy, Norway, Rumania, Russia, Spain, and Sweden. In France and Switzerland, *Marie* is the preferred form. Croatia, Lithuania, and Serbia prefer *Marija*, while in Lapland and Poland it is *Marja*. The Irish use *Muire* for the Blessed Virgin, but call their daughters *Maire*, feeling *Muire* is too sacred.

The meaning of Mary is thought by most authorities to be "bitterness," although some interpret it as "wished-for-child" or "rebellion." Many other definitions have been advanced, most of them highly fanciful. The first known bearer of the name was Miriam, the sister of Moses and Aaron, a Hebrew form which is a favorite name among the Jews.

The Virgin Mary made the name the most honored of feminine names. Although it was popular in the East, it was surprisingly slow in creeping into the Western church. The Crusaders first brought the name to Europe about the middle of the twelfth century, although the earliest instance appears to be a Spanish maiden who was martyred by the Moors at Cordova in 851. Only in the last three hundred years, with the increased attention by the Catholic church to the cult of the Virgin, has the name attained overwhelming popularity.

George M. Cohan, in 1905, wrote the song hit "Mary's a Grand Old Name." The sentiment was not new. More than three hundred years ago the French poet Théophile de Viau expressed the same idea in a single line, "Le plus beau nom du monde est celui de Marie" (the world's most beautiful name is that of Mary). It was Oliver Wendell Holmes who inquired,

> Where are the Marys, and Anns and Elizas,
> Loving and lovely of yore?

Lord Byron, in *Don Juan*, wrote:

> I have a passion for the name of Mary,
> For once it was a magic sound to me:
> And still it half calls up the realms of fairy,
> Where I beheld what never was to be:
> All feelings change, but this was last to vary,
> A spell from which even yet I am not free.

MEANING OF NAMES

In times past an infinitely small number of names have been applied without some awareness of their meaning. It would have been impossible for Adam to have named the woman God gave him without some consciousness of the meaning of the name. "And Adam called his wife's name, Eve [living]; because she was the mother of all living." Actually, it is safe to allege that all personal names have meanings.

In present-day life we seem to have lost all feeling for the meaning of names. When a person is asked what his name means, the answer will often be that it is just a name and has no meaning.

The Egyptians, Hebrews, Greeks, Romans, and all ancient peoples were highly conscious of the meanings of their names. All Greeks knew *Thucydides* (to the divine glory), *Demosthenes* (power of the people), *Polycrates* (to great power), *Alexander* (protector of men)—there was manna in names in those days.

MEANINGFUL NAMES IN LITERATURE

In writing fiction, since all the author has to put his ideas across to the reader are the words he uses, he cannot waste any by selecting names for his characters that do not have connotations that help to describe the character. Even the sound may be used to convey an impression of the one named. Colonel Blimp's name, for example, clearly hinted at the windiness of a cartoon character during World

War II. Dickens was an expert in selecting names that contained a subtle half-suggestion of other words in our language which are associated with the traits embodied in the characters he delineated.

A glance at the *Dictionary of Fictional Characters*, compiled by William Freeman in 1963 from over two thousand works of British and American writers, discloses that unusual names given to the fictional characters far exceed the proportion of such names found in ordinary life. The common, colorless names were reserved by most writers for minor characters and for common, colorless persons.

During the eighteenth and nineteenth centuries in England many playwrights and novelists gave names to characters baldly indicative of character or actions. Calling attention to a few of the well-known ones, there is *Squire Allworthy* in *Tom Jones* and *Mrs. Slipslop* in *Joseph Andrews*, both novels by Henry Fielding. *Lady Sneerwell* appears in Sheridan's play, *The School for Scandal*. *Sir Giles Overreach* is used by Massinger in his play, *A New Way to Pay Old Debts*; and *Sir Courtly Nice* is a character in a play of that name by John Crown. Colley Cibber wrote about *Sir Francis Wronghead* in the comedy, *The Provoked Husband*. *Thomas Aimwell* did aim well as the young hero of George Farquhar's play, *The Beaux' Stratagem*. *Tony Lumpkin* is well described in Goldsmith's comedy, *She Stoops to Conquer*. *Adam Overdo* is prominent in Ben Jonson's *Bartholomew Fair*. *Paul Pry* pries in the short play of that name by John Poole.

Professor Kemp Malone correctly wrote, "Fictitious characters with characterizing names are to be found in all literatures known to me." As a good Greek example he mentioned *Mentor* (counselor) of *The Odyssey* whose function was that of giving counsel to young Telemachus. Plautus, the Roman playwright, was aware of the significance of personal names and selected most appropriate ones, sometimes suggestive in several different respects. *Widsith* (long journey), the chief character of the seventh century English poem of that title, refers to the far and wide travels of the minstrel. Chaucer and Bunyan introduced characters with clear, meaningful names such as *Delight, Beauty, Desire,* and *Peace*. The Russian novelists employed many meaningful names.

Indeed, one characteristic of the author whose works survive throughout the years is the close attention given to the significance of the names of the characters. This use of appropriate names is one of the elements that makes the ancient Greek and Roman writers,

116

and the English-language authors, Chaucer, Fielding, Smollett, Scott, Dickens, Thackeray, Bernard Shaw, Faulkner, Sinclair Lewis, and many others giants in literature. The exception that proves the rule is none other than Shakespeare. He took many of his characters from history, but for his minor ones he was most careless. For example, the three Danish soldiers in the opening scene of *Hamlet* are Francisco, Bernardo, and Marcellus, hardly typical names for Danes. The other man, a friend of Hamlet, possibly a German, was called *Horatio*, neither German nor Danish.

METRONYMICS

Most surnames from a parent's name are from the father's name, but a few are derived from the mother's name and are called metronymics. However, surnames produced from feminine names are far from rare. There are *Ibbs* and *Ibbott* from *Ibb*, a pet form of *Isabel*, *Lett* and *Letson* from Letitia, *Sara* and *Sare* from Sarah, and *Alison* from a pet form of Alice. *Marion* and *Marriott* indicate descent from little Mary. *Margary* and *Margetson* and their variant forms are derived from Margaret. The surnames *Till, Tilley, Maud*, and *Mawson* arose from pet forms of Matilda. All the common feminine names of the Middle Ages are found in surnames. Some names could be either a patronymic or a metronymic. *Emmerson* could be the son of Emma or the son of Emery. Some metronymics have other derivations. *Mayson* is explained as the son of May, although it is also a variant of Mason.

Some authorities have declared that metronymics indicate illegitimate birth, but this is not true generally. Some acquired their surnames from the mother as the more important, wealthy, or dominant parent, or the one with a markedly higher social status. In other cases the husband died and the posthumous child was brought up by the mother by whose name the child became known. Lengthy absence on the father's part due to military service tended to cause the children to be identified with the mother. A few metronymics were the result of adoption by female relatives. Some apparent metronymics were the result of female names applied as nicknames to effeminate men. Many Ashkenazic Jews took the names of mothers or wives as surnames, as *Sarasohn* (son of Sarah) and *Perlmann* (husband of Perl).

117

MEXICAN NAMES

Mexican names are little different from Spanish names. In modern Mexico, however, the *y* and *de* names have all but disappeared.
See also SPANISH NAMES

MIDDLE INITIAL

The use of an initial between the Christian name and the family name is a distinctly American custom. In today's busy life it serves a useful purpose in identifying an individual among others with the same forename and surname. Harry Cohen of Chicago found that he was receiving the mail of other Harry Cohens, and they were getting his letters. So he had himself listed as Harry N.M.I. Cohen to indicate that he had No Middle Initial.

At school the small boy gave his name as Henry H. Richardson. "What does the 'H' stand for?" asked the teacher.

"Henry" was the reply.

"But that is your first name."

"When my mother calls me, she yells, 'Henry, Henry'; and that is my name," explained the lad.

MIDDLE NAMES

Middle names throughout the world are of two principal types, (1) the patronymical form, designating the father, and (2) an additional given or Christian name. The patronymical form is the father's given name to which is added the proper national word, prefix, or suffix which designates the son. Both types have their merits and use in identification.

Everyone in our present complex civilization should have a middle name now that all that tedious work is being done by automation and the electronic machine is geared to note the middle name. The army and navy used the term "no middle initial," abbreviated *NMI*, for those rare individuals whose parents had been so thoughtless as to fail to provide them with one.

Spain was probably the first country to encourage the custom of giving more than one Christian name. There, double Christian names were not unknown as early as the year 1000 among the nobility.

Germany found the custom agreeable before the close of the fifteenth century. In England in 1628, Sir Edward Coke asserted that a man cannot have two names of baptism and what Lord Coke said was considered to be English law. No one on the *Mayflower* had a middle name. The custom in England of more than one given name became common only in the nineteenth century, although a few are found as early as the fourteenth century and several can be noted in the sixteenth century.

Before the middle of the eighteenth century, the use of middle names was quite rare in America. Among our first seventeen presidents only three had middle names; but among the last eighteen only three did not have middle names. In the United States about three-fourths of the men have middle names, and this has been true from the middle of the nineteenth century. The proportion seems to be growing. The German immigration, beginning more than a century earlier, gave impetus to the rise of middle names, as most of the Germans coming to America bore two or more given names. Many persons choose their own middle names. Jacob M. Arvey, when running for alderman in a predominantly Jewish ward in Chicago, adopted the middle name of *Meyer* when his rival spread the word that he was a Syrian. Middle names are useful when a parent wants to scold a child. Simply shouting "George Brown" is not enough to make him squirm. but if "George Washington Brown" is screamed, in rising accents, he will be set back on his heels good and proper. The sensible custom of giving a child the maiden name of its mother as a middle name is widespread in America and common elsewhere.

People with short first names and common last names are likely to insist on using their middle name. There is *John Quincy Adams, John Paul Jones, John Philip Sousa,* and *John Foster Dulles.* Others adopt the style of the first initial as *J. Pierpont Morgan* and *J. Edgar Hoover. John W. Davis* is the exception that proves the rule, and did the uninteresting form of his name have anything to do with his failure to secure election to the presidency in 1924?

Especially among girls there is a tendency to give a short middle name and use it constantly with the first name, as *Betty Jane, Mary Ann,* and *Barbara Sue.* Sometimes the two names are joined by a hyphen, as *Ruth-Ann, Mary-Margaret,* and *Sarah-Louise.* In other cases they are joined together, as *Roseanne, Joanellen, and Saralee.*

Like many parents, Sam Ealy Johnson, Jr., and his wife, Rebekah

Baines Johnson, could not agree on a name for the boy who was to become President Lyndon Baines Johnson when he was born on August 27, 1908, and he went nameless for three months. His grandfather, Sam Ealy Johnson, was known as Big Sam and his father as Little Sam, so there was no room for another Sam. He was finally named after Judge W. C. Lindon of San Antonio (his mother insisted on the variance in spelling) with a middle name, following the American custom of using the mother's maiden name.

When Mr. and Mrs. John Schulz were first married they decided to allow their children to choose their own middle name inasmuch as they had no choice over their first and last names. Their daughter, Mary, aged thirteen, finally made her selection in 1965—*Dontyaweep-dontyamourn*. She explained that she liked folk songs, and her favorite was "Don't Ya Weep, Don't Ya Mourn."

There was the child who acquired nine first names through the mistake of the clergyman baptizing him. The name selected by the parents was on the back of the paper listing the nine names considered by the parents which was handed to the rector, and he read off all of them before he could be stopped.

MOSLEM NAMES

Moslem (also spelled Muslim) religious custom requires that the personal name be drawn from the roster of the immediate members of the family of the Prophet and from the names in the Koran. This roster of names would seemingly tend to limit the total number of names in Islam, but the number is increased immeasurably by the custom of coupling a common word such as *Asad* (lion), *Nur* (light), or *Rahimat* (grace) with another word referring to Allah, religion, or the Prophet, such as *Asad Ullah*, *Nur Elahi*, and *Rahimat Ul-Islam*.

Muhammad, together with its many variant forms, is the most popular name for men among the Moslems. *Muhammad*, like Jesus, was a name that had been borne by other men both during and before the time of the Prophet and the Saviour. The name is from the root *hamida* and means "the praised one." The Prophet sometimes changed his name. Upon occasion he used *Abdullāh* (servant of God), *Ahmed* (the most praised), *Nabi Ulmalhamah* (prophet of war), and *Moukib* (last of the prophets). More than five hundred names have been applied to Muhammad some of which were in use during his lifetime.

The custom of naming children after the Prophet started even during his lifetime. *Ahmad* was sometimes given to children as an alternative to Muhammad. There is a belief that angels pray in every house where there is an Ahmad or a Muhammad. Some other variations of the name are *Hāmid, Hammād, Hamdan, Hamdūn, Humayd, Mahmoud, Mahmud, Mehemet* and *Mohamet*. With its variants, *Muhammad* is the most common name in the world. For girls, *Fatimah*, the name of the Prophet's daughter, is used by many. Converts to Islam generally take the name of an Islamic saint.

It is an old Moslem custom in many countries, especially the more backward ones, to let a man get by with just one name. Really, one name was sufficient in most cases. Children were seldom registered unless they were sent to school. Few families bothered to register their dead; marriages were made official with a family party.

In Tunis, a couple of years after freedom from France was gained, a law was passed that family names had to be adopted by September 1, 1960. Those who balked were offered a year in jail. Before the Tunisians gained their independence many an *Aly* avoided conscription because the *Aly* next door had already served. And *Aly* just did not come forward to volunteer to pay taxes.

In India the titles *Sayad, Saiyyid,* and *Syad* before the personal name indicate that the bearer is descended from the Prophet, or would like to be thought such. As the Moslem religion is prominent in *India, Turkey, Egypt, Persia, Jordan,* and *Arabia,* and subject to the laws of the land, the Moslem names vary somewhat.

To the religious Arabs Ramadan is the month when every good Mohammedan must fast during daylight hours. A man named Ramadan, making a journey through the Sahara, stopped for the night at a tent, asking for shelter. The owner took him in and, giving him food, asked his name. Never having heard the name before, the ignorant tent owner thought that Ramadan was the cause of the annual month's fasting. While the guest slept the Arab killed him. A few months later a sheik told the Arab, "Next month is Ramadan, and you must fast." "No," replied the Arab, "I don't have to fast any more because when Ramadan was in my tent I killed him; now there is no more Ramadan."

Ernest Brown of Jersey City adopted the Moslem religion and petitioned to change his name to *Nasir Ibnu-D-Din*.

See also ARABIC NAMES; IRANIAN NAMES

MOVIE NAMES

It has been estimated that more than 75 per cent of all performers in the entertainment field—screen, stage, television, and radio—appear under names especially selected for box-office appeal. Four principles are usually considered—brevity, clarity, euphony, and alliteration. Short names are important because they can fit well on theater marquees and credit notes. *Gary Moore* is better than Morton Goldpaper. Names must be easily understood when first heard. They must be pleasing to the ear. Alliteration aids memory. One writer has noted that among entertainers' names used at the present time the letter R has been prominent, as witness *Roy Rogers*, *Kathryn Grayson*, and *George Burns*.

Unlike singers, many from other countries have adopted Anglo-Saxon-type names. Dino Crecetti became *Dean Martin*; Margarita Cansino changed to *Rita Hayworth*; Anna Maria Italiano is now *Anne Bancroft*. Anthony Benedetto changed to *Tony Bennett*. But some movie personalities have kept their foreign names successfully instead of adopting easily remembered Anglo-Saxon names. There is *Horst Bucholz*, *Maximilian Schell*, and *Rossano Brazzi*.

There seems to be no valid reason for many changes of name among movie stars. Why should Edythe Marrener change to *Susan Hayward?* A nice name like Harriette Lake is just as good as the adopted name of *Ann Sothern*. *Shirley Booth* is no better than Thelma Ford. *Barry Sullivan* is no improvement over Patrick Barry. *Jennifer Jones* is not more sparkling than Phyllis Isley. *Dennis O'Keefe* is no more glamorous than Edward Flanagan. Why would Julie Wells become *Julie Andrews?* *Sally Rand* would achieve no more than Helen Beck. Diane Belmont would have been just as popular if she had not changed to *Lucille Ball*. When Kim Reid became *Kim Stanley* and Virginia McMath became *Ginger Rogers*, what did the change do for their careers?

The change from Issur Danielovitch to *Kirk Douglas*, Tula Ellice Finklea to *Cyd Charisse*, Judy Tuvim to *Judy Holliday*, and Frances Gumm to *Judy Garland* are readily understandable. Some with names too grandiloquent have found it advisable to adopt simpler names. Lucille Le Sueur achieved success among movie fans as *Joan Crawford*. Do some names require toning up? Ruby Stevens becomes *Barbara Stanwyck*, Peggy Middleton upgrades to *Yvonne De Carlo*, Norma Jean Daugherty converts to *Marilyn Monroe*. Some real names just do not describe the bearer and thus need alteration. William Henry Pratt had to become *Boris Karloff* to frighten people. Rose Louise Hovick could not do the things that *Gypsy Rose Lee* could; Joe Yule, Jr., must become *Mickey Rooney* and Diana Fluck must become *Diana Dors*.

The *Marx* brothers were in a poker game one night with Fred Fisher, a talented monologist, when he suggested that Julius, who then was playing the role of a strict school teacher, should call himself *Groucho*; Adolph, who played the harp, should become *Harpo*; Herbert, who then had his hair shaved off and resembled a monkey, should become *Zeppo*; Leonard, who liked to chase "cute chicks" should be referred to as *Chico*; and Milton, who wore his rubbers in rain or shine, should call himself *Gummo*. The suggested names were adopted and they became famous.

Henry Willson, a film agent, probably created more names for movie celebrities than any other man. His first coinage was *Lana Turner*. He said he named *Rock Hudson* (formerly Roy Fitzgerald) after the Rock of Gibralter and the Hudson automobile which he then was thinking of buying. He thought that Timothy Francis McGowan looked like the kind of man who could roar, so he named him *Rory Calhoun*; *Guy Madison* (Robert Mosely) was so called after the Dolly Madison cupcakes. He was also responsible for *Rhonda Fleming, Tab Hunter, Race Gentry, Chance Gentry, Tara Ashton, Jon Hall,* and *John Saxon*. Willson expressed his opinion: "I believe a new actor needs an unusual name to get him attention. A name must have flair and flash. Like Rex Reason. Most of the kids who come to me have names that are just dull."

Zsa Zsa Gabor, the actress, was named Sari after a Hungarian actress who was famous about the time Zsa Zsa was born. Zsa Zsa is said to be a Hungarian nickname for Sari. When a personality of the screen adopts a stage name there is almost always some previous connection with the name. Martha Janet Lafferty became *Janet Blair*, having been born in Blair County, Pennsylvania. Jesse Lasky was in a plane during a storm while searching for a name for Josephine Cottle; he landed with *Gale Storm*.

But some have resisted all temptations to change names. There are Hume Cronyn, Gregory Ratoff, Kuldip Singh, Alec Guinness, Danielle Darrieux, Elvis Presley, Yul Brynner, and Ernest Borgnine. Of course Rip Torn is Elmore (Rip) Torn the son of Elmore (Rip) Torn. *Rip* is an inevitable nickname for anyone with the surname of Torn.

Some other well-known cinema personalities are:

Movie Name	Real Name
Fred Allen	John Florence Sullivan
Eve Arden	Eunice Quedens
Desi Arnaz	Desiderio Alberto Arnaz de Acha III
Fred Astaire	Frederick Austerlitz
Jack Benny	Benny Kubelsky
George Burns	Nathan Birnbaum
Red Buttons	Aaron Chwatt
Eddie Cantor	Isidore Itzkowitz
Dennis Day	Eugene Denis McNulty
Doris Day	Doris Kappelhoff
Sandra Dee	Alexandra Zuck
Cary Grant	Archibald Leach
Kathryn Grayson	Zelma Hedrick
Jon Hall	Charles Locher
Tab Hunter	Arthur Gelien
Boris Karloff	William Henry Pratt
Danny Kaye	David Daniel Kominsky
Janet Leigh	Jeanette Helen Morrison
Jerry Lewis	Joseph Levitch
Frederic March	Frederick Bickel
Mary Pickford	Gladys Mary Smith
Edward G. Robinson	Emanuel Goldenberg
Ginger Rogers	Virginia McMath
Roy Rogers	Leonard Slye
Soupy Sales	Milton Hines
John Saxon	Carmen Orrico
Robert Taylor	Spangler Arlington Brugh
Danny Thomas	Amos Jacobs
Rudolph Valentino	Rodolpho d'Antonguolla
John Wayne	Marion Michael Morrison
Shelley Winters	Shirley Schrift
Natalie Wood	Natasha Gurdin
Ed Wynn	Edwin Leopold

Mary Ellen Powers, the movie starlet, glamorized her name to *Mala Powers*, saying that, "*Mala* is a little bit of everything; in Eskimo it means 'brave'; in Latin it is 'bad'; in Russian it is 'little'; in Dutch it is 'peculiar'; and in Burmese it is 'good.' "

MULTIPLICATION OF SURNAMES

The number and variety of surnames in use have been greatly increased through corruption in numerous ways. Some of the more important, as outlined by Arthur Folkard, in 1886 are:

Corruption by scribes' use of Latin. A Latin termination was added to proper names. Also there being no *w* in the Latin alphabet, that letter had to be omitted.

Corruption by the use of abbreviations. When all writing was in longhand, many proper names were abbreviated, as *Thomas* to *Thom̄.* When personal signatures began to be used extensively (about the end of the fifteenth century) one might refer to documents for guidance to see how his name was written, and might adopt the abbreviated form.

Corruption by changed national pronunciation. For example, the final *e* of a name might retain the accentuation and the *r* be dropped as an excrescence, as *Folker* becoming *Folke.*

Corruption by synonymous employment of letters. In older times *e* and *y* were given similar pronunciation and *Dorothy* might be spelled *Dorothe; Carre* for *Carey.*

Corruption by use of the plural form. *Folke* could easily be corrupted to *Folkes* and *Brigg* to *Briggs,* with no patronymical connotation.

Corruption due to lack of arbitrary spelling. Before the wide use of dictionaries, every man spelled as he chose at the moment.

Corruption due to local pronunciation. Dialectal variations change the spelling. For example, the soft *l* has not been maintained in the northern counties in England and in Yorkshire. *Folk* has become *Fawke* and *Fock.*

Corruption due to use of various languages. In England, the contemporaneous use of Saxon, Latin, and French has given the same name various forms. We have *Fairfield, Belfield,* and *Bonfield,* all with the same meaning.

Corruptions due to indiscriminate use of vowels and consonants. In earlier times the clear distinction between vowels was not in vogue as it is today. Among others the consonants *P* and *B* were interchangeable as in *Bullinger* and *Pullinger.*

125

MY NAME IS A POEM CLUB *See* NAME ORGANIZATIONS

NAME AS REPUTATION

"Name" is synonymous with reputation in most of the languages of the Western world. Perhaps they have been influenced by the Hebrew. In the Old Testament the "Name" of God is used many times to designate His exalted reputation, attributes, or presence. In I Kings 9:3, God says, "I have hallowed this house, which thou hast built, to put my name there for ever; and mine eyes and mine heart shall be there perpetually." In Proverbs 22:1, it is said that "a good name is rather to be chosen than great riches," and, in Ecclesiastes 7:1, it "is better than precious ointment." In most languages there are common folk sayings attesting to the value and importance of a good name. The Chinese say, "He who does good hands down a fair name for a hundred generations."

When one makes a reputation for himself it is said that he has made a name for himself. There is no better way to describe a good or bad reputation. The Lincoln National Life Insurance Company advertises, "Its Name Indicates Its Character." That names could be intertwined with personal behavior is evidenced by our speaking of a "bad name" when we mean a name that has been borne by one who acquired a bad reputation.

It was Shakespeare, in *Othello*, III, iii, 156, who wrote:

> Good name in man and woman, dear my lord,
> Is the immediate jewel of their souls:
> Who steals my purse steals trash; 'tis something nothing;
> 'Twas mine, 'tis his, and has been slave to thousands;
> But he that filches from me my good name
> Robs me of that which not enriches him
> And makes me poor indeed.

Bardsley, that early onomastic authority, said, "A good name is as a thread tyed about the finger to make us mindful of the errand we came into the world to do for our Master." An old English proverb crudely sets out the use of a good name: "He who but once a good name gets may piss abed and say he sweats."

After the Civil War General Robert E. Lee was invited to become president of a life insurance company at a salary in five figures, but he explained that he knew nothing about the insurance business. His prospective employers replied that they did not need him for his knowledge of the insurance business but that what they really wanted was the use of his name.

"Well," replied the General, "if my name is so valuable, don't you think that I should be very careful how it is used?" He rejected their offer and became president of a small college at a salary of $1,500 a year.

NAME CALLING

In these days when one is called a *dirty Red*, it may mean that he is thought to be an unclean Communist or maybe just one who is so indiscreet as to disagree with the speaker. If one is a Communist, it is better to call another person a *dirty Fascist*, particularly if sanitation is important. Some of the worst controversial names you can call a man relate to his spiritual beliefs or lack of beliefs, such as *infidel, romanist, ritualist, dissenter, deist, atheist,* and *evangelist.* Other terms of disrespect which can be applied to one who takes issue with one's opinions are *liberal, radical, conservative, isolationist, extremist, warmonger, do-gooder, agitator,* and *Nazi.* In Franklin D. Roosevelt's day some of the opprobrious terms were *capitalist, constitution-wrecker, demagogue, dictator, economic royalist, rabble-rouser, Tory, plutocrat,* and *utopian,* all capable of being enunciated in a throaty way which nestled about them all the opprobrium they contained. With the decline in recent years of the colorful cuss word these terms of vilification have come to the fore.

All these words and phrases are demons; the dictionary meanings are not important. One who can coin a few colorful, vigorous epithets can exert great influence in a democracy. Future generations will come up with other hate labels just as nebulous and just as evil to which can be attached the pejorative "dirty" or "damn." In years past the labels were *mobocrat, doughface, barn-burner, cane-bully, copperhead, carpetbagger,* and *scalawag.* These terms have lost their force. Labor's demon words were *anarchist* (after the 1886 Chicago Haymarket riots), *capitalist,* and *fink.*

Archie Cameron, the speaker of the Australian Parliament in 1952, compiled a list of names covering seven foolscap pages, which, he declared, members could not call him or each other. All had previously

127

been used in parliamentary sessions. He listed such beauties as *blatherskite, gasbag, chattering jackass, jabbering nincompoop, knave, idiot, lapdog, liar, skunk, slimy reptile, body-snatcher, cad, ignoramus, imbecile,* and *insect.* Some thought that he should have compiled a list of names which members could call each other.

The enthusiastic use of impressive epithets is an old habit that has flourished from time immemorial among politicians in England and the United States and elsewhere. The practice must be somewhat effective else it would not be used so much. Of course, the victim can always reply primly that calling names is proof that one has run out of logical arguments. Elbert Hubbard said, "If you can't answer a man's arguments, all is not lost; you can still call him vile names." Others have pointed out that you cannot properly hate a man or group of men until you have labeled him or them with some unpleasant epithet.

Since they have been successful in inducing people to capitalize the initial letter of *Negro,* several minor Negro groups have crusaded for some term to replace *Negro* with a definite, adequate name for their people in America, but have not been able to come up with a satisfactory substitute. They have suggested *colored American,* and *Afroamerican.* Those favoring the latter term have urged the use of the over-all name *African* for all indigenous people of Africa.

When the proper dowager instructed her new maid before the big reception, "From six to six-thirty I want you to stand at the door and call the guests' names as they enter," she received the reply, "Oh, I've wanted to do that for a long time. Some of them deserve it."

NAME COLLECTORS

Many follow the hobby of collecting unusual names. One can ride it at any time and follow the quest within doors or out. Indoors the only equipment necessary is a telephone directory. If one is satisfied without extensive travel in foreign countries, the hobby is inexpensive.

Henry Ladd Smith, who calls himself a namephomaniac, or "nut about collecting names," came across Dr. *Pacifico D. Quitiquit.* He observed, "There, I thought sadly to myself, but for the grace of God goes Henry Smith." Others interested in namesmanship have been called onomatologists, onomasts, nomenclaturists, and nomenclators. C. J. Furnas described himself as a namester. Clare Booth Luce, the writer, former congresswoman and former ambassador, also has a hobby of collecting odd names. Some of her favorites are *Lala Legattee Wiggins, Stanley Toogood, Effie Bowleg,* and *Polycarp Pridgen.*

Dave Garroway, the television personality, reported that he had received letters from *Merriweather Trivelpiece, Aspidia Snitch, Tabaca Blacksheep, Iva Headache, Marietta Avenue Jeeter, Vaseline Malaria, Soda Waters,* and a big happy-birthday card from the Green family who had named their children, *Bee, Ivy, Lettuce, Myrtle, Olive, Sage,* and *Paris.*

E. V. Durling has gathered odd names, such as *Ten Million* of Seattle, Washington, and *St. Elmo Bug* of Beverly Hills, California.

Stanley Walker, the late, noted Texas journalist, collected the odd names he encountered in newspapers. Some of them are: *Fice Mook, Trammer W. Splown, Gulley Cowsert, Buckshot Magonicle, Teemer Furr, Sepnoress Gorce, Phoebe Beebe, Heathcliff Heimerdinger,* and *Honeysuckle Ginsberg.*

One observer noted with regret the death of *Ah Fatt,* the Malay Communist leader in 1957. *Ah Fatt* he had hoped some day would be photographed with Vietnam official *Mee Thinh.*

Many odd names are listed by Nathaniel Bowditch in his *Suffolk Surnames* (three editions, Boston, 1857, 1858, and 1861), such as *Nothing New, Mama Mason, True Scales, Miss Submit Nutting, Napper Tandy,* and *Coplestone War Bampfylde.* Several other writers have compiled collections of odd and unusual names.

See also ODD NAMES

NAME-DROPPERS

Casually mentioning the name of a prominent person with whom one has had some contact in order to impress one's hearers is an ancient and well-documented practice indulged in by all, but especially by the natives of New York, Hollywood, and Miami. The name-dropper's biggest worry is accuracy. If he refers to Bernard Baruch as "Barney" when some present know that his real intimates called him "Bernie," the results could be embarrassing. Charlie Rice (we must mean Charles) has called name-dropping the most hazardous sport in the world next to Russian roulette.

If one knew President Johnson before he became chief of state, or Marilyn Monroe before she became shapely, or Richard Nixon before his school days ended, it is all right to refer casually to them in talking with acquaintances and thus fatten one's ego. Entertainers and announcers are fond of the practice. When they speak of a famous man he is never just an acquaintance. He is always an old friend. Most writers are guilty of name-dropping. The practice appears to exude authority to the uninitiated. One accused name-dropper defended himself with the plaintive assertion, "Last week Bob Hope told Hubert Humphrey that I'm NOT a name-dropper."

A particularly obnoxious form of the habit is the casual dropping of first names only. The person who refers to lunch with Bobby and means Robert Kennedy, or Harry when he means Truman should be ignored in any polite society. There was the man who spent the evening talking about Adlai. Finally when Stevenson entered the room, a heckler asked the fellow to introduce the man. "Oh, I didn't mean Adlai Stevenson," the dropper said, "I was talking about Adlai Sponitz."

There is nothing a girl enjoys more than name-dropping—especially her maiden name. Mel Allen once remarked that a Hollywood name-dropper is an actress who keeps getting divorced.

A legitimate exercise of the practice of careful name-dropping is often observed on the letterheads of charitable committees and organizations soliciting funds. Unless the "Big Names" sponsoring the organization are listed, little support can be expected from most people. They need assurance that their contributions will be used properly, and they are relieved to see names they recognize. For example, the campaign put on by the Crusade for Freedom was successful because of the skillful collection of the "right" names used in the successive drives. The directors enlisted an important sponsor from every dominant opinion group in America and carefully excluded names not the "best" ones, that is, the controversial ones. In England the names of the nobility are most useful because the title exudes importance even though the particular man may not be known.

See also USE OF FIRST NAMES

NAME GAMES

There are many games built around names. One of the best known is the old one of "Knock-knock." One says to a friend, or bored companion, "Knock, knock." He inquires, "Who's there?" The answer might be "Sarah." The friend asks, "Sarah who?" and the punch line comes, "Sarah doctor in the house?" This is pretty funny to children under the age of eighty-two.

Or, "Who's there?" "Morris." "Morris who?" "Morris Saturday and then comes Sunday." Again, "Felix who?" "Felix cited."

Another, "Hello, this is Mr. Zark." "Which Mr. Zark?" "Noah— Mr. Noah Zark."

Charlie Rice reported that the French have doubled the names required to produce something like the following: "Hello, this is Mrs. Warner-Cracker." "Which Mrs. Warner-Cracker?" "Polly— Mrs. Polly Warner-Cracker."

Orson Bean is alleged to have come up with, "Hello, this is Mr. Buggy." "Which Mr. Buggy?" "Orson—Mr. Orson Buggy."

Or, "Hello, this is Mr. Peace." "Which Mr. Peace?" "Warren— Warren Peace."

A diversion, also promoted by Charlie Rice, is to marry well-known personalities to others, to produce new names. Thus if the late King Farouk's former wife, Narriman Sadik, married former Governor Harriman, her name would be Narriman Harriman. Sally Ann Howe might be married to Rudy Vallee to become Sally Vallee. Rhonda Fleming would have to marry Henry Fonda to become Rhonda Fonda. If Tuesday Weld married Hal March's son, who would be Hal March the 2nd, she would become Tuesday March the 2nd. While waiting for him to grow up she might marry the grandson of the late great evangelist Billy Sunday to become Mrs. Tuesday Sunday. That would confuse people.

Another game, called Improbable Authors, is to attach famous people as authors of famous songs, books, plays, or slogans. Thus it could be "Charley's Aunt" by Immanuel Kant; "Ivanhoe" by Brigitte Bardot; "Huckleberry Finn" by Bambi Lynn; "Tom Sawyer" by Charles Boyer.

Rearranging the letters in a name to form a slogan or phrase relating in some way to the person is an interesting game. For example, when Franklin Delano Roosevelt ran against Alfred Landon, a Republican supporter twisted the president's name to "Vote for Landon, ere all sink."

Another recreation is drawing a picture or caricature of a person merely by printing or writing the letters of his name one over the other. More complicated is to draw a church or house using only the names of the members or residents.

See also ACRONYMS; ACROSTICS; ANAGRAMS; NAMES AND AD-DRESSES FORMING COMPLETE SENTENCES

NAME ORGANIZATIONS

American Name Society

This is an organization formed by a group of scholars in a conference on onomastics at the meeting of the Modern Language Association of America in Detroit, December 29, 1951, for the purpose of promoting and encouraging the study of all categories of names—geographical, personal, scientific, commercial, and popular—and the dissemination of the results of such study.

At the annual meetings, which are held at the same time and place as the meetings of the Modern Language Association, important papers are read by members. Some regional meetings are also held. The affairs of the society are administered by a president, three vice presidents, an executive secretary, and a treasurer elected for one-year terms and a board of managers consisting of the three most recent ex-presidents together with six managers elected for three-year terms.

At the present time there are about eight hundred members, including library members. Most of the individual members are engaged in academic pursuits, but anyone interested is eligible to join. The dues are $6.00 per year ($8.00 for library members) which includes a subscription to *Names*, a quarterly journal, published by the society.

International Congress of Onomastic Sciences

The International Committee of Onomastic Sciences is composed of one or more scholars interested in onomatology from all the important countries where work has been done on names. The secretary-general of the group is Professor Doctor H. J. van de Wijer of Louvain, Belgium. The committee was formed at the Third International Congress of Toponymy and Anthroponymy held at Brussels in 1949 for the purpose of organizing international congresses of onomastic sciences to be held about every third year at a time and place designated by the committee.

The following congresses have been held or are planned:

I Paris	1938	VI Munich	1958
II Paris	1947	VII Florence	1961
III Brussels	1949	VIII Amsterdam	1963
IV Uppsala	1952	IX London	1966
V Salamanca	1955	X Vienna	1969

At these congresses papers are read and discussed by internationally known onomatologists.

Lucy Stone League

This is a society founded in 1921 by Ruth Hale, consisting of aggressive feminists who insist on keeping their maiden names after marriage. The organization took the name of Lucy Stone, a militant American advocate of women's rights, who died in 1893. The members asserted that there was no law requiring the use by the wife of the husband's name. In 1925, after four years of struggle, one of its members, Doris E. Fleischman (Bernays), forced a passport from a reluctant State Department in her maiden name. Then after twenty-six years of frustration, trouble with hotel clerks, embarrassment at cocktail parties, and refusal of her parents and her children to use her maiden name, she gave up and took her husband's name. She said the fight had been "like swimming upstream through molasses."

The story is told that before Betty Smith, the novelist, divorced Joseph Jones, they used to travel extensively. When the trip was in connection with her work, they registered as Mr. and Mrs. Smith, but if it was just a pleasure trip, they used the husband's name. One time they were undecided as to the exact nature of their trip. A startled hotel clerk heard her question her husband, "Which shall it be this time dear—Smith or Jones?"

My Name Is a Poem Club

This is an informal group of persons whose first and last names rhyme, promoted by E. V. Durling, the newspaper columnist. In 1950, Hugh Blue was president of the club. It has been decided, facetiously, that a woman whose first name rhymes with the last only because of marriage is ineligible as otherwise a woman might marry an inappropriate man just to get into the club. The club governing body is deeply conscious of its social obligations.

133

There is *Jesse Lesse* of Boston, Massachusetts; *Merry Berry* lives in Chicago and so does *Max Wax*. *Hollie Jolley* calls San Bernardino, California, home. *Della Stella Serritella* comes from Chicago. *Jane Cane* is from Wheaton, Illinois, and *Newton Hooton* hails from Cambridge, Massachusetts. E. V. Durling cites his favorites as *Nancy Clancy* and *Truly Dooley*. *Kenny Tenny*, of San Francisco, together with his daughter, *Penny Tenny*, achieved membership. *Dick Vick* of San Diego has a son *Dick Vick, Jr*. Miss *Trudy Moody*, a bowler, lives in Newburgh, New York.

NAME STYLE

There are seven common, distinct styles in setting forth one's name. They are:

1. John Baker
2. John William Baker
3. John W. Baker
4. J. William Baker
5. J. W. Baker
6. Jack Baker
7. J. Baker

Most people definitely prefer one of the above styles. The first style (John Baker) is the simplest and least formal. It is preferred by ordinary people who go in little for frills; politicians use it as they like to be thought of as "just folks." Those who want to be noticed by the full name (John William Baker) are ones who put both feet forward; they are sometimes clergymen who desire to be recognized. The use of style 3 (John W. Baker) indicates mature, conservative, middle-of-the-road traits. Persons who affect style 4 (J. William Baker) are thought to be individualists who have a high opinion of themselves, perhaps inclined to be somewhat vain. Those in the fifth category (J. W. Baker) are likely to be self-contained people who know what they want, shrinking somewhat from publicity. The sixth style (Jack Baker) is affected by persons who are friendly and easygoing, somewhat unobtrusive, and who give the matter little thought. On the other hand, some politicians often deliberately use this style to emphasize their folksy ways and to show that they are just common people who have the interests of the ordinary voter close to their hearts. The seventh style (J. Baker) is used by men with a self-derogatory attitude, and implies a feeling of unimportance or exaggerated modesty.

Of course there are grounds for adopting a certain name style other than the effect of certain personality traits. The principal one is the use of one or two initials to conceal a disliked Christian name. Another is because of a desire for more accurate identification, as when the surname is a common one, or a father or cousin is locally known by the same name. Initials may often be used to conceal sex, and sometimes nationality. One's attitude toward his name is sometimes affected by admiration for, or dislike of, another with the same or similar name. One named after a father who is loved and admired may tend to adopt the same name style.

A very slight, almost unrecognized, prejudice against people who use the initial of the first name with the middle name spelled out in full, does exist. Shortly before W. Averell Harriman was mentioned as a possibility for the Democratic presidential nomination in 1952 he dropped the W. As the head of New York State he was usually styled Governor Averell Harriman. W. Somerset Maugham, the late English novelist and playwright, reduced his name to Somerset Maugham. Many have dropped their first name to be known by just the middle name and surname. James Branch Cabell dropped his first name and then later resumed it. William Cabell Greet became Cabell Greet. George Bernard Shaw in his later career was just Bernard Shaw.

The custom of three-decker names was popular among literary men of the nineteenth century in America; there is William Cullen Bryant, Ralph Waldo Emerson, Henry Wadsworth Longfellow, John Greenleaf Whittier, Edgar Allan Poe, James Russell Lowell, William Dean Howells, and James Fenimore Cooper.

The use of a forename and surname separated by a middle initial (style 3) is now a definite American style which is sometimes ridiculed by our English brethren. This is the style used by almost half of the men in America. With married women the middle initial stands for either the middle name or the former surname. A much larger percentage of people in America receive the mother's family name as a middle name than anywhere else. Another American tendency, not common elsewhere, is to use the initial of the forename, the middle name, and the surname. Many Americans commonly use all three names in full. In England, the prevailing custom is to use the initial letters of both the first name and the middle name with the family name. There is H. G. Wells, G. K. Chesterton, A. E. Housman, D. H. Lawrence, and W. H. Auden. A well-known American who followed the English in this respect was H. L. Mencken. A surname preceded by only one initial is very seldom seen, possibly because it does not properly identify the bearer. Hyphenated names are common in England, very rare in America. Pet forms of names with surnames are common in the Midwest and South.

The style used in signing letters depends almost entirely on the degree of intimateness with the person to whom the letter is addressed. If it is a close friend of either sex, the signature is likely to be the first name only, or if known by an approved nickname, that form would be used. To strangers or important persons the usual name style would be employed.

The style in oral communication is quite different from that in formal writing. In introducing oneself to a stranger quite often only the first and last name are enunciated. On the telephone the efficient style would usually be *John Baker*, *J. W. Baker*, or *Mr. Baker*, although the Christian name or a nickname alone is used in calling a close friend. An efficient businessman may use only the surname. The full three-name form would be used only in an oratorical or flowery introduction or in a humorous way.

In 1953 in Greensboro, North Carolina, an attorney asked a witness to spell her name. She replied "P-E-O-P-L-E-'S." "What is the apostrophe for?" he asked. "That's so folks can distinguish me from other Peoples," she explained.

NAMES AND ADDRESSES FORMING COMPLETE SENTENCES

Another line of useless endeavor is finding persons whose names and addresses form complete sentences. Some, which could be more than slightly fictitious are: Wenn Knight Hood, Wuzzin, Fla.; Doan B. Sow, Finny, Ky.; and S. Topp York, Illing, Me. Bennett Cerf has collected many, some of which are: Hans R. Dirty, Jr., Goan, Wash.; G. Thereza Mighty, Pretty, Miss.; Ide Lamy, Down, N.D.; Lettice Finder, Shady, Del.; I. M. Phelan, Slightly, Ill.; C. U. Sunday, Early, Mass.; Daniel Inner, Lyons, Tenn. Go thou and do likewise.

NAMES DISCLOSING AGE

Some Christian names are definitely linked to age. Girls born around 1915 or 1916, when Zita, the Empress of Austria and Queen of Hungary, was crowned, sometimes received the name of *Zita*. During World War I boys became *Joffre* and girls *Joffrette*. Numerous French children during the Revolution were registered as *Marat, Robespierre,* and *Danton*. Others received such names as *Plein d'amour pour la patrie* (full of love for country), *L'ami du peuple* (friend of the people), *La mère du peuple* (mother of the people), and *L'aurore de la liberté* (dawn of liberty). It was not until 1803 that the French authorities adopted a law regulating the registration of given names. A provincial registrar in 1892 was shocked to learn that one man desired to register his daughter as *Syphilide* and refused to reconsider until the old 1803 law was brought forth to save the baby from a catastrophe she could never live down.

People do insist on naming children after names in the news. When Khrushchev came over in 1959, Mr. and Mrs. Eugene Fleming of Belzoni, Mississippi, named their eighth child *Nikita*. In Hope Mills, North Carolina, Mr. and Mrs. Walter Street burdened their sixteenth child with *Nikita Khrushchev* Street. Girls with the names of *Invasia* (June 6, 1944, landing in France) or *Pearl Harbor* advertise their age. Whenever a president is elected, many of the babies born that day carry his name. At the end of World War II, some babies were named *V-J* and *V-E*. Others were named *Victor* or *Victoria* which, although commemorating the surrender, were not so blatantly precise.

A girl named *Comet* was told that she was born in 1910 because it was remembered that Halley's comet made an impressive appearance that year. A gentleman in Detroit was named *Halley Comet*. *Alma* had a temporary vogue following the battle of Alma in 1854. *Balaklava* and *Sebastopol* produced names for English infants unable to make their objections heard.

When people bear certain names connected with some outstanding public event, their age is forever known. Such persons as *Herbert Hoover* Schmidt, *Dempsey Tunney* Miller, and *Armistice* Jones carry their age in their names—something like keeping the price tag on their coats. Other names quite clearly disclose the generation of the persons who bear them. Many *Shirleys* were born when Shirley Temple was popular. Naming after a celebrity does definitely date one because

137

such names are usually adopted when the famous one has just been in the front-page headlines. Some names date the bearer by reason of the shifting winds of fickle fashion. Many women named *Pearl, Rose, Ruby, Jewel,* or *Violet* were born before World War I.

Mamie Eisenhower's middle names are *Geneva Doud.* Her mother took Geneva from the song "Lovely Lake Geneva," popular at the time the former president's wife was born. At the bottom of the sheet music, in tiny Roman numerals, is the date the song was published. Boys named *Dwight* are likely to have been born about the time Eisenhower was first elected president. Boys named *Franklin Delano* (Roosevelt) are all about the same age.

NAMES THAT ARE NOT WHAT THEY SEEM

The origin of many surnames is not what it appears to be. Many derived from place names, especially, are corrupted into other names and are given erroneous derivations. Sandhurst becomes *Sanders,* Plumbergh becomes *Plumber* and *Plumer,* Luckhurst reduces to *Lucas,* and Dickleston has become *Dickson.* Smeeth, the place name from Old English *smēthe* (level field) produces *Smith,* the occupational name. *Waters* does not refer to the thin fluid found under bridges, but to the son of Walter, from the common, early pronunciation of the name. The pet form was *Wat. Rainbow* is a corruption of the Old English *Reginbeald,* while *Rainbird* comes from *Rambert* and *Raginbert. Bedward* does not refer to a lord of the bedchamber but derives from the Welsh patronymic *ap-Edward. Bride* is from Old English *bridd,* a bird, a dweller at the sign of the bird, or one with birdlike characteristics.

Deadman and *Dedman* had these names long before they passed to the other world. The bearers or their ancestors merely came from Debenham, in Suffolk. *Quarterman* was not a fraction of a man; the name comes from the French *quatremains* (four hands, i.e., mail-fisted). *Gotobed* might be what it says (there was the Early English name *Gotokirke*), but it probably is a corruption of the Teutonic names *Godbert* or *Godeberd. Godbehere* is probably a corruption of good beer, although some authorities think that it may be a nickname from habitual use of such a phrase as "May God be here [in this house]," and that explanation cannot be ruled out entirely. Illogical and capricious fashions play so conspicuous a part in name-giving that accurate interpretations are most difficult.

138

Names derived from other languages are sometimes words in English. *Kiss* is a very common name in Hungary describing the small man. *Grass* designates the large or fat person in France. Other names are corrupted from various languages to the sound and spelling of English words. *Twopenny* is from Tupigny in Flanders; *Littleboys* is from French Lillebois. *Grumble* is a corruption of Old German Grimbald (helmet, bold).

Lieutenant Daniel Litt was a chaplain at a naval district headquarters in California when a telephone call came for another chaplain. The secretary answered, "We only have one chaplain here just now, and he is Litt." She realized what she had said when the caller quietly hung up after an embarrassed silence.

See also ORIGIN OF SOME ODD NAMES

NAMESAKES OF THE FAMOUS

Individuals bearing the names of famous people are often the butt of amateur gagsters. The Washingtons are not an extremely small group, and some of them are baptized George. They are sure to have someone call them on February 22 at about 3 A.M. to wish them a happy birthday, and to ask about Martha. Harry Truman tells of a nephew named after him, a sergeant in World War II, whose name almost deviled him to death.

Claus is found in all the large city directories. Every Christmas people surnamed Claus receive telephone calls from youngsters wanting to talk to Santa. Some of the Clauses go along with the caller and carefully explain that Santa is busy and take a message for him. That seems to satisfy some children who feel that talking to the relatives of the great man may get their wants relayed to Santa himself.

A baby born on April 4, 1888, near Marshall, Missouri, to Mr. and Mrs. William Claus was christened Santa, and Santa Claus was duly registered at the Saline County courthouse. He broke his leg in 1929 and came to national prominence, after which he was deluged every year with the familiar "gimme" letters from children. When he tries to register at a hotel, he has trouble. Calling a stranger on the telephone is likely to result in a slammed receiver when he discloses his name, and cashing a check in a strange place is most difficult.

Some persons with renowned names have been forced to take an unlisted telephone number to avoid annoying telephone calls from practical jokers. Paul Revere, of Boston, actually a direct descendant

139

of the original, was compelled to adopt this remedy for a while because wits (or at least those who had attained half that status) would dial his telephone number in the middle of the night and, after the admission that his name was Paul Revere, shout, "Quick, get on your horse, the British are coming."

Many persons who have names made famous by others report that they are an asset. People remember them longer. Robert E. Lee, for example, is today a popular name in the South. In introductions, the ice-breaking potentialities are rife. With particularly well-known but uncommon names, such as Julius Caesar, people think the bearer is jesting, and then a driver's license or other identification card is a necessity.

Following an old Texas ranch-country custom, Lyndon Baines Johnson has been giving calves to boys and girls named *Lyndon* and *Lynda* after him. A white-faced Hereford heifer is separated from the herd. When it is ready for the market, it is sent to the slaughter house, and the money is presented as a gift to the child.

There was the famous football player named Edgar Allan Poe. One Saturday when the stands were cheering his play, an absent-minded professor touched a student and asked, "Is he any relation of the famous Poe?"

"Great guns," exclaimed the astonished student, "He *is* the great Poe."

Theodore Bear, of Brooklyn, received so many calls from teen-aged wits that he took his number out of the directory.

See also IDENTICAL NAMES

NAMING BABY

In choosing a name for a baby, the only consideration to be kept in mind should be the welfare of the child, and the selection of an appropriate name that can be borne with pride and pleasure for a lifetime. Pleasing an adult should be no part of the process. Only if an adult's name is satisfactory in all respects should it be used. Zasu Pitts, the late character actress, had her name from the last two letters of Eliza and the first two of Susan, her nicest aunts. Children are likely to confuse the name with the person and thus find playmates attractive who have pleasant names. An unattractive name condemns the child to veiled social disapproval.

One Pasquale wrote of trying to induce his sister to name her baby boy after him. He admitted that the kid might have to fight his way through school, and would be called *Pocky, Pasky, Pat, Porky, Packey*—everything but Pasquale—and that he would be embarrassed because others would have trouble pronouncing the name in making introductions. No consideration was given to the troubles the poor boy would encounter with the name—the uncle's pride was uppermost in his mind. Parents seeking to honor themselves by giving their names to their children often succeed only in producing a reflection of their immaturity. For responsible parents, naming a baby is more than just choosing a name one likes. To bestow a name that will be satisfactory for upwards of a hundred years is the goal.

Parents, even among primitive peoples, usually evince an interest in giving a child a "good" name, one that will benefit the child in infancy and in later life. Even when, through superstition, a child is named *Dirt* or *Filth*, it is with the object of protecting the child's life by convincing the evil spirits that it is not worth their trouble to injure it. The distressing names which were applied by the Puritans, such as *Hate Evil, Humiliation,* and *Dust,* were bestowed with the child's religious good in mind.

Naming children after political characters still in office is somewhat risky. If they become involved in a scandal, their names are tarnished. Even an ordinary change in regime may evoke second thoughts about the desirability of the use of their names. In Communist countries where a change of administration often involves the banishment and disgrace of the outgoing official, the name may prove a source of embarrassment to the child. Parents must sometimes hurry to change the children's names. After King Farouk of Egypt was forced into abdication and exile, many Egyptian fathers sought to change the names of sons who had been given the king's name.

Which parent selects the name? Often there is disagreement. Some follow the old-fashioned idea of letting the wife name the newborn child if a girl and the husband if a boy. There is the boy in the backwoods of Kentucky named "Either-One." The male parent wanted to name him Ulysses while the mother held out for Simon. To settle the matter they agreed to leave it to the local teacher who said, "Just name him either one," and they did.

An odd name holds a child up to ridicule by his classmates. The young person is sensitive to ridicule and feels impotent to retaliate. If the child matures early, his attitude is likely to mellow. As he is introduced to people throughout his life, he hears the same sophisticated repartee time after time and gradually ceases to begrudge new acquaintances the apparent enjoyment they derive from an observation they think is original. Nothing so advertises the ignorance or mental oddity of a parent as a queer or awkward name given to the offspring. Cute names may fit the baby but will be a millstone around his neck when he decides to run for judge of the supreme court or other position of honor. Trick spellings bring on the burden of causing him to have to spell the name for every new acquaintance throughout his lifetime. One sage has observed that giving a boy a name subject to ridicule is like painting a bull's-eye on his back. He must fight to defend himself. Names commonly borne by girls or commonly used for both sexes are embarrassing for boys. Boys' names for girls are less troublesome to them.

It is sometimes difficult to avoid trouble such as future ridicule when some cartoonist or comedian chooses a name for a character or connects a popular anecdote to what was an innocent name. When Mr. and Mrs. Duck named their son Donald in 1931, before Disney's cartoon character became famous, they had no way of knowing that Donald, a perfectly sensible and harmless name, might prove to be embarrassing. Mrs. Haskins named her baby *Exzema*. She explained that she saw the name in an advertisement and thought it a "purty" name.

In achieving euphony the following rules might well be considered:

1. Family names of two or three syllables should have two given names of one and two syllables in either order.

2. Family names of one syllable should have two given names of three and two syllables in either order.

3. Family names accented on the last syllable may have given names so accented.

4. Family names starting with a vowel should not be preceded by a name terminating in a vowel.

5. Overlapping consonants or combinations of consonants should be avoided, as Kathleen Norris, Bernard DeVoto, James Stevens, and Ruth Thurman.

6. Rhyming, or repeated syllables, should be avoided, as Charlotte Lott and Rosebud Dudley.

An illustration of the family tugging and pulling for their favorite name for the baby is the choosing of the name for that man who became president of the United States under the name of Ulysses S. Grant. His mother favored Albert, supported by her sister, Mary. A younger aunt voted for Theodore. Grandfather Simpson spoke up for Hiram, while his wife argued for Ulysses. The names were put in a hat, and Ulysses was drawn out. Thereupon the father, desiring to please his in-laws, proclaimed that the baby would be named Hiram Ulysses. It was at West Point that the name became Ulysses Simpson Grant.

Folklorist George C. Grise, after querying seven hundred students at Austin Peay State College in Tennessee to find out whom they had been named after, learned that 35 per cent of the boys had been named for their fathers and 17 per cent for their grandfathers. More girls were named after their grandmothers than mothers. About 60 per cent of all babies in America are named after close relatives, mostly parents and grandparents.

Parents with wealthy relatives have little difficulty in selecting names for the baby. Many Christian names are chosen to propitiate a solvent aunt or uncle, or with a desire to commemorate an important ancestor or honor a friend. Sometimes both parents seek to honor themselves by combining their names. Edward and Ina might beget *Edwina*, Charles and Eveline could produce *Charline*. Even John and Mary might produce an ugly *Joma*, and that would be no worse than Thomas and Catherine coming up with *Tomcat*.

Naming a baby after a medical term seems to be in the nature of cruelty to children, but there might be extenuating circumstances. On January 17, 1847, Dr. James Young Simpson delivered a baby painlessly to a mother rendered unconscious by ether, the first case of its kind. That baby was named *Anaesthesia* by the grateful mother.

The parents of the entertainer, *Eartha* Kitt, were farmers who reaped a good crop (after many barren years) the year before the singer was born, and expressed their gratitude to the land by naming her Eartha. Mr. W. J. Weaver, of Birmingham, Alabama, explained his initials: "My mother and daddy had eleven daughters in a row. When I came along they called me Welcome John."

The newspapers reported that Mrs. *Luquincy Raine Martha Jane Eldorado Julie Dean Delma Ruthie Matilda Felma Jacka Cina Sophi Husky Charlotte Moss Stone* Banks died at the age of 100 in Jasper, Alabama. She was known as *Lu-Ma*. Judge J. E. D. J. N. S. W.

143

E. D. Henderson observed his seventy-sixth birthday in Charlotte, North Carolina. His mother named him for his uncles, Jackson, Ezekiel, David, James, Nathaniel, Sylvester, Willis, Edward, and Demosthenes, in the hope that they would will him something, but they all passed on without leaving him a dime.

Those who have surnames that are common given names, such as the Welsh family names of *John* and *George*, have their troubles. When Delbert George attended the University of Arizona, a clerical mistake listed him in one class as both Delbert George and George Delbert. Although his attendance was regular, George Delbert appeared on the dean's list for failure to be in his proper seat in the classroom. It took him hours to straighten out the matter and clear his name as Delbert George. A Pennsylvania lad named Schwartzmeerkosaken Ralph always has to remind people that his family name is Ralph.

One father explained the name *Encore* for his new baby, saying, "Frankly, he wasn't on the program at all." J. John B. B. B. Brownlie said that he was christened by a minister who stuttered. Mr. Maximilian, a resident of Stafford, England, was so angry at the registrar that he named his son *Chusan Rishaithaim Maher-Shalal-Hash-Baz Dodo* Maximilian in order to provide work for the arrogant official. Hazel McMillin, a police officer in Spartansburg, South Carolina, and his wife, Hazel, could not think of any other name but Hazel, Jr., when their son was born in 1953.

One mother named her child *Verily* after consulting her Bible where Jesus said, "Verily I say unto you." Earl William "Madman" Muntz, a television manufacturer, and his wife, Joan Barton, a television actress, named their daughter *Tee Vee* in 1952. The William T. Day family of Gahanna, Ohio, named their two sons *Stormi Day* and *Raini Day*.

An Iowa couple told the attending doctor they wanted their thirteenth child named James, and he so noted it on the birth certificate. Later the father frantically telephoned the doctor saying, "Please change that name to Kenneth. We just realized we've already got a James."

There was the ancient history professor who took a long disapproving look at his newborn son. Upon being asked by the attending doctor what name would be bestowed, he answered, "We'll call him Theophilus."

"Isn't that a bit strong for the poor tyke?" asked the medical man.

144

"No," said the professor, "he's Theophilus looking baby I ever saw."

This article will end with "no mo," as the probably fictitious parents thought who named their boys *Eeny, Meeny, Miney,* and *George*— they didn't want no Mo.

When selecting a name for a baby twelve principles, or rules, should be closely followed:*

1. It should harmonize with the family name.
2. It should be easily spelled.
3. It should be easily pronounced.
4. It should carry with it only pleasant nicknames or pet forms.
5. It should not evoke unpleasant connotations or associations.
6. It should fit the nationality of the bearer.
7. It should have a pleasant meaning.
8. It should produce initials with a good meaning or pattern.
9. It should not create confusion with the namesake.
10. It should clearly identify the bearer.
11. It should not be so odd or unusual as to evoke constant comment.
12. It should designate the sex clearly.

See also FANCY NAMES

NEGRO NAMES

Not many Negro slaves were known to whites in America by the names they bore before they were captured and sold in Africa, and very few first-generation Negroes had African names, such as *Cuff, Juba, Mingo,* and *Mamadoe.* Before attaining freedom the Negroes in this country were known generally only by a single, simple name. The most common of these names, as compiled by Professor Newbell N. Puckett, who has made comprehensive studies of Negro names, were *John, Henry, George, Sam, Jim, Jack, Tom, Charles, Peter,* and *Joe* for males. For women the common names were *Mary, Maria, Nancy, Lucy, Sarah, Harriett, Hannah, Eliza, Martha,* and *Jane.* Additional epithets such as *Big, Old,* or *Fat* coupled with the other usual descriptive nicknames were used when necessary to distinguish one John or Mary from another on a big plantation. If further identification were needed, the master's name was used. If *Tom* belonged to a white man named

*These rules are discussed and explained in Elsdon C. Smith, *Naming Your Baby,* New York, 1943.

Henry, he would not be called *Tom Henry,* but *Henry's Tom.* The names were utilitarian, usually selected by the master in the same way in which he named his mules and cows. Among themselves the slaves were often known by a more intimate name, generally African in origin.

Present-day Negro names are not too much different except that instead of *Sam, Jim, Tom,* and *Bob,* it is *Samuel, James, Thomas,* and *Robert.* The favorite minstrel names of *Rastus* and *Sambo* are and have been extremely rare, practically nonexistent, in actual practice. Names like *Caesar, Pompey,* and *Plato* were not rare in slave times. Peculiar, unusual, and odd names found in the South are borne by both Negroes and whites. Researchers have found that there is not much difference between the given names of white and Negro women college students in the South.

The Negroes are the largest group to acquire family names in this country. Upon gaining freedom one of the first things they did was to assume a surname, to be like white people. They did not consider themselves to be perfectly free until they had taken a surname. The newly freed Negro wanted a name which indicated status. Such names as Tom C. Lincoln or Sam S. Douglas might be selected. The middle initial often did not stand for a name, but was considered to be an imposing decoration. The choice was limited to the family names of the whites they knew and admired, and the names of their former masters, although these latter ones were by no means emphasized, except for those who set them free. Before emancipation they just did not have surnames. The free Negroes in the North had surnames chosen from those of the whites around them.

As surnames were casually chosen by Negroes after Lincoln's Emancipation Proclamation set them free, they were as casually changed from time to time as the bearers came across one they liked better. In the early scattered Negro schools students adopted surnames or changed the ones first chosen. Booker T. Washington entered school as Booker Taliaferro. Negro children were often given complete names at baptisms in the many Negro churches which sprang up after liberation. But, particularly in the South, many Negros lived in illiteracy and temporarily adopted a surname only on the few occasions in their lifetime when it seemed important to have one.

During and after World War I many Negroes emigrated to the North, and the acquisition of jobs and service in the army stimulated more stable family names. Later, the Social Security Act, passed by

Congress in 1935, was a major contribution to the fixing of their surnames. The dominant position of the mother in Negro families often brought about transmission of the mother's surname to the offspring rather than the father's name.

Washington is a popular name among the Negroes, although the reason for the first president's popularity with them is not entirely clear. It is said that four-fifths of the persons using that surname are Negro. On the other hand, the names of *Lincoln* and *Grant* were not adopted by many Negroes. White benefactors of the Negro race have not been memorialized in the names chosen by the freed slaves, with the possible exception of General Oliver O. Howard, commissioner of the Bureau of Refugees, Freedmen, and Abandoned Lands, and founder and president of the Negro school, Howard University in Washington, D.C. A substantial proportion of those bearing the name Howard are colored.

Brown, Johnson, Jones, and *Williams* are much more popular among Negroes in proportion to the population than among Southern whites. Other common surnames among Negroes are *Harris, Jackson, Robinson,* and *Thomas.* The Negroes have a tendency to put a final *e* to names like *Browne, Clarke,* and *Greene.* Place names, descriptive terms, and occupational names were not particularly popular with the Negroes; they leaned much more to the well-known English patronymics.

NICKNAMES

A nickname is a name or epithet added to, or substituted for, the usual or proper name of a person, mainly applied in pleasantry, ridicule, or even opprobrium. The word *nickname* comes from coalescing the Middle English words "an eke name," that is, "an also name," into a *nekename* which became *nickname.* According to Professor John A. Wilson, the famous Egyptologist, many in ancient Egypt were known to each other by such nicknames as *Mouse, Ape, Cat, Donkey, Frog,* and *Grasshopper.* Others were known as *Big Head, Baldy, Happy, Gloomy, Lazy,* and *Nosy,* not different in signification from common, present-day epithets.

Many early nicknames were crudely accurate in description. Those that became family names tended to be altered or changed for others with a more pleasant connotation. Eilert Ekwall, the great Swedish onomatologist, has found the following in London records of the

147

twelfth and thirteenth centuries: *Agodeshalf* (for God's sake), *Bredhers* (with flat posteriors), *Carles* (careless), *Forfot* (pig feet), *Gos* (goose), *Holebagg* (hollow bag), *Holebuc* (hollow belly), *Hore* (dirt or filth), *Huniteil* (honey tail), *Illefoster* (bad offspring), *Lambesheved* (lamb's head), *Milksop* (piece of bread soaked in milk), *Nagod* (no good), *Pudding* (a kind of sausage), *Pullegos* (plucked goose), *Quachehand* (shaky in the hands), *Scerehog* (lamb between shearings), *Smud* (dirty mark), *Stunch* (smell), and *Wigga* (beetle). In the Middle Ages almost every man was known among his neighbors by a nickname more or less harsh.

Studies conducted at several colleges show that people who have acquired nicknames, such as *Spike*, *Butch*, *Bud*, and *Mac*, tend to be more popular and better adjusted socially than persons who are without nicknames. Also people who are known by the pet forms of their Christian names have been found to have more outgoing personalities than those known only by their precise first names. A study at Harvard University disclosed that boys were more likely to flunk out if they had unconventional or peculiar-sounding names. People who are nicknamed are not the colorless, mediocre people, but persons distinguished by their prominent mental or physical qualities or by their outstanding actions.

Long or difficult names are likely to be shortened into a nickname, and this practice has been going on almost since time began. There was Pepiseshemsenefer, the royal treasurer in Egypt in 2600 B.C., whose tomb contained his picture and the fact that he was called *Senni* for short.

To one with an eye for status, nicknames are flattering from above and insulting from below. They can be affectionate, familiar, or contemptuous. They are given to pull people down, or to get closer to people, or even to reach them on an even keel. Some psychologists say that all nicknames are subconsciously meant to be belittling, an effort to bring others down to what one fears is his own level. Others contend that by applying a nickname to an important person a man is trying to move up rather than drag the other down.

Mrs. Eleanor Roosevelt said that as a child she was sometimes called *Totty*, and her father's pet name for her was *Little Nell*. After her husband attained the White House some old friends called her *Lady*, but to most of her friends she was Mrs. Roosevelt. She observed, "I would give much to inspire less respect and more sense of familiarity

148

and warmth." When asked if she thought the public would like to have its presidents and governors referred to more respectfully than by familiar nicknames, Mrs. Roosevelt replied, "I think anyone speaking to the President or to a governor always refers to him respectfully by his title. However, sometimes the nicknames are expressions of affection, and then I think anyone would be pleased and would not consider it lack of respect." When Queen Elizabeth II of England visited the United States, in October 1957, she was greeted with love and affection by people anxious to see and hear a "real queen"; the newspapers displayed their blasé sophistication by headlining her as "Liz."

One can do little about a nickname. Mrs. Lyndon Johnson, as first lady, only accepted *Lady Bird* as a nickname when she found that she could not shake it since her husband always liked it, and that Mrs. Claudia Alta Taylor Johnson, her real name, was unknown, except to a few very close friends. In *Who's Who in America* she is listed as Lady Bird, although the President, in his sketch, admits only that he married Claudia Taylor.

In regard to nicknames it can be said that people do not treat human beings any worse than they do dogs. They may call their dog *Pickleheimer* or *Einstein* and call their fellow weirdos *Saphead*, *Waterhead*, and *Scarecrow*. People just don't call their dogs *Fido* anymore. Nicknames used to be reserved for family and close friends. Nowadays no comedian, crooner, or screen star can be a success until he has acquired a nickname. In some cases it is even necessary to hire a press agent, adopt a nickname, and hope that fans will take it up.

Most of the radio, television, and screen stars have nicknames and as such they are known and called by the staff workers and their fellow actors. Many performers use nicknames and pet forms professionally, as *Rudy* Vallee, *Red* Skelton, and *Kay* Francis. *Bob* Hope reported that when on his first day in school in Cleveland he said his name was Les Hope the other kids quickly switched it to *Hopeless* which brought about several fights by the future comedian in defending his name, causing him a few bloody ski-snoots.

Society debutantes are just as likely to be known among their friends by a nickname as the ordinary workingman. Many debutantes are known by cuddly sounding nicknames such as *Itty*, *Fifi*, *Pinky*, *Tish*, and *Bunny*.

Psychologists have discovered that an inferiority complex can sometimes be traced to an offensive sobriquet. Nicknames that do not wear

149

well for children are *Sonny, Junior, Lefty, Fuzzy, Boo, Buttercup, Precious,* and *Goo Goo.* These should be avoided for babies. Names like *Cookie, Peanuts, Rusty, Red,* and *Speedy* are not particularly disliked. Children are attracted to the sport of attaching nicknames to others by their generally uncomplimentary nature. Boys are fond of applying nicknames from comic strip characters to their associates. They use them often without conscious effort and without mercy. Don't call a baby girl Daphne if you object to the nickname *Daffy,* or Celia if *Silly* is not pleasing to you. Young Peter Jenkins-Codd of Maidenhead, England, changed to his mother's maiden name of Hayward because he was about to get married and he did not want his future children teased as he had been. "At school, I was called Fishface and Codears," he said. "Kids even grabbed my hand and said 'Fish Fingers.' No child of mine will have to face that."

Often nicknames arise from the inability of a younger brother or sister to pronounce correctly the name given at birth. One Aloysius Hanlin had a brother who pronounced it *Aly,* and that name stuck. Queen Elizabeth II used to be called *Lilibet,* which was Princess Margaret's childhood way of lisping the name Elizabeth. Dame Edith Sitwell was called *Dish* by her younger brother, Osbert, who could not pronounce the last syllable of Edith.

Admiral William (Bull) Halsey, a mild-mannered man, is said to have acquired his nickname because a newsman hit the *u* on his typewriter instead of the *i*. The nickname caught on and the officer became Admiral *Bull* Halsey instead of *Bill.* The Indian religious woodcarver of Quito, Ecuador, Manuel de Chili, was better known by his nickname *Caspicara,* meaning "wooden face" in the Quechua language. Louis Kriloff, campaigning against archaic letter forms such as "Dear Sir" and "Respectfully Yours," earned the nickname of "The Dear Slayer." *Vera* Dull, of Wichita, Kansas, of course, became *Very* Dull. What else? A girl attending Oberlin College a few years ago acquired the nickname of *Bug.* A short time before there had been a play and a movie in which an invisible character named Harvey was a rabbit. When Bug dated Harvey in college he became known as Bug's Bunny, a reference to one of Disney's cartoon characters.

Some of the more common disagreeable nicknames are *Stinky, Jughead, Creep, Fatso, Bub, Hey, Big Mouth, Birdbrain, Fleabait, Numbskull, Horseface, Skinhead,* and *Gabby.* An Argentine court ruled that it was not defamatory to call President Frondizi, a tall thin man,

Skinny. Few tall men greatly resent being called *Longfellow, Long,* or *Longshanks*. As nicknames, *Freckles* and *Buddy* are generally unobjectionable. Persons with initials *K. C.* are likely to be nicknamed *Casey*. Every descriptive word or phrase is a possible nickname. E. V. Durling found nicknames very interesting. One of his favorites was the baseball star *Cool Papa* Bell. Others were *Mysterious Billy* Smith, *Wee Willie* Keeler, *Last Race* Cook, *Harlem Tommy* Murphy, and *Terrible Terry* McGovern. Berry and Van Den Mark, in their monumental *American Thesaurus of Slang* devote fourteen pages to a selection of nicknames under various classifications.

Criminals' Nicknames

A hoodlum has not been generally considered to have "arrived" in mob circles until he has acquired a colorful nickname from police, news reporters, or associates. In modern times the best publicized American hoodlum was *Scarface Al* Capone. He would never explain how he received the wounds on his left cheek and forehead except to say that they were "war wounds." It is believed that he got the scars in a knife fight in Brooklyn before making Chicago his headquarters.

Many criminals are better known by their nicknames than their given names. A hoodlum may go through a dozen aliases, shedding one name after another, but to his cronies he is often known consistently, and sometimes only, by his nickname. Often contact between members of the group is so casual that many never bother to learn last names. Sometimes a nickname spoken during a crime is heard by a witness, and the clue is a valuable one. At its Washington headquarters the FBI has a Nickname File of about 150,000 picturesque monikers used by criminals. There one finds such desperadoes as *Carbolic Kid, Clothesline Slim,* and *Gold Tooth Frenchy*. The "ladies" have even better titles: *Babbling Bess, Wild Cat Alma,* and *Iron Foot Florence*. The Detroit and Omaha police have nickname files which contain such entries as *Foot in the Grave, Stack of Dollars, Talcum Powder, Fire Cracker, Gospel Pat, Rigor Mortis, Water Dog, Popcorn, Lampblack,* and *Salty Dog*. An up-to-date roster of nicknames of lawbreakers is an important aid in apprehension. Sometimes these nicknames give a hint to the bearer's criminal specialty. *Fire Alarm* Brown would turn in a false alarm and then pick the pockets of the gathered crowd. *Step Ladder* Lewis, disguised as a painter, used the tool to get into second stories.

151

Smaller police departments such as that of Greensboro, North Carolina, have found a card index of criminals' nicknames very helpful.

Criminals' nicknames are likely to be more descriptive than ordinary citizens' monikers. *Shaky* will probably tremble; *Toad* or *Owl* may have some facial resemblance to the animal. A physical deformity is especially likely to give rise to a bluntly descriptive name. One who limps is *Limpy*; an ugly man is *Ape-face* or *Horse-face*. Some nicknames give a clue to the surname, as when one named John Crosby acquires *Bing* as a nickname, after Bing Crosby the actor.

The late and unlamented Arthur Flegenheimer, known as Dutch Schultz, complained of his nickname, regarding it as the chief source of his notoriety, as it made such a colorful headline in newspapers. If his real name had been used, he might have escaped the spotlight more often.

George Spelvin

In the theater this name is employed for an actor who is used for a mere walk-on role, or plays two parts in one play, or one part in each of two plays performed the same evening. Some authors use the name for the average American, or in writings where there is a policy against disclosure of the real author's name.

The name originated about 1905 at the Lambs Club in London when Edward Abeles, the late English comedian, obtained the role of Brewster in the play *Brewster's Millions*. Because of difficulties with the play the sponsor became discouraged, and the whole idea was about to be dropped. Abeles liked the part he was to play and suggested calling in an outside drama expert, exclaiming, "Oh, if George Spelvin were only here!" He was asked to get him. Considering how he could manufacture a mythical Spelvin, he went to the bar, where he found a young man, William Stone by name. Quickly outlining his plan he asked Stone to be Spelvin and pronounce the play to be a good one that should be produced. Stone joined in the plot, and the sponsor was induced to put up more money. Stone was given a small role as George Spelvin, and the play went on to a most successful run.

Inevitable Nicknames

Some nicknames inevitably attach themselves to certain surnames, especially in England. All men named Rhodes seem to acquire *Dusty* as a nickname, Millers are also known as *Dusty*; Clarks or Clarkes become *Nobby*; *Tug* is the nickname of all Wilsons.

152

According to Eric Partridge, A *Dictionary of Slang and Unconventional English*, these inevitable or inseparable nicknames came into being in the nineteenth and twentieth centuries, first in the British Navy, and then quickly spreading to the army. For example, calling Martins *Pincher* arose, he said, after Admiral Sir William F. Martin, a strict disciplinarian, "pinched," i.e., arrested many for minor offenses. These inseparable nicknames quickly spread to America, where many athletes acquired them. The origin of most of them is obvious from their relation to the surname, as *Shorty* Long, *Tippy* or *Sugar* Kane, *Trader* Horn, and *Spud* Murphy. Nicknames of this type are applied to men; they are rarely bestowed on women.

Some others of the most frequently heard nicknames with their surnames are: *Chalky* White, *Buck* Taylor, *Busky* Smith, *Chippy* Carpenter, *Cock* Robins, *Dan* Coles, *Darky* Smith, *Dickie* Bird, *Dodger* Green, *Fanny* Fields, *Foxy* Reynolds, *Ginger* Jones, *Gunboat* Smith, *Happy* Day, *Hooky* Walker, *Jack* Shepard, *Johnny* Walker, *Kitty* Wells, *Knocker* Walker or White, *Cottie* Collins, *Muddy* Waters, *Nutty* Cox, *Pony* Moore, *Sandy* Brown, *Shiner* Black, Bright, Green, White, Wright, *Shoey* Smith, *Spokey* Wheeler, *Timber* Wood, *Topper* or *Tupper* Brown, and *Wiggy* Bennett. Almost all of the common English family names have their inevitable nickname.

Nationality Nicknames

Every nation has numerous nicknames, or slang terms, usually unfriendly and opprobrious, to designate men of other nations. Following are some of the most common of these in English:

American: *Yank* (*Gringo* is used among Spanish-Americans)
Australian: *Aussie*
Canadian: *Bluenose* or *Canuck*
Chinaman: *Chink*
Czech and some other Slavic people: *Bohunk*
Englishman: *Limey* (*Gringo* by Spanish-Americans)
Filipino: *Fip* or *Flip*
Frenchman: *Frog*
German: *Fritz*
Hungarian: *Hunky*
Irishman: *Mick* or *Paddy*
Italian: *Dago* or *Wop*
Japanese: *Jap*
Malayan or Polynesian: *Brownie*
Mexican: *Greaser*
Pole: *Polack*
Russian: *Ivan*
Scotsman: *Jock, Mack,* or *Sandy*
Swede: *Olaf*
Welshman: *Taffy*

In 1951, in an effort to cement friendship with the United States, the Spanish Press censorship forbade the press from using the nick-name *Tito Sam* (Uncle Sam) on the ground that it might offend American sensibilities.

A. A. Roback collected many of these names, and pejorative words and phrases in A *Dictionary of International Slurs*, Cambridge, Massachusetts, 1944.

Presidential Nicknames

Washington had no intimate pet nickname. Various sobriquets have been applied to him, the best known being *The Father of His Country*. This term was first used by Francis Bailey, a printer who published an almanac in 1779 so describing Washington because he had taken such an active part in forming this independent nation. The two Adamses as presidents did not bring forth any particular nicknames, although, of course, various writers have come forth with some apt sobriquets. Jefferson was known as *The Father of the Declaration of Independence* and *The Sage of Monticello*. A tall man, his associates sometimes called him *Long Tom* or just *Tom*. Madison and Monroe were not known by affectionate nicknames.

Andrew Jackson was widely known as *Old Hickory*, a nickname first applied to him by his soldiers who said he was as tough as hickory when in 1813 he turned his horse over to ill or disabled men, and walked on a march back to Nashville, Tennessee. Martin Van Buren acquired the name of *Fox* from his shrewd handling of political matters. William Henry Harrison was dubbed *Old Tippecanoe* in commemoration of his victory over the Indians in the Battle of Tippecanoe. Neither Tyler nor Polk was particularly known by nicknames. Zachary Taylor was known as *Old Zach*. Fillmore, Pierce, and Buchanan did not rate familiar nicknames. Lincoln was well known as *Abe* and *Honest Abe*. Grant was sometimes called *United States Grant* and other epithets that were a play on his initials, *U. S.* Hayes, Garfield, Arthur, Cleveland, and McKinley did not acquire significant nicknames.

Theodore Roosevelt was affectionately known everywhere as *Teddy*; running for president he was often referred to as *Bull Moose* be-cause in answer to a question about how he felt, he assured the re-porters that he felt "like a bull moose." His children called him the *Old Lion*. Taft, Wilson, and Harding appeared not to have acquired really popular sobriquets. Because of Coolidge's reticence about his plans and politics he became known everywhere as *Silent Cal*. Possibly because of the troubles caused by the Depression, Hoover did not become well known by a nickname. On account of his long name, Franklin Delano Roosevelt was habitually mentioned in newspaper headlines as *F.D.R.*, the first of the popular presidential initialisms. He was also designated the *Boss* by his appointees. Truman, succeeding Roosevelt, became *H.S.T.*, even though the *S* did not require a period because it did not stand for any name other than the letter.

The mother of President Eisenhower did not like nicknames and did not like to have her son Arthur called *Art* or Edgar called *Ed.* Earl Eisenhower has said that no nicknames were used around the house. Mrs. Eisenhowever gave her third son the one-syllable name of Dwight. Edgar Eisenhower was first called *Ike* because the name *Eisenhower* was entirely too long. When Dwight came along to play in the same group as Edgar, he was called *Little Ike* and Edgar was dubbed *Big Ike.* Edgar went to the University of Michigan, leaving his childhood friends behind, and so lost the nickname. Dwight went to West Point and there admitted that his nickname was *Ike.* His classmates so referred to him and continued to do so in the army, and the affectionate nickname stuck for life.

President John F. Kennedy passed the word that he didn't like *Jack* in headlines but that he would have no objection to "JFK," and the newspapers generally respected his wishes. As Lieutenant Kennedy he was known to his crew as *Shafty*, due to his penchant for using the military slang phrase, "I was shafted," i.e., tricked. Mrs. Kennedy, the mother of the former president, always called her sons, *Jack, Bobby,* and *Ted*, not John, Robert, and Edward. When Lyndon B. Johnson came to the presidency the newspapers naturally used "LBJ." In contrast with Kennedy, President Dwight D. Eisenhower once commented, "So long as I live, I shall most readily answer to the name of Ike." Mrs. Mamie Eisenhower commented that she thoroughly enjoyed being called *Mamie* by friendly strangers during the campaigns for the presidency. She hoped that the newspapers would stick to *Ike* in headlines and not refer to the President by his initials, as D.D.E. sounded too much like DDT, the insecticide.

Presidents throughout our history have all been given cumbersome appellations, but not many have been universally known by friendly, even affectionate, nicknames. It may be noted that, in general, the stronger presidents acquired well-known nicknames while the others were only referred to in the newspapers by various sobriquets.

See also **ALIASES; PET NAMES**

NOM DE GUERRE

A *nom de guerre* is a French term for a name assumed in fighting or some other war activity to conceal the real name. When failure to serve in the French army was a capital offense a *nom de guerre* was a necessity to conceal identity when evading service. At one period it was the custom for men entering the French army to become known by a war name for the duration of their military service. The phrase is now synonymous with *nom de plume,* pen name, or pseudonym.

Many of the old Bolsheviks in Russia used "party" names to disguise their underground activities. Some of these are *Lenin* (formerly Ulyanov), *Stalin* (formerly Dzhugashvili), and *Trotsky* (formerly Bronshteyn).

In war periods nowadays some assume another name to avoid the draft. Refugees in occupied countries must take an assumed name for protection. Spies have often found it expedient to use an assumed name.

See also PSEUDONYMS

NORWEGIAN NAMES

The idea of a permanent family name rather than one that varied with each generation arose in the urban parts of Norway as early as the sixteenth and seventeenth centuries due to the influx of people to the cities, but the custom did not spread to the country districts until quite late in the nineteenth century. The first family names were borne by the aristocracy and important military officers, possibly in imitation of the nobility in Germany. Clergymen were next to adopt family names. The surname of the children of Halvor Knutsen would be *Halvorsen* or *Halvorsdatter* according to sex. Outside of the cities a man was identified by the addition of his father's name; and if more were needed, the name of the farm on which he resided was added. A countryman had, formally, three names, a given name, a patronymic, and a farm name.

As among their Swedish neighbors, there were some soldier or army names used by the Norse. These were short, somewhat warlike, names by which the man was known in the Norwegian army and which he sometimes kept as a family name upon his discharge.

Many surnames that appear to be common German or English

names are really Norwegian names with a different meaning, as *Bakke* (hill), *Bratt* (steep bluff), and *Holland* (rounded hill farm).

Farm names are unique features of the Norwegian system of nomenclature. Villages were few and unimportant. The farms were large, running sometimes from seashore to mountain top, and composed of woodland, mountain pasture, lakes, and marshes as well as cultivated fields. Farm names were seldom changed; some can be traced back to the Early Iron Age. People were known by the names of the farms on which they resided. If they moved to another farm, their name changed to that of the new residence.

Farm names were considered higher in social rank than other names, especially those of the larger, more important farms. Topmost in the social echelon were the uncompounded names without the definite article such as *Lie* and *Lund*; also high in rank was *Hof* (each patriarchal family had its hof or pagan temple, its religious center) and names terminating in *-vin* (meadowland), *-heimr* (dwelling), *-boer* (homestead), *-sœtr* (dwelling place), *-land* (cultivated field), *-stadir* (farm or place), and *-rud* (clearing) which denoted smaller habitations owned by individuals. Very few trade names arose in Norway, even in the cities, because each man considered himself to be a farmer. The Norwegians used nicknames, but they seldom became family names.

Christian names gave some indication of the family to which one belonged in a small community. By custom, names were handed down in a fixed order. The eldest son was given the grandfather's name on the father's side and the eldest daughter the father's mother's name. The next children were named after the parents of the mother. Other children were given the names of other relatives. The given name of the eldest son alternated generation after generation, and it was easy in a small community to tell to which family a child belonged from its forename.

In 1964, the Norwegian Parliament passed a new comprehensive Name Act, which provided that children of a married couple take the father's family name, children born out of wedlock take the mother's name, adopted children take the family name of the adopter, and married women take the husband's name. The act also provided that a woman could retain her maiden name after marriage by serving advance notice or could, with official approval, retain the surname acquired in a previous marriage.

Many Norwegians today have the common European names of

157

Biblical and Teutonic origin such as *John, Peter, Jacob, Paul, Albert, Henry, Anna, Marie, Esther, Edith, Evelyn,* and the like. But today it is fashionable to bestow names on boys which appear to have a strong Norse flavor such as *Arne, Leif, Odd, Olaf, Einar, Sven, Harald, Haakon, Bjorn, Ragnar, Hjalmar, Lars, Jens, Arnulf, Brynjulf, Ottar, Thorbjorn, Asbjorn, Thorvald, Ingvald, Frithjof, Thorleif, Hallvar, Halfdan,* and *Knut.* Similar good Norwegian names for girls are *Aase, Agna, Alfhild, Ambjorg, Aslaug, Asta, Borghild, Brynhild, Dagny, Magnhild, Gudrun, Gunda, Gunvor, Hedvig, Helga, Hjordis, Ingrid, Ragnhild, Rigmor, Signe, Svanhild, Thea,* and *Thordis.*
See also AMERICANIZATION OF NAMES

NUMBERS INSTEAD OF NAMES

Computers are tending to drive out names, substituting numbers, and may soon take over the direction of our lives. They can handle numbers with ease, but not names. The Internal Revenue Service has forced the adoption of social security numbers as a much better means of identifying the harassed income taxpayer than names. Banks run the numbers of their depositors through their machines. License numbers are assigned to auto engines, and to operate them one must have a numbered driver's license. Auto license plates are only numbers, sometimes with letters added. Athletes and team players have numbers on their backs. To add complications even an address today boils down to a zip code number, and in prison numbers replace personal names. Telephone companies drop the prefixes in favor of all-number dialing. Gasoline, telephone, and other credit cards are numbered. Club members use a number for credit purposes. Montana law since January, 1949 provides for the assignment of a serial number to each baby which will be carried for the rest of his life.

The first thing that happens when a man is inducted into the armed forces is the assignment to him of a number to replace his name. A number is just an abstraction; it carries no picture. Even an unusual or previously unknown name conjures up some sort of picture. There may be music in the sound of a name, not in a number. It has been pointed out that the universal adoption of numbers instead of names would do away with the embarrassment suffered when it comes to spelling or pronouncing another's name incorrectly. Only the person with a prodigious memory could be expected to remember the numbers of his friends. A name can achieve a reputation, a standing among men; a number cannot become good or bad.

The change from names to numbers was reversed when, in 1957, the army announced its new policy of naming its eight types of helicopters and light airplanes after Indian tribes to replace numerical designations.

Conspicuous for his name was Willie ⅝ Smith, likewise 4 E Chittenden who was an electrical contractor in Stanford, California. George Leisher of Powder Springs, Georgia, found that when he printed his name with his pen in longhand with the proper flourish and turned it upside down it became the numbers 6345137 366036. One wit asks if we can have "nicknumbers" when all our names are replaced by numbers.

NUMEROLOGY

This is the pseudo-science that contends that one's destiny is revealed by one's name. In addition it is claimed that the number value of the name discloses one's attitude, thought, ability to work, worldly gain, art appreciation, intuition, spirituality, and manifold attributes and conditions. Each numerologist appears to set out his own system of arriving at the meaning for each name, though none claims originality but attributes the interpretation to ancient wisdom.

A number from one to nine is assigned to each letter of the English alphabet. In many systems A is 1, B is 2, and so on. After nine is reached one starts over again with 1. J is 1, K is 2, and so on. Then the numbers ascribed to each letter of a name are added. The digits of the total may be again added to produce a single digit or key number, and the special values, powers, and vibrations of that number are the attributes and destiny of the person so named. Sometimes the numbers of the vowels and consonants are combined separately to produce two final numbers, the first being allocated to "the inner soul quality" and the latter to "the person's exterior." Various permutations and combinations are supposed to disclose different esoteric secrets. Much is made of the harmony of names.

These theories as to the influence of numbers on one's destiny were first promulgated by Pythagoras, the Greek philosopher and mathematician of the sixth century B.C., and extended by his early followers. Pythagoras made the important discovery of the dependence of the

159

musical intervals on certain arithmetical ratios, which doubtlessly contributed to the idea that "all things are numbers." The Pythagoreans developed the theory and attributed all sorts of fanciful meanings and values to numbers. Numbers were assigned to letters of the Greek and Egyptian alphabets.

Elda Furry said that she was pushed around like a little house kitten. She married the late DeWolf Hopper, American actor, which brought some numerological improvement to her name. But he confused her first name with those of his four previous wives, Ella, Ida, Edna, and Nella. She then went to a numerologist who picked out Hedda. Life took on new meaning, and she became the distinguished Hedda Hopper, radio and television commentator and newspaper columnist internationally known as *The Hat*.

A bank clerk in Taipei, Formosa, named Tseng Yun-ting, meaning "bad luck," changed to Hsieh Yung-sheng, meaning "good luck," and then stole 125,000 Taiwan dollars. But the name change did not help, and he was quickly found and arrested.

One numerologist told a prolific papa that if he gave all his children three-letter names, they would be lucky. So he named them *Jon, Fay, Max, Eva, Hue, Ona, Hes,* and *Ima.*

See also MAGIC NAMES; ONOMANCY OR ONOMATOMANCY; SUPERSTITION

ODD NAMES

Since one can pick almost any word out of the dictionary and find it a surname somewhere, derived through the English or other language, the number of names which may be regarded as odd or queer is almost infinite. Workers on telephone and other extensive lists of names have come across so many peculiar or unusual names that they have learned to take them in their stride without further thought. As for meaning, one can expect to find names as far apart in idea as the German name *Manteuffel* (man-devil) and the French name *L'Hommedieu* (the man-God).

The family seat of the Dysart family for three hundred years has been Ham House near London. One of the family is a gentleman named *Lyulph Ydwallo Odin Nestor Egbert Lyonel Toedmag Hugh Erchenwyne Saxon Esa Cromwell Orma Nevill Dysart Plantagenet.* (The initials of this strange collection of names for some obscure reason, spell *Lyonel the Second,* followed by *Plantagenet.*) A lady in the family sports the name of *Mabel Helmingham Ethel Hunting Tower Beatrice Blazenberie Evangeline Vize De Lou de Orellana Plantagenet Toedmag Saxon.* Others of the clan have included *Cuthberga, Esyth, Ethelswytha, Fredgunda,* and *Wenefryde.*

People who become drunk and disorderly get their names in the newspapers if their names relate in some way to the charge on which they were arrested. If Mr. *Booz* is arrested for drunkenness (and he sometimes is), he is certain to read of his disgrace in the papers (and he does). James R. *Aikenhead* was dismissed in a Hartford, Connecticut, police court when charged with drunkenness in 1954. Mike *Badboy* pleaded guilty to being drunk and disorderly in Park Rapids, Minnesota. *Margaret Folds Quick* was apprehended for drunkenness in Tallahassee, Florida. Heywood *Tipsy* was arrested for drunken driving in Los Angeles, December 26, 1962.

Two policemen operated together in Long Beach, California, in 1953 under their names of *Goforth* and *Ketchum.* People named *Sherlock Holmes* or *Jesse James* are sure of a little publicity if they are careless enough to get themselves arrested.

Undertakers who have names that call attention to their business are sources of merriment. M. *Balmer* was an embalmer in Fort Collins, Colorado. Mr. W. A. *Coldflesh* operated as an undertaker in Jenkintown, Pennsylvania. In 1958 in Malden, Missouri, the *Day* funeral home merged with the *Knight* funeral home to become the Day and Knight funeral home offering a twenty-four hour ambulance and undertaking service. *Knight* and *Day* are two common surnames, and when they get together they make headlines.

When Mr. *Central Still* of Danville, Virginia, answers the telephone to say, "This is Central Still speaking," the other party is likely to retort, "I didn't know you had begun and besides, I don't want Central; I want Mr. Still." People calling the morgue in Washington, D.C., in 1951 were often startled by hearing a voice say, "The morgue, St. Peter speaking," until they learned that Joseph F. St. Peter was merely the morgue attendant. Mr. *Eleven Moore* of Coalgate, Oklahoma, called the doctor who advised him to go to a hospital. When the doctor made the reservation there was consternation at the hospital when the news spread that they were bringing in eleven more.

Some names are unusual because of the paucity of different letters

161

they contain. *Willi Willis* uses only four different letters. *Otto Ott* and *Bob Bobo* each use only two.

According to the Veterans Administration, *Love'n Kisses Love* is a deceased sailor, formerly from Bremerton, Washington. In 1949 *Dill L. Pickle*, a pickle salesman for Paramount Foods, of Louisville, Kentucky, achieved the title, during National Pickle Week, of all-time "Man of Distinction."

A Russian lady named *Abbie Sidi Iyef Giyech* living in Los Angeles is said to sign her name merely as *Abcdefgh*. In 1949, when Major General *Choi Yong Duk* was Korean Army chief of staff, some wit suggested that he had obviously escaped from the menu of a Chinese restaurant offering choice young Long Island duck. When James *Vice* became town marshal in Mulberry, Indiana, it was reported that vice had taken over the town. In 1956 when the first shipment of Australian eggs arrived in London, guests of honor to celebrate the event consisted of Henry *Egg*, Mrs. Elizabeth *Chick*, and Thomas *Henn*.

Johnny *Yesno* is a Canadian. The United States has several persons whose names include these two words, but the names are usually spelled *Noyes*, and the sound conceals the indecisiveness. John R. *Wellbeloved* sued for divorce in Savannah, Georgia, in 1951. In Kentucky, one of the legislators was elected with his nickname included on the ballot. He was listed as Earl "Dirty Ear" Rogers. Mr. *Thomas Todd Teedle Tabb* formerly lived in Todsbury, Virginia, in the eighteenth century.

The *Wrong* family of Canada has produced many *Wrongs* who are right. *Sandy Mae Burby* of East Sparta, Ohio, is a close friend of *Burby Mae Sandy* of Columbus, Ohio. *Luci Puci* is a Chicago hat designer (1956). *Carbon Petroleum Dubbs* was formerly president of the village of Wilmette, Illinois. His father, Jesse Dubbs, invented the thermocracking process for making gasoline, revolutionizing the art of petroleum refining. *Oofty Goofty Bowman*, named after a circus clown, died in Racine, Wisconsin, in 1951 at the age of seventy-five. He always said he liked his name and never attempted to hide it by using initials. The related *Icenogles* and *McSnapberrys* of LaSalle County, Illinois, held a family reunion August 6, 1961, in Nerpp's Grove.

The family of *Lucques*, in France, named their son *Noxxvi*, which when the proper space is noted, would show him to be No. XXVI, the twenty-sixth son in the family. The French boast of a family with the surname of 1792 who named their four sons *January, February, March*, and *April*. In Pittsburgh, Pennsylvania, in 1954, Mr. *I. Will Love*, 80 years old, ran afoul of the law after determinedly battling it out with a 46-year-old rival for the hand of a 40-year-old woman.

I. M. Rood added to his business cards the words, "By name, not by nature." And *I. M. Cross* followed Mr. Rood's example. *Penny Cash* worked for the Internal Revenue Service in Cheyenne, Wyoming. *T. Hee* was a story and gag writer for Disney films. Disney also employed *X. Atencio* and *Ub Iwerks* as animators. In 1962, Professor *Harvard*, Professor *Cornell*, and Professor *Yale* all taught at Yale University. Roger *Wypyszynski* in 1959 was a football player for the Washington Redskins. Including his name he weighed 275 pounds, and it is pronounced *Wih-pih-zin-skee*. The administrative chief of staff appointed by Governor Rockefeller of New York in 1960 was General *Cortland Van Rensselaer Schuyler*, a real mouthful. In shows in which *Durward Kirby* had a part, producers tried to capitalize on his unusual name by advertising in the personal columns, offering prizes for the best answer to the question, "What is a Durward Kirby?"

Both *Leo Smart* and *Leo Dumm* made the dean's honor roll at St. Francis College in Pennsylvaina in 1953. Walter Sippey of Zanesville, Ohio, finds that he must always have a river for a wife— Mrs. *Sippey*. *Vermont Connecticut* Royster is editor of the *Wall Street Journal*. *J. Schuyler* Smith would obviously have more status than Joe Smith. *Outerbridge Horsey* was named ambassador to Czechoslovakia early in 1963. *Tommy Tophat* is a bartender at the Malibu Shore Club on Long Island. *Sixkiller* is in the Dallas, Texas, telephone directory, while *Kilboy* is in the Chicago directory. *Gisella Werberzerck Piffl* became a character actress in Australia and Hollywood in 1948. She acquired the last name by marrying Mr. Piffl. When Mrs. *Rum* of Chicago divorced her husband she was allowed to resume her maiden name of *Cork*.

There was Henry *Arft*, a former baseball player, whose name sounds like what dogs say in comic strips. The famous firm of *Batten, Barton, Durstine & Osborne* has been described as sounding like a trunk tumbling down a flight of stairs. *Mary Will Ketchum* was a truant officer in Seymour, Indiana, in the late nineteen forties. In 1954

163

she was elected president of a truant officers' group. Keenan Wynn's real name is said to be *Francis Xavier Aloysius James Jeremiah Keenan Wynn*. A psychiatrist in Vienna is named *Hans Hoff*. Mr. and Mrs. *Parlor Piano* of San Francisco, California, named their child *Grand*. Dr. *Yellapragada SubbaRow* was an Indian scientist living at Pearl River, New York. Werner *Schnurrpusch* was appointed Mundelein sanitation superintendent in 1960. When a man by the name of *Lawless* is elected judge (as he was in Pasco, Washington), the matter is publicized throughout the country. In 1957 *John Minor Wisdom* was named a federal judge in New Orleans.

The social security lists include 330 persons surnamed *Jesus* and fifteen named *God*. Others are *Bandit, Murder, Money, Honest, Killer, Alias, Cutie, Pain, Agony, Doubt, McZeal, Quy, Moron, Ape, Skunk, Slob, Goon, Ghoul, Oaf, Joker, Frump, Ghost, Boob, Lout, Dam.* Social Security lists them all. A count, a few years ago, disclosed 40 workers named *Ha* and 133 named *Ma*.

A few more odd names culled from the author's collection, all names of real persons, are *Christ Altergott, Adam Smart, Original Bug, Ephraim Very Ott, Gladys Whysoglad, Park A. Carr, Hardy Hollers, Creekmore Fath, May June July, Great Scott, Slow Burns, Pork Chop, Safety First, Melody Tunes, Rae Wray, Ann Ant, Fairy Duck, Vito d'Incognito, North Western, Napoleon N. Waterloo, Peter A. Damit, Tressanela Noosepickle, Osbel Irizarry, Athelstan Spilhaus, Weikko Tinklepaugh,* and *Twilladeen Hubkapiller.* Some peculiar family names are *Barefoot, Drybread, Lonesome, Outlaw, Watchpocket, Godbehere, Applewhite, Swindle, Thyfault, Outhouse, Manypenny, Scissors, Quattlebaum, Qazzaz, Underdown, Sickafoose, Schmittschmitt, Dumjohn, Wiszowaty,* and *Wosk,* names with no more tidiness than a cold scrambled egg.

Many follow the hobby of collecting unusual names. One can search through any large city telephone directory and find a collection of peculiar names. The Chicago telephone directory is the largest one-volume list, and it probably contains more different names than any other single volume.

People do talk about names. There was the member of the Blackfoot Indian tribe from South Dakota whose name was a conversation piece at the San Diego naval training center. It was Leroy *Everybodytalksabout*. A Chinese telephone directory contains a thousand *Wong* numbers.

A Canadian society, SVEFNAP—the Society for the Verification and Enjoyment of Fascinating Names of Actual Persons—was founded by Clyde Gilmour of the Toronto *Telegraph* a few years ago. *See also* NAME COLLECTORS; NAMES THAT ARE NOT WHAT THEY SEEM; ORIGIN OF SOME ODD NAMES

OLD GERMANIC NAMES

The principles of name-giving among the various Germanic kingdoms in England and on the continent cast considerable light on many of our present-day names. Most Germanic names are dithematic, that is, they are composed of two name-themes. The same elements and principles are used for both men and women. Compound names are typical of all Teutonic names, although in very early times uncompounded names do appear with some frequency.

Three well-defined principles, discernible in the Old Germanic royal and other families in the bestowal of names on children, are alliteration, variation, and repetition. Alliteration is simply the use of the same sound, generally the same letter, at the beginning of names, as *Hengest* and *Horsa*. Variation is forming a new name by using a name-theme of another to which a new element is added, as *Eadgar* from *Eadmund*, or through the transposition of both name-themes, as *Beorhtwulf* from *Wulfbeorht*. A famous instance of double variation is *Wulfstan*, the Bishop of Worcester, the son of *Ethelstan* and *Wulfgifu*. Repetition is the use of identical names for different persons.

Germanic name-themes are limited in number. Some of the most common, generally found only as the first element, are: *Ælf-*, *Æthel-*, *Ceol-*, *Coen-*, *Cuth-*, *Cyne-*, *Ead-*, *Eald-*, *Ecg-*, *Ger-*, *Leof-*, *Mild-*, *Os-*, *Theud-*, and *Wil-*.

The common ones usually found only as the second element are: *-beald*, *-frith*, *-fric*, *-gar*, *-gifu*, *-helm*, *-mund*, *-red*, *-stan*, *-swith*, *-thryth*, *-weald*, *-wealh*, *-weard*, *-wine*, and *-wyn*. Some are found either as the first or second part of Teutonic names: *beorht*, *burg*, *heard*, *hild*, *ric*, *sige*, *wig*, and *wulf*.

By the ninth century these compound names had lost all meaning. This is evidenced by such meaningless formations as *Frithwulf* (peace, wolf) and *Siegfried* (victory, peace). The casual combination of these themes to make a person's name indicates that little or no attention was given to the meaning of names although the meanings of the elements were common knowledge. Such names as *Hedwig* and

165

Hildegund mean war or battle in both component parts. Others even have contradictory meanings, such as *Wigfrith* (war, peace).

The pattern of name selection can be observed in royal lines of the small kingdoms of preconquest times. Thus *Eadweard* in the tenth century in Wessex had two sons, *Eadred,* and *Eadmund,* and three daughters, *Eadburg, Eadgifu,* and *Eadgyth.* Then in the eleventh century King *Æthelred,* the Unready, of England, son of *Eadgar* and *Ælfrida,* and the brother of *Edward,* the Martyr, had sons *Æthelstan, Eadred, Eadweard* (the Confessor King of England 1042–66), *Eadwig, Ecgbeorht, Eadgar,* and *Eadmund* (Ironside, became king of England, 1016), and three daughters, *Ælfgifu, Wulfhild,* and *Eadgyth.* In a few cases brothers were given identical names, and even brother and sister have received identical names. Similar genealogies can be found in nonroyal families. With the limited names among the families it is easy to see why many were referred to by some descriptive epithet.

Identity of name-themes is thus some indication of relationship. Certain families used only a very few name-themes over a period of many generations. Repetition of a name-theme or the entire name may have originated from some vague belief in the transmigration of souls. The repeated name may have helped the soul to enter into the new body once the old body had expired. Giving the child the name of the grandfather may have been meant to give an extension of life.

See Henry Bosley Woolf, *The Old Germanic Principles of Name-Giving,* Baltimore, 1939.

ONOMANCY OR ONOMATOMANCY

This is the belief that a man's name could be used in deciphering his fate. The abilities of two competitors, for example, could be compared by calculating the numerical values of their names and dividing them by nine. If the two were of the same type, that is, followed the same trade or profession or possessed the same degree of knowledge or followed the same religious beliefs, the one left with the larger number was the superior. If they were not of a similar type, the one with the smaller number was the better one. Study of the texts found in the Egyptian pyramids reveals that even before 2000 B.C. belief in the power of a name to determine the behavior and destiny of its possessor was commonly held.

Some have carried names indicative of some future event in their lives. Diocletian was told that he would become emperor by killing a wild boar, and as a famed hunter he killed many. In 284 A.D., he stabbed to death the assassin of Emperor Numerianus and became emperor of Rome. The man he killed was named *Aper*, meaning, "wild boar."

Some have believed that the identity of a thief could be divined by writing the names of those suspected on small balls of clay and dropping them into the water. The prayer of Psalm XVI might then be recited, with its reference to the name of God, and the ball with the name of the thief would rise to the surface.

William Camden, the celebrated English scholar, relates how Theodatus, King of the Goths, curious to learn the outcome of his wars with the Romans, consulted a Jewish name-wizard who advised him to pen up a number of hogs after marking some with Roman names and others with Gothic names and leave them for a certain length of time. On the appointed day the king and the name-wizard went to the sty, where they found the ones with Gothic names dead and those with Roman names alive but with their bristles more than half lost. Whereupon the name-wizard foretold that the Goths would be defeated but that the Romans would lose a large part of their forces. The Romans believed that a person's name was an omen of what that person's future would be, as shown by their folk saying, *Nomen est omen*.

Sometimes the prophetic, mystical significance of names could be ferreted out, it was believed, by transposing the letters of the name into words which appeared to have some relation to the person named, that is, by the judicious use of anagrams.

See also ANAGRAMS; MAGIC NAMES; NUMEROLOGY; SUPERSTITION

ORIGIN OF A SURNAME

Men did not consciously choose their family names. They merely placidly accepted the name by which they became known in the village. Almost all of our family names were in existence before the beginning of the fifteenth century.

Assume that in the year 1184 a baby boy was born to Ann and her husband Robert, called Hob, and they named him Henry after the king. How did Henry get a surname and what was it? Let us first have a brief look at the place where the three lived. Perhaps it was in the village of Cuxham, held by Walter Foliot, lord of Cuxham, Sheriff of Oxfordshire. The house of Ann and Robert was situated just south of the church on a small hill near the west-field boundary mark. Robert was the reeve, but when young Henry was only four the father died, and Ann had to operate the lord's oven for the villagers in order to make a living for her son and herself. Henry was apprenticed to Walter, the local tanner, to learn the trade. He grew up to be a tall, strong, red-headed youth with bow legs, interested in taking the part of the king in the annual village pageant.

Now, perhaps you are a direct descendant of this Henry, in the male line, and if so, what is your family name? Let us see, it could be *Henry* or *Harris* (from Henry your ancestor). Or it might be from the surname that Henry acquired. That could be *Roberts* or *Robertson* or *Hobbs* or *Hobson* (from the father's name), *Reeves* (from the father's occupation), *Cuxham* (from Henry's birthplace), *Oxford* (the county), *Church* or *South* (shortened from Bysouthofthe-church), *Hill, Westfield, March* (boundary mark), *Widoson* (son of the widow), *Annett* (descendant of little Ann), *Baxter* (from the mother's occupation), *Prentice* (the apprentice), *Walters* or *Watson* (transfer from the master's name), *Tanner* (from the trade learned), *Long* (being tall), *Strong* or *Armstrong, Read* (from being red-headed), *Foljambe* (from his crooked legs), or *King* (from the part played in the annual pageant).

Any of these names, and a thousand others, could achieve a great variety of dialectal forms and spellings. Over the centuries since Henry was born there could have been several changes of name, and there you are.

ORIGIN OF PERSONAL NAMES

Names first began in the dim shadow of remote antiquity. The origin of language was so early in man that linguists can only offer various inadequate theories on which they cannot agree. Language has been referred to as a "gift of God" which sets man apart from animals. It has slowly developed by a long, complicated process over many eons. Names undoubtedly originated during the very earliest beginnings of the birth of language, after our lovable ancestors got tired of pointing. No savage tribe has been discovered so primitive that its members did not have names. Man never lived so alone as not to have need for names. When he had a mate there were in-laws to be mentioned. Whether the very first names were common nouns or proper nouns can only be conjectured. There has even been a dispute as to whether the first names denoted concrete things or abstract qualities.

Certainly primitive savages must have designated different members of the tribe by some vocal sound soon after the first elements of language or conscious production of sound appeared, especially when the man referred to was not present and could not be designated by the pointed finger. Were the first names a roar, a howl, a purr, a whisper, a grunt, a click, a whistle, a high or low note, a seemingly senseless babble, even a hum or snatch of song, a chant, or some other noise or even gesture possibly imitative in some vague way of the person intended? As a possible example, *Barbara* might be considered. It is derived from a Greek word meaning "barbarian" or "foreigner" which was formed from a mocking imitation of the "baa-baa" or babble of foreigners speaking a language alien to Greek ears.

The first names are so far back in the dim and distant antiquity that even modern man with his superior scientific knowledge cannot fathom them. The names we know that were used by primitive man give no hint as to origin.

ORIGIN OF SOME ODD NAMES

Odd names are often simple corruptions of ordinary names. Most of them have prosaic origins. When a name sounds somewhat like a common word, it is likely to be altered in sound and spelling to that word. Mr. *Onion* comes from Ennion (anvil), an old Welsh name. The ancestor of Mr. *Pickle* originally came from Pickhill (Pica's nook) in Yorkshire. *Angel* earned his name by acting as a messenger in a religious play or was one, perhaps, who had an angelic disposition. It is also a variant of Angle (dweller at an angle or corner). *Blood* is a Welsh name for the son of Lloyd. *Good* is a descendant of Goda or Gode (good), while *Bad* (generally spelled *Bade*) is from the old English *bada*. *Love* is from Anglo-French *louve*, feminine of *loup* (wolf). In some cases it refers to a descendant of Love or Lufa, a popular Early English feminine given name. *Guess* is a softening of Guest, a newcomer.

Some of these odd names, though, are just what they appear to be. *Goodenough* was easily satisfied, although in some cases the name comes from *Gudknave* (the good boy or servant). *Golightly* was originally a slang term for a messenger. *Fullilove* was one who was full of love for his compatriots. John W. *Turnipseed* lives in Lake Forest, Illinois; his name is a translation of the German *Ruebsamen*. *Unthank* describes a man from Unthank, the name of several villages in England and means a squatter's farm. *Riding* is a dweller in a clearing in the wood.

To ferret out all the origins and subtle significations of the personal names in use is a task only a little more complicated than putting a cabbage together again from finely chopped cole slaw. Because there are so many different nationalities in this country there is more significance in names here than elsewhere. Mr. *Forget* is a Frenchman, the name being from *Fargeau*, a popular form of *Ferreolus*; as *Forgette* it refers to the little forge. *Toothaker* is the dweller at, or in, the lookout field. People were not named after quick snacks: *Frankfurter* as a surname designates one whose family originally came from Frankfort in Germany, while Mr. *Hamburger's* ancestor came from Hamburg, and most of the *Wieners* left Wien (Vienna).

Mr. Arthur M. *Getsick* lives in Cambridge, Massachusetts, while Dr. *Stasick* in 1956 was a physician in Hammond, Indiana. Both are German names which were spelled in accordance with their sound. *Getsick* is merely a respelling of *Kützig* from Godizo (God) and *Stasick* is the pronunciation of *Staschik*, a surname from *Eustachius*.

A man approached the manager of the Duchess Hotel in Ogallala, Nebraska, saying, "Coldsnow checking out." "I certainly hope so, I have had enough of this weather," replied the clerk. But the guest persisted, "That's my name, Coldsnow, and I want to check out." The managed got the slip from the files, and there it was: E. O. Coldsnow, Wichita, Kansas. *Coldsnow* merely designates the man who came from Cowlishaw in Lancashire.

See Richard Stephen Charnock, *Ludus Patronymicus, or the Etymology of Curious Surnames*, London, 1868. James Pennethorne Hughes, *Is Thy Name Wart? The Origins of Some Curious and Other Surnames*, London, 1965.
See also NAMES THAT ARE NOT WHAT THEY SEEM

PALINDROMES

These are words or names reading the same from beginning or end, forward or backward. Palindromes are not uncommon as personal names, and even double palindromes are not unknown. Harrah Reynolds, in the nineteenth century, married Hannah Wells and the twelve children born of that union were all given palindromic names: *Hannah, Asa, Emme, Iri, Aziza, Anna, Zerez, Axa, Atta, Alila, Numun,* and *Harrah. Otto Laval* lived in Evansville, Indiana. *Anna Renner* resided in Chicago, as did *Otto Rentner,* a former master-in-chancery. A few other common palindromic Christian names are, *Ada, Ava, Ede, Hamah, Nun, Odo, Ollo, Uddu,* and *Ziz.*

Some people give as a Christian name the surname spelled backward. *Revilo Oliver* was formerly a classics professor at the University of Illinois. *Opal Lapo* resided in Concordia, Kansas. *Marba Abram* has been discovered. *Nebelow Woleben* was a native of Marengo, Illinois, in 1939. In Chicago there lived *Ronnoc Connor.*

There is the story of the four-year-old who was so smart, it was claimed by his parents, that he could spell his name backward as well as forward. This was considered quite a feat until it was disclosed that his name was *Otto.*

PATRONYMICAL NAME ELEMENTS

Almost every nationality has one or more prefixes or suffixes or words which indicate the patronymical name. These either have a definite meaning "son of" or are diminutives or other suffixes with a patronymical connotation. A diminutive may easily acquire the meaning of "son of" or "descendant" and thus become a patronymical affix.

Nationality	Patronymical Forms	Meaning	Example
Anglo-Saxon	–ing	Beorming	Beorm's people
Arabic	Ibn	Ibn Ezra	son of Ezra
	bin	bin Abdullah	son of Abdullah
	binte	binte Aḥmad	daughter of Aḥmad
Armenian	-ian	Simonian	from Simon
Basque	-ez	Ibañez	son of John
Byelorussian	-enok, -anok	Semcanok	son of Sëmka'
Bulgarian	-off, -eff	Georgieff	from George
Chinese	-tse, -se	Tao–tse	son of Tao
Czechoslovakian	-ov, -ek	Pavlov	son of Paul
Danish	-sen	Hansen	son of Hans
Dutch	-se, -sen, -z, -szen, -en	Pieterse	son of Peter

171

Nationality	Patronymical Forms	Meaning	Example
English	-son, -s	Johnson	son of John
Finnish	-nen	Heikkinen	son of Henry
French	de	Dejean	son of Jean
Frisian	-sen, -s, -inga	Sieuwerts	son of Siegfried
German	-sohn, -s, -zohn	Mendelsohn	son of Mendel
Greek (modern)	-antis, -poulos	Georgantis	son of George
Greek (ancient)	-ides, -idas	Aristides	son of Ariston
Hebrew	ben	ben David	son of David
Hindi	walad	walad Tugral	son of Tugral
Hindustani	-putra	Brahmaputra	son of Brahma
Hungarian	-fi, -f	Petöfi	son of Peter
Icelandic	-son, -dottir	Magnusson Magnusdottir	son of Magnus daughter of Magnus
Irish	Mac-, O' (grandson)	O'Reilly	grandson of Raghallach
Italian	de, di, d', degli	d'Alberto degli Alberti	son of Albert of the Albert's
Lapp	-dotter	Larsdotter	son of Lar
Latin	filius, -ilius	Quinti filius Hostilius	son of Quinti son of Hostis
Lithuanian	-aitis	Adomaitis	son of Adam
Navaho Indian	Begay	Denae Nez Begay	tall man's son
Norman	Fitz-	Fitzgerald	son of Gerald
Norwegian	-sen, -son, -datter	Knutsen	son of Knut
Old Babylonian	mâr	mâr-Ishtar	son of Ishtar
Old Persian	ebn bent (daughter)	ebn Khāled	son of Khāled
Persian	zade	Muḥammad zade	issue of Muḥammad
Polish	-wicz	Janowicz	son of John
Portuguese	-es, -az	Pires	son of Peter
Rumanian	-escu	Adamescu	son of Adam
Russian	-ovich, -na, -ovna	Pavlovich Pavlovna	son of Paul daughter of Paul
Saxon	-ing	Dunning	son of Dunn
Scottish	Mac	MacDonald	son of Donald
Slovak	-ak, -ek, -ic	Matuščak	son of Matthew
Spanish	-es, -ez	Gonzalez	son of Gonzalo
Swedish	-son	Jonsson	son of Jon
Turkish	oğlu	Budakoğlu	son of Budak
Ukrainian	-enko	Ivanenko	son of Ivan
Welsh	ap, -s	ap-Lloyd	son of Lloyd
Yugoslavian	-ovich, -evich	Stefanovich	son of Stephen

172

PATTERNS IN CHRISTIAN NAMES

Some families give all of their children names beginning with the same letter. Mr. and Mrs. W. O. Prince, of Peoria, Illinois, selected the letter D. Their thirteen children were named, *Darrell, Delmar, Donald, Dallas, David, Dale, Delbert, Doris, Darlene, Dorothy, Duwayne, Dora,* and *Deva.* Not knowing they would have sixteen children, the *Mayards,* of Abbeville, Louisiana, selected the challenging O as the initial letter. They came up with *Odile, Odelia, Odalia, Olive, Oliver, Olivia, Ophelia, Odelin, Octave, Octavia, Ovide, Onesia, Olite, Otto, Ormes,* and *Opta.* If they had another baby, what name would you suggest? The James Hickok family of Bellingham, Washington, named their children *Zarnell, Zane, Zorin, Zellum, Zale, Zolund, Zerrill, Zatha, Zorina, Zelpha,* and *Zella.*

Others use the characters in a popular book or story, as the Robin Hood saga with its *Robin Hood, Little John, Maid Marian,* and *Friar Tuck.* Some name the first-born with a name beginning with A, and the next with a name beginning with B, and so on throughout the alphabet. A Mormon family named their children in order: *Abigail Bertha, Caroline Daisy, Edward Frank, George Harold, Ida Jane,* and *Katherine Libby.* Mr. and Mrs. A. W. Bowlin of Bonifay, Florida, covered the alphabet. Their children were named *Audie Bryant, Curtis Drue, Era Fay, Grady Hampton, Ida Jennette, Knola Leantha, Millard Nathan, Olevia Penelopa, Quincy Ruth, Sarah Thelma, Ulysses Venson, Wilson Xana,* and *Yon Zirckle.*

The family of the president of the United States has followed the L.B.J. pattern. Lady Bird has the same initials as Lyndon Baines. Their children are Lynda Bird and Lucy Baines. Pets and ranch animals also carry the same matching initials.

A Frenchman, Alphonse Durand, a music teacher, named his children, *Doh, Ray, Me, Fah, Soh, Lah, Te,* and *Octave* to advertise his profession. Mr. and Mrs. Henry Drabik of Chicago named their seven daughters, in order of birth: *Marybeth, Marykay, Marysue, Marylynn, Maryjan, Marypat,* and *Maryrose,* and of course they were featured in the newspapers. Then in 1953 a son showed up and they named him *John Henry.* A popular television program names its family of girls *Bobbyjoe, Bettyjoe,* and *Billyjoe.* The Robert C. Tai family of Honolulu named their girls *Dodo, Rere, Mimi, Fafa, Soso, Lala, Sisi,* and *Octavia.*

An English parson called his first-born *Primus,* the second *Secunda,*

173

the next *Tertia,* and so on up to *Decima.* Then the following girl was recorded as *Ultima.* Mr. and Mrs. Spike Nail of Tulsa, Oklahoma, named a daughter *Penny* and a son *Rusty.* Mr. Jack Trees, son of *Forrest Trees,* lives in Firwood Place in Forest Park, Ohio, and has three children, *Merry Christmas Trees, Jack Pine Trees,* and *Douglas Fir Trees.*

Mr. and Mrs. Jackson of Ardmore, Oklahoma, named their two sons *Tonsillitis* and *Meningitis.* The four girls were named *Appendicitis, Laryngitis, Peritonitis,* and *Jakeitis.* The last one must have signified the end of their medical knowledge. The family pattern came to public notice when Tonsillitis in 1955 signed up for a second six-year hitch at the amphibian base in San Diego and was sent to the naval hospital with tonsillitis.

PERSIAN NAMES *See* IRANIAN NAMES

PET NAMES

The pet-name epoch began in England just before the rise of hereditary family names based on patronymics, as is conclusively shown by the large number of English surnames based on pet forms. About the beginning of the fourteenth century there were about twenty Williams, fifteen Johns, ten Roberts, and ten Richards in each community of a hundred people. By the middle of the fourteenth century John passed William. Pet forms and nicknames had to be produced to distinguish one Richard from another.

In the thirteenth and fourteenth centuries every man was familiarly known as *Watte* or *Thomme* or *Gibbe* or *Will* or *Grigge* or *Hobbe* or *Hudde* or *Judde* or *Tebbe,* not Walter, Thomas, Gilbert, William, Gregory, Robert, Roger, Jordan, or Theobald. Girls throughout the years even up to the present, in ordinary speech, were *Meg* or *Cis* or *Prue* or *Pen* or *Ib* or *Pris,* not Margaret, Cecilia, Prudence, Penelope, Isabel, or Priscilla. Almost any name can give rise to one or more pet forms. In almost all countries from very early times pet or diminutive names have been very popular.

Pet, or hypocoristic, names are formed from familiar given names in many ways, the more common of which are:

1. By the addition of a diminutive suffix, as *Johnnie* from John and *Peterkin* from Peter

2. By apocope, or shortening the name to its first one or two syllables, as *Will* from William, *Sim* from Simon, and *Alex* from Alexander

3. By syncope, the contraction by omission of one or more letters, as *Gib* from Gilbert, *Wat* from Walter, *Bab* from Barbara, and *Ted* from Theodore

4. By rhyming, as *Hob, Dob, Nob,* and *Bob* from *Rob* for Robert, *Dick* and *Hick* from *Rick* for Richard, *Peg* from *Meg* for Margaret

5. By sound softening, as *Harry* and *Hal* from Henry, and *May* from Mary

6. By corruption, as *Jack* from John, *Doll* from Dorothy, and *Sally* from Sarah

7. By aphesis, or dropping of the first part, as *Bert* from Herbert and *Beth* from Elizabeth

8. By taking a syllable from the middle, as *Liz* for Elizabeth and *Mab* for Amabel

9. By adding N to the first syllable of names beginning with a vowel, as *Nan* for Ann, *Ned* for Edward, *Nam* for Ambrose, and *Nol* for Oliver

10. By a combination of the above, as *Jackie, Gibbon,* and *Watkin*

New and fantastic formations are constantly increasing the number of recognized pet forms. The usual laws of sound change fail to explain many pet forms.

In colonial America, where the Old Testament names were common, various pet forms arose, as *Abe* for Abraham, *Eben* for Ebenezer, *Jake* for Jacob, *Jed* for Jedidiah, *Seph* for Joseph, *Lish* for Elisha, *Nat* for Nathaniel, *Rube* for Reuben, *Zak* for Zachary, and *Zeke* for Ezekiel. In later times these were regarded as country names.

Elizabeth has more widely recognized variant or pet forms than any other name. Variant forms are *Elisabeth, Elisheba, Elisabetta, Elspeth, Isabel, Isabelle, Isabella, Isobel,* and *Isbel.* The Isabel forms first developed in France and Spain but became popular in England at an early period. Some of the pet forms are *Alisa, Bess, Bessie, Bessy, Bet, Beth, Bethia, Betsey, Betsy, Bettie, Bettina, Betty, Elisa, Elissa, Eliza, Elsie, Elspie, Libby, Lisa, Lisbeth, Lise, Lisette, Liz, Liza, Lizzie, Lizzy, Tetsy, Tetty,* and *Tibbie.* Other pet forms have arisen in other countries. Some of these hypocoristic forms are so common that they are often regarded as independent names, such as *Bethia, Elsie, Elisa* and *Lisa.*

Some people dislike nicknames and try to give their children names

175

that have no common pet form. Others in an attempt to forestall the practice bestow a nickname to start with. At the baptismal font they name the baby *Davie* or *Kathy*. This is not always successful as the child may end up as *Bud, Buster,* or *Bootsie.* Any boy can be known as *Sonny* throughout life by doting parents.

Many new and original pet forms are used by people reaching after exotic and unusual appellations, but such forms are seldom taken up by others to become well-known and accepted spellings. A pleasant one that could attract the fancy of people is *Mia*, pet form of Maria, used by Mia Farrow, the television actress, whose formal name is Maria de Lourdes Villiers Farrow.

One known by the pet form of his name is admired and loved. Mark Twain's Tom Sawyer beseeched, "Call me Tom; Thomas is the name I get whipped by." The man known by the full baptismal name is serious, gifted, successful, and respected. He is chairman of the board, is director of many companies, wins Nobel prizes, is highly solvent, a dignified official in the church, the man who is always assigned a prominent seat on the platform. On the other hand, the man known by the pet form of his name is more fun-loving, the athletic and sporting type who places a modest bet on the game; he may have a university degree and own his own home and even hold an important position, not the top one, in his company. There are Samuel Johnson and Sam Snead; William Shakespeare and Billy Eckstine; Robert E. Lee and Bob Hope. Entertainers who want to be liked tend to become known by the hypocoristic forms of their names.

Many nicknames which arose as pet forms of regular Christian names are now being chosen as the true given name, and accepted in their own right. Many men are named *Jack*, not John, *Harry*, not Henry, as former President Truman can testify. For girls there is *Betty* and *Bette,* not Elizabeth, *May* not Mary, and *Mamie,* not Mary or Margaret, as Mrs. Eisenhower can vouch for. Pet forms can even produce a string of acceptable Christian names. There is *Ann, Anna* or *Anne*, the common Western form of the Hebrew *Hannah*, and we have *Annie, Nan, Nancy, Nanette,* and *Nina* among others. Some are named *Billie* and not William. Billie Farnum, who has held various political offices in Michigan recently, likes his name but rankles when he receives mail addressed to Miss Billie Farnum.

PET NAMES FOR BEAUTIFUL GIRLS

Charlie Rice, the *Punchbowl* columnist, realized that it was necessary to know what to call a beautiful girl when one is outside the country on business, besides *Hello Beautiful* and quickly did the necessary research. He observed that a French girl might be addressed as *Mon Petit Loup* (my little wolf), or *Petit Chou* (little cabbage), or *Petite Gazelle*. German girls will not object to *Schnuckel-Putz* (translates to something like American snooky-wookums), and they will coo upon being called *Puppy-Dog*, *Kitty-Cat*, or even *Mein Schweinchen* (my piglet). Russian girls react favorably to *My Little Pop-Over*; Italians say *My Star*; Peruvians call the beautiful one *My Sweet Potato*. In Lebanon one may say *My Little Moon* and in Greece, *My Eyes*. Turkish girls are satisfied with *Sugar*. The British do not hesitate to employ terms such as *My Good Old Sausage* or *My Tough Little Bundle*. And the expert Irish go all out with *My Share of the World*.

One observer has pointed out that you can call a girl a *kitten*, but not a *cat*; you can refer to her as a *mouse* but not a *rat*; call her a *chicken* or *chickie*, but never call her a *hen*; speak of her as a *doll*, but carefully avoid *dummy*.

PET NAMES FOR HUSBANDS

Henrietta Ripperger, the newspaper writer, warned wives against allowing an undignified pet name for a husband to become public and hurt him in his business. When you engage a man to represent you, you don't want one known as *Honey Duck*. Hearing a doctor or dentist called *Poopsie* does not inspire confidence. Other terms for husbands are *Pops*, *Daddio*, *Sweetie Pie*, and *Snookums*. Most conservative are *Honey*, *Darling*, *Dear*, and *Sweetheart*.

Robert S. Harris in his divorce hearing in Brookline, Massachusetts, testified that his wife had the habit of addressing him in public as *Sassafras*. Phyllis Diller, the comedienne, divorced the husband whom she referred to as *Fang*, on the stage and on TV, in many sketches depicting their married life.

The first day at school a teacher asked, "What's your father's name?"

"Daddy."

"What does your mother call him?"

Little Jacqueline was silent for a moment, then spoke up, "She doesn't call him anything. She likes him."

PET NAMES FOR WIVES

A New Yorker called his spouse *Snooky-Ookums*. E. V. Durling, the human interest commentator, said it called a once-popular song to mind, "All Night Long He Called Her Snooky-Ookums." Other names for wives are *Baby Cuds, Button Nose, Bunny, Pinky-Dinky, Princess, Dolly, Cookie, Schnickel* (short for Schnickelfritz), *Patty-cake,* and *Mommio*. Most conservative are perhaps *Honey, Darling, Dear,* and *Sweetheart. Baby, Dearest,* and *Precious* are also heard frequently. Nicknames are in as frequent use among high-society ladies as in the dregs of our land. A few years ago an investigator quickly turned up *Cupcake, Squeezie, Pookins, Maycat,* and *Gaga* among the wives of the carriage trade.

Charlie Rice, the columnist, observed that disillusioned Americans refer to their wives as *My Ball and Chain, The Boss,* or *My Better Half;* French husbands say, *My Legitimate One;* with the English it is *My Trouble and Strife* or *My Old Dutch;* the Russian husband says, *My Cashier;* and among the Greeks, the word is *My Operator.*

There was the husband who called his wife Peggy, although her name was Esther. He explained that Peggy was short for Pegasus, the immortal steed, and an immortal steed is an everlasting nag.

See also DIMINUTIVES; NICKNAMES

POLISH NAMES

The most characteristic termination of Polish names is the suffix *-ski,* sometimes *-cki.* About six hundred years ago this was an adjectival suffix used by wealthy landowners to connect the family with its landed estate. One living in Adamov would first be called Lord *Adamowski;* one in Rudnik or Rudnica would be Lord *Rudnicki.* Due to phonetic processes *-ski* and *-cki* sometimes change into *-dzki,* such as *Zawadzki* (from Zawada "obstacle," originally possibly *Zawadski*). A simplified spelling may be *Zawacki.* Later Lord was omitted, but the name continued even though he moved to a different place. By the year 1500, 75 per cent of the Polish nobility possessed names ending in *-ski* or *-cki.* Kings of Poland often granted the right to use this suffix as a mark of honor. When the peasants began to use this suffix with Christian names, it came to be regarded as meaning "son of." Many Polish

178

immigrants on coming to this country adopted the termination to achieve prestige.

Women's family names end in -a although their husbands' names may end in -ski or some other suffix. Madame Curie's original name was Marya Skłodowska, the daughter of Professor Wladisłav Skłodowski. Her brother was Józef Skłodowski. The Polish endings -yk, -ak, -ek, -czyk, -czak, and -czek indicate the diminutive, as Stasiak (little Stanisław), Cieślak (little carpenter), and Włodarczyk (little steward).

Gomulka, the first secretary of the Communist party, derives his name from gomółka (head of cheese). Moskwa designates the man from Moscow. Pietrusiewicz is the descendant of Piotruś (little Peter). There are many short Polish surnames, such as Bialy (white), Dobry (good), Krol (king), Szewc (cobbler), Gora (mountain), Kon (horse), Koza (goat), Krowa (cow), Lis (fox), Ptak (bird), and Sowa (owl).

Since World War II many in Poland have changed their names. Many Poles had German names due to the German influence. German names and any names reminiscent of Germany in later times were an anathema, and bearers hastened to change them. Many German Müllers, for example, found it advisable to take the Polish equivalent of Mlynarski. Large numbers adopted Polish-sounding names or any name ending in -ski. Recent legislation discouraged name-changing unless the name was ridiculous, had a foreign sound, or was in the form of a Christian forename.

Early kings of Poland have popularized such Christian names as Boleslaw, Kazimierz, Stanislaus, and Wladyslaw. The word -sław (glory) ends boys' names while -sława ends girls' names. Stanisław, Bronisław, and Czesław, together with the above kingly names, are popular for boys. Many girls answer to Stanisława and Wladysława. Most of the children in Poland are known only by diminutives or nicknames.

See also AMERICANIZATION OF NAMES

PORTUGUESE NAMES

As in many other countries the Portuguese nobles and wealthy landowners were the first to use surnames, and among them this started as early as the eleventh century, but family names did not become hereditary until the fifteenth century. The wealthy nobles first began to be known by the names of their estates. Among the common people in Lisbon surnames, then mostly patronymical, became current about the early part of the fifteenth century. They were transformed into fixed family names in the sixteenth century.

By far the most common Portuguese family name is *Silva* which means a wood, or thicket, of briars. Other very popular family names are *Santos, Ferreira, Costa, Pereira, Oliveira, Almeida, Rodrigues, Carvalho,* and *Martins.* The number of different Portuguese surnames is relatively small. The common suffix *-eira/-eiro* is derived from the Latin *-ariu* and *-aria* used in the formation of nouns and some adjectives, with a vague meaning of "derived from" or "related to." In Portugal many surnames referring to trees and village names have this suffix.

A great many Portuguese surnames represent place names, such as the village names of *Cunha, Lisboa, Porto, Miranda,* and *Alencar. Ferreira* is the name of numerous small towns. Many people are named after trees, such as *Oliveira* (olive tree), *Pereira* (pear tree), *Teixeira* (boxwood), *Moreira* (mulberry), and *Carvalho* (oak), some of which are also town names. Other names of natural features are *Ribeiro* (river), *da Rocha* (of the rock), *da Costa* (of the hillside), *do Vale* (of the valley), *Cruz* (cross), and *Madeira* (woods).

Many Portuguese have patronymical surnames, but these are not the most common as in many other countries. Some of them are *Duarte, Simões, Luis, Enes* and *Pires. Martins* is the most frequently found.

Surnames from nicknames are very common. They were often quite frank, but were usually applied without malice. Many resulted from incidents arising while people were working together. There is João, whose surname means *Fathead,* which came about because he had a deformed head. Very few Portuguese family names have come from the occupations of their bearers, possibly because when family names became fixed, much of the labor was performed by African slaves, Moors, and Jews.

An unusual kind of family name found in Portugal is that in which the names refer to religious devotion but are not the names of saints. Monks and nuns were the first to use them and then others followed. Some of these names representing invocations to Christ and the Virgin Mary are *de Christo, do Nascimento, das Chagas, da Santa Maria, da Conceição, da Graça* and *dos Passos.*

180

In many cases there is evidenced the Portuguese desire to include the mother's maiden name. For example, if *Eulália Rebelo* marries *João dos Santos*, she becomes *Eulália Rebelo dos Santos*, and their son may be *Joaquim Rebelo dos Santos*, or *Joaquim R. dos Santos*.

Some common boys' names are *Antonio, Carlos, Edwardo, Eugenio, Francisco, Jorge, Henrique, Jaime, João, Jorge, José, Luiz, Miguel, Pedro* and *Reinaldo*. For girls there are *Ana, Carlota, Francisca, Inês, Isabel, Joana, Leonor, Manuela, Margarida,* and *Maria*.

PRESIDENTIAL NICKNAMES *See under* Nicknames

PRIMITIVE NAMES

Among primitive peoples there are numerous methods of selecting a name for the newborn child. The child may be given the name of the last to die in the village. The name of an ancestor other than the parents is selected. Various names are recited, and when the child cries or sneezes or smiles, that is the name chosen. Or sticks with names inscribed on them are offered the baby, and the one grasped by the child is the name preferred. The name of the first object to come to the father's attention after being apprised of the birth of the child may be chosen. Some are given disgusting names like *Ugly* or *Pig* or *Dung* to fool the spirits into thinking the person is not worth bothering about. Physical peculiarities or defects are frequently the basis for names. Disagreeable habits are referred to in some names. Few primitive peoples name children after the father or mother.

In many savage tribes the earliest form of the family or clan name was the totem name, usually some animal, as a wolf or kangaroo, or perhaps a snake. The primitives regarded the animal as an emblem because they thought themselves to have sprung from it or be related to it, and it thus became an object of worship. It is probable that no sound devoid of meaning was ever applied as a name for men by primitive people.

Among the Penan of northwestern Borneo there is a complicated system of death-names, that is, the custom of adopting a new name upon the death of a grandparent, father, mother, uncle, aunt, child, husband, or wife. The name indicates the particular relative, as when, in our culture, we call a woman *widow* we designate that her husband

181

died. A person known and addressed by one death-name may drop that and take another upon the death of another relative.

In Samoa a male starts out with a "boy's name," then gets a "man's name" and if he becomes a chief, a "title name." Names are applied sometimes to show disrespect or to punish for crime. As a punishment, one who stole a bag of rice was officially renamed *Bag of Rice*.

PRONUNCIATION

There is just one way to pronounce correctly the name of any living person, and that is the way he himself pronounces it. Of course sometimes when you ask a person how to pronounce his difficult name he will reply that in Greece it is so and so, in Germany it is . . . , and in the United States they pronounce it . . . The correct way is the pronunciation he affects in the locality where he lives. If the person changes the pronunciation of his name, the correct way is changed.

Christian names which terminate in the same letter as the initial of the surname are likely to be slurred in American speech, thus *Esthe Restall, Phili Pope, Herber Tietema,* and *Nichola Schilling.* A curious pronunciation is the Italian name spelled *Sganga* and pronounced *S C angar.* Mr. John B. Sganga found in the army that when his friends learned the pronunciation of his name they seemed to enjoy saying it, and repeated it every chance they got. They would say, "S C angar," instead of "Hello." The name has a ring to it; people remember it.

There are various names well known in history, literature, or the arts over which people stumble or which they hesitate to pronounce in public, such as *Van Gogh, Goethe,* and *Tschaikovsky.* The simple-appearing, straightforward name of *Chopin,* the composer, is said to be the most mispronounced surname. Many verses have been written to indicate the correct way of enunciating difficult names. One of them, printed in the London *Graphic* in the last century, about Samuel Pepys is:

> There are people, I'm told—some say there are heaps—
> Who speak of the talkative Samuel as Peeps;
> And some, so precise and pedantic their step is,
> Who call the delightful old diarist Pepys;
> But those I think right, and I follow their steps,
> Ever mention the garrulous gossip as Peps!

Mark Twain once wrote a quatrain to explain the pronunciation of the first name of Adlai Stevenson, vice-president of the United States, 1893–97:

> Philologists pray; lexicographers bray,
> But the best they can do is call him Ad-lay.
> At political clambakes where accents are high,
> Fair Harvard's not present, and they call him Add-lie.

The pronunciation of many names is a nerve-racking crisis. In Oss, Holland, the cuckoo clock in a polling place was stopped during elections for councilmen because the cuckoo sounded like the name of the Agrarian Party leader, H. Koekoek. Pelagia *Wrzecz* and Dr. Casimir F. *Przypyszny* died in Cook County, Illinois, in 1959 and 1960 respectively. Michael *Hrynyszyn* lived in Illinois. A Chicago advertising agency attempted to put callers at ease by leaving in its reception room a little booklet telling the pronunciation of the names of its executives.

Some of our easily pronounced English names are difficult for other nationalities. Elias *Harlampopoulas*, a Chicago meat dealer, changed his name to Louis Harris. A short time later he was back in court asking to change his name back to Harlampopoulas, explaining that most of his customers were Greek and could not pronounce Harris. Kasavubu, of the African Congo, remarked in 1961, "Isn't *Kennedy* a hard name to pronounce?" During the run in New York of Franz Werfel's play, *Jacobowsky and the Colonel,* playgoers had great difficulty in pronouncing the Slavic name *Jacobowsky.* A Pole standing outside the theater was once heard to remark to his friend, "How on earth do you pronounce this word, 'Colonel'?"

An unknown limerick writer called attention to the Chinese infant who recited,

> If-itty-teshi-mow Jays
> Haddee ny up-plo-now-shi-buh nays; ha! ha!
> He lote im aw dow,
> Witty motti-fy flow;
> A-flew-ty ho-lot-itty flays! Hee!

which he translated,

> Infinitesimal James
> Had nine unpronounceable names;
> He wrote them all down,
> With a mortified frown,
> And threw the whole lot in the flames.

Prime Minister Solomon West Ridgeway Dias Bandaranaike (pronounced Bahn-drah-NIK-ah) of Ceylon, said that he had spent four years at Oxford, "and that at the end of that period there were hardly two people who could pronounce my name correctly." People who are born with names difficult to pronounce are among the first to complain of others with unpronounceable names from a different language.

Most names in America have standard or generally recognized pronunciations, and are usually pronounced as spelled within the limits of the English language. Americans just will not stand still for the many unusual and absurd pronunciations given to many English surnames. Mr. *Onderdonk*, with a good old Dutch name, may be asked to repeat his name several times only to be met with the reply, "Sorry, I don't seem to get it. It sounds just like Onderdonk to me." *Clough* and other names terminating in *-ough* have many prouncia-tions. They can rime with through, cough, bough, dough, hough, and tough. People can just take their choice, even use the sound of hic-cough, and what's wrong with cloth?

Sometimes pronunciation is not so clear to the small fry. There were two families, the Spragues and the Smiths, whose children were attending a small Sunday School. The superintendent, after the closing reading, followed with the statement, "You are dismissed." After one session a small Sprague complained to her Daddy, "He always says 'you are de-Smiths.' Why doesn't he say sometimes, 'You are de-Spragues'?" When a little Mexican boy in an American school was told to write the first verse of *The Star-Spangled Banner* he began it, "Jose, can you see?"

See also ENGLISH PRONUNCIATIONS

PSEUDONYMS

Pen names, or pseudonyms, have been adopted by writers, throughout recorded history, to conceal their identity for a number of reasons. The most common of these are:

To conceal sex. George Eliot (Mary Ann Evans) found publication easier if she wrote as a man.

To indicate character of the writing. Crackerbox philosophy was written by Henry Wheeler Shaw under the name of Josh Billings.

To protect academic dignity. Lewis Carroll desired to protect the mathematician Charles Lutwidge Dodgson.

To escape the past. O. Henry did not admire his past as William Sydney Porter, and mailed his manuscripts first to a friend to conceal his address at the Ohio State Penitentiary.

To enter another field. Christopher Crowfield wrote *House and Home Papers* whereas Harriet Beecher Stowe might have aroused other thoughts.

To avoid loss of job. Johnston Smith wrote the sensational *Maggie, a Girl of the Streets* that might have cost Stephen Crane his job as a newspaper reporter.

To amuse oneself. Théophile Wagstaff was a name used by William Makepeace Thackeray.

To conceal the number of authors. Frederic Dannay and Manfred B. Lee use the name of Ellery Queen.

To protect relatives. Grace Zaring Stone wrote a novel *Escape*, denouncing the Fascists under the name of Ethel Vance to protect her relatives abroad.

To avoid having too many stories in the market at one time.

To arouse interest. Charles Dickens published *The Pickwick Papers* and a series of sketches under the name, Boz.

To avoid immodesty. Charlotte Brontë published *Jane Eyre* under the name of Currer Bell.

To avoid possible suits for libel.

To protect reputation when selling in a second-class market.

Ted Malone, the radio pseudonym for Alden Russell, registered at a most respectable hotel in San Francisco with his wife, signing the register as Ted Malone. Confusion arose when his wife, not knowing it, called from the room for service as Mrs. Russell.

See also NOM DE GUERRE

PSYCHOLOGY OF NAMES

Another's name may be just a statistic, but to the person bearing it, it is of prime importance. To that person it is more than a name;

it is his or her very self. Everyone is deeply interested in his own name. He will carry around a newspaper clipping mentioning his name, even in a minor way, for years until it literally falls apart. The hometown paper is of interest because it contains names of people we know. Even a child feels that its name is a symbol of the Self. Children, particularly the shy ones, try hard to shield that Self from prying eyes of people they don't know. Most children dislike having to tell their names to strangers. Forcing a young, timid child to tell his name out loud before strangers is one of the most fearful moments such a child may experience.

It is sound psychology to name children after famous men. Dr. George W. Crane, the well-known psychologist-writer, said that throughout his childhood he took pride in being named after the first president. He was the third generation of the Crane family so named and conferred the name on his first-born son.

If some names could call up visions only of common peasant people, they would be considered most unattractive. For example, *Hogg*, *Bacon*, *Lamb*, *Shakespeare*, *Dickens*, and *Bunyan*, may be crude and uncouth names except that their association with eminent characters keeps us from noticing the fact.

Psychologists contend that unconscious motivation strongly influences parents in naming their children. They say that people who give their children the father's name or the mother's maiden name are fulfilling a self-perpetuation wish. Middle-income people tend to give their children unusual or foreign names in an attempt to go up a rung on the status ladder. Parents who bestow the common, accepted names are conformists who do not want their children to develop too much individuality. So say the psychologists.

That names affect one's life and behavior can scarcely be doubted, but insufficient research has been conducted to ascertain the extent of the influence of a name. A name may influence in subtle ways which are not recognized. A name may affect choice of occupation, but it is not known how much is coincidence of name and occupation and how much the name affected the choice. The same is true concerning the effect of the name on the choice of love object. Professor T. Percy Nunn called attention to the Greek poet Philodemus (lover of Demus) who fell in love with four persons named Demos in succession. Schiller loved Charlotte von Wolzogen, Charlotte von Kalb, and Charlotte von Lengefeld. The poet Shelley loved Harriet

Grove, Harriet Westbrook, and Harriet de Boinville. Byron had many attachments to women named Mary.

Albert Ellis and Robert M. Beechley have discovered that boys with peculiar given names are more likely to be emotionally disturbed than boys with ordinary first names; yet no such tendency was found in girls. Most persons think that *other* persons with long or peculiar names should change them. Dr. John W. McDavid, of the University of Miami, has found that the more attractive the name a youngster possesses the more likely he or she is to be popular with classmates. Children tend to associate names with stereotyped images formed from movies, radio, television, and reading. Names seem to be attractive if they call to mind people who are admired and liked.

Dr. Crane advised a girl who was in love with a sailor, but did not know how to write him an interesting letter, to use his name frequently, saying that everyone wants to feel important and see his name on paper. He wrote, "In writing letters to your sweethearts, therefore, you must remember that they get a greater thrill if you include their names in almost every paragraph."

Some people deeply resent any slur on their names even though they are very common given names designating millions. Witness the flood of protest when the weather forecasters began identifying hurricanes by women's names. Some said they must use feminine names because men's names would not be appropriate, there being no "him"icanes. People are influenced by surnames. People who are prejudiced against other races, nationalities, and religions tend to be influenced by what is suggested to them by the surnames.

Calling a man by another name is a sure way to ruffle him. Shakespeare put the words into the mouth of an arrogant, newmade knight in his *King John*: "If his name be George, I'll call him Peter." The deliberate distortion of a name is generally intended to annoy the owner. The insistent use by a wife of her maiden name after marriage can cause trouble to the marriage if the husband has little confidence in himself. While we commonly use only the Christian name or surname of a person when speaking to him, we are likely to use both names when we are provoked.

That we often react emotionally, even unconsciously, to a name rather than the thing itself is easily seen when we note that New Jersey's Hazard Hospital changed its name to Doctors Hospital. Chicago has a "Home for Incurables." Does that name help the patients? Words like cancer and leprosy have ominous connotations.

That a name is really an intimate part of our being, even among civilized people of today, is evidenced by the distaste many feel when addressed by their Christian names by persons of short acquaintance, people of lower status, or younger persons.

See also INFLUENCE OF NAMES

PUNS

Puns on names are found from the earliest times. As names in all countries have a meaning, the clever have been eager to find and make a pun on names. Jesus said (Matthew 16:18), "Thou art Peter [rock], and upon this rock I will build my church." Abigail, speaking of her husband to David (I Samuel 25:25), said, "Nabal; for as his name is, so is he; Nabal [fool] is his name and folly is with him." Naomi exclaimed, "Call me not Naomi [pleasant]; call me Mara [bitter]; for the Almighty hath dealt very bitterly with me" (Ruth 1:20). In two of his sonnets (CXXXV and CXXXVI), Shakespeare rings all the changes on Will. By calling himself Noman, Ulysses outwitted the Cyclops. Thomas Hood was probably the most prolific of English punsters. His last pun was "Now the undertaker will earn [urn] a livelihood [lively Hood]."

People with punnable names like *Saint* are condemned to go through life hearing the same worn-out witticisms and trying to pretend that they are amused for the zillionth time. William Feather tired of the remarks people made when introduced; after listening painfully to their weak wit, he would top them with, "Call me Feather, but please don't call me down." That silenced them. It is a good idea when meeting the bearer of an easily punned name to be the unusual person and ignore the matter. Puns on personal names are tactless. Many great writers and speakers resort to puns only occasionally and then generally with an apologetic air.

Weare Holbrook, a free-lance writer, claims that he always laughs politely when acquaintances come up with tired witticisms about "Weary Willy," "underwear," or "wear and tear." He does not need to laugh; a swift poke in the snoot would be a more efficacious cure. When meeting the glamorous Mrs. Wright one can gallantly quote "I'd rather be Wright than be president." The poet Shenstone thanked God that his name was not liable to a pun.

When General Lewis Cass ran for president in 1848 against

188

Zachary Taylor the puns on his name helped defeat him. References were made to the Democratic nomination of "C. Donkey, vulgarly known as C-ass." The riddle was asked, "Why is it necessary to go to Europe to understand the true character of Lewis Cass?" The answer: "Because it is necessary to pass over the C."

Family mottoes and the crest or coat of arms are often allusions to the surname. The motto of Lord Fortescue was *Forte scutum salus ducum*. The arms, called canting arms, of the Dobells represents a doe among three bells; Bolton's arms are a crossbow driven through a tun; Castile and Leon had for their bearings a castle and a lion respectively. Bishop Alcock, of Jesus College, Cambridge, has his crest, the cock, painted in its windows.

Tradespeople have used punning signs to encourage the public to remember their names, and some went to extremes. *Chester* had a chest with a star over it; *Lionel* used a lion with an L on its head; Mr. *Handcock* in London adopted a hand and a cock; Mr. *Drinkwater* imitated his name with a water fountain.

Punning by bestowing a name on a baby because of its relation to the family name is clever for fifteen minutes, but it is cruelty to the child. Such names as *Manly Fellows, Jay Bird*, and *Penny Nichols* will bring about the same inane remarks repeated so often that the bearer is bored to tears.

After John Gottfried Von Herder, in a note to Goethe, made a play on his name, the poet expressed his resentment in his *Autobiography*: "It was not polite, indeed, that he should allow himself this jest on my name: for a man's name is not like a cloak, which merely hangs about him, and which, perchance, may be twitched and pulled with impunity; but is a perfectly fitting garment, which has grown over and around him like his very skin, and which one cannot scratch and scrape without wounding the man himself."

Jeremiah Tax of New York says that he gets tired of jokes about his name, especially around April 15. The worst joke usually comes after he walks through a door and some wise guy exclaims, "Well, the door opened and in come Tax."

PURITAN NAMES

During the sixteenth century the Puritan movement developed in the Church of England. The Puritans practiced or affected great purity of life and were most strict in their religious observances. They

189

were opposed to all Catholic church reverence for the saints, martyrs, and virgins and sought to replace their names with Old Testament names and phrases and words from the Bible. The popular saints' names encouraged by the church were not sufficiently godly for them. They hated the Devil, and they hated the saints.

Starting about 1590, in the reign of Elizabeth I, the more fanatical Puritans began to baptize their children by scriptural phrases, pious ejaculations, and godly admonitions. The Presbyterian clergy baptized with such names as *Stedfast, Renewed, Safe-on-Highe, Much-merceye, Increased, Accepted,* and *Thankful.* Some of the more extreme, not to say colorful, are *Search-the-Scriptures, Job-rakt-out-of-the-Ashes, Zeal-of-the-land, Help-on-high, Flie-fornication,* and *Sorry-for-sin.* Best known is *Praise-God* Barebone whose name is associated with the Barebones Parliament of 1653.

About Cromwell's time a jury is said to have been impaneled in the county of Sussex with the following Puritanical names: *Accepted, Redeemed, Faint-not, Make-peace, God-reward, Standfast-on-high, Earth, Called-Lower, Kill-sin, Return, Be-faithful, Fly-debate, Fight-the-good-fight-of-faith, More-fruit, Hope-for, Graceful, Weep-not,* and *Meek.* This panel has been called a forgery and a hoax, but the names are real enough. They are an authentic collection of the names existing in Sussex villages at the same time. Some of the actual persons can be found in the church registers. Most of the names used by John Bunyan in his *Pilgrim's Progress* can be found to have been in use during his lifetime.

Many Puritan names were those of abstract virtues. Some of the more common were: *Abstinence, Affability, Amiable, Blessed, Chaste, Comfort, Constant, Diligence, Gracious, Happy, Humility, Obedience, Patience, Placid, Polite, Perseverance, Prudence, Righteous, Silence, Sober, Temperance, Worthy,* and *Zeal.* Other names were *Admonition, Advice, Agony, Deliverance, Humiliation, Repentance,* and *Trial.* On the one hand there was *Enough, Last,* and *Omega;* and *Welcome* on the other. Abstracts derived from the Greek were *Alethea* (truth), *Philadelphia* (brotherly love), and *Sophia* (wisdom). Others were: *Felicity, Veracity, Unity, Verity,* and *Grace. Discipline* and *Acceptance* had a short life.

Even during the height of the Puritan name eccentricity, those with the peculiar names had to suffer much good-natured raillery and ridicule. On the stage they were roughly handled by such dramatists as

Ben Jonson, Cowley, and Beaumont and Fletcher. Many of the names were, of course, shortened in the day-to-day battle of life.

After the Restoration in 1640 the use of these peculiar Puritan names began to die out. The religious apathy of the early eighteenth century was also responsible for driving out the Puritan names except for a few which lingered until the beginning of the twentieth century like *Prudence, Faith, Hope,* and *Grace.*

Many Puritans fled England and came to America where their Old Testament names and peculiar system of nomenclature continued longer than in the mother country and the permanent effects were greater. Richard Mather left for New England in 1635; and his son, *Increase* Mather, is well known to students of American history. *Preserved* Fish was born in 1766. Practically all of the Puritan names mentioned are also found in New England, together with all the unusual Old Testament names, which persisted for a century after the epidemic had subsided in England. The Frederick Lindloff family in Clinton County, Iowa, registered the birth of a child, in 1880, as *Through-Much-Trial-and-Tribulation-We-Enter-the-Kingdom-of-Heaven.*

Through-Much-Tribulation-We-Enter-the-Kingdom-of-Heaven Clapp, called Tribby for short, was a sea captain sailing out of Gloucester, Massachusetts, a blunt man using simple language. *Faint-Not* Wine became a freeman in 1644. *Hate-Evil* Nutter is listed in Massachusetts records in 1649, along with *Search the Scriptures* Mabb. Other given names common in early days were *Accepted, Elected, The Lord Is Near,* and *Joy Again.*

See Charles Wareing Bardsley, *Curiosities of Puritan Nomenclature,* London, 1897.

REMEMBERING NAMES

The importance of remembering the names of the people with whom one comes in contact was recognized by the great leaders of antiquity. Agamemnon is disclosed in the *Iliad,* our earliest Greek literary work, as fully aware that one honors a man when he calls him by name and exhibits a knowledge of his lineage. Xenophon records how Cyrus the Great took particular pains to address his army officers by name in an assembly. Several authors have contended that Cyrus knew the names of all of his soldiers, not just the officers. The

Athenian statesman Themistocles is supposed to have known the names of all the citizens of Athens. Crassus was said to greet all Roman citizens by name no matter how humble their station. Cicero could recall the names of thousands of his villagers and soldiers.

Our present-day politicians and candidates for elective office strive to remember names. Former Postmaster General James A. Farley could remember the names of 50,000 persons he met. Napoleon III, of France, claimed that he could remember the name of every person he met. The Romans employed nomenclators—slaves who accompanied candidates for office and other distinguished men in order to whisper the names of the people they met.

Once a haberdasher named Kaskel shook Teddy Roosevelt's hand and reminded him, "I made your shirts—"

"Oh yes, Major Schurtz," interrupted Teddy, "I'd have known you anywhere!"

When Henry Clay was reproached by a young lady for failing to call her by name, he gallantly excused himself by responding, "When last we met I was sure your beauty and accomplishments would very soon compel you to change it."

Authorities on memory generally emphasize the following rules for remembering names:

1. Get the name correctly the first time it is given, asking, if necessary, that it be repeated.

2. Repeat the name as often as possible in conversation.

3. Associate some real or fancied meaning or some unusual or ludicrous word or act with the name and the person involved.

There was the man who couldn't remember the rules for remembering names, so he just called all the ladies "Sister" and all the men "Doc." Mr. Walter A. Humphrey of Lancaster, Ohio, had his stationery printed in the shape of a camel. He says if you think of a camel, you should think of a hump and if you do, it's easy to recall the name Humphrey. A well-known doctor in Memphis addressed all acquaintances as *Benny* to avoid the embarrassment of a faulty memory. But his plan backfired when he received a lot of Christmas cards, each one signed "Benny." In some places *Darling* is the popular form of address in speaking to a person of the opposite sex whose name at the moment cannot be brought to mind.

There are 181,360,729 people, give or take a few, who have trouble remembering names. Ability to recall people's names is a talent that will carry one far in all lines of endeavor. To remember Bobby Burns, the poet, one might fix in his mind's eye a picture of a British policeman lighting a match. See! Bobby Burns! Yes, but how is one to know that it doesn't represent Robert Browning?

One who had trouble remembering Mr. Attic's name associated it with the upper part of a house. The next time he met Mr. Attic he called him Mr. Garret. One woman had trouble remembering the name of Mr. Pallas. It was suggested that she associate his name with a large and fine house—which she did. The next time she met him she was self-confident and exclaimed, "How do you do, Mr. Castle." When buxom Mrs. Dressler went to the market to purchase her meat she was told that it was not ready and she must come back. Upon being asked her name she explained, "Mrs. Dressler, just think of dress plus 'ler.' The biggest part of me is my dress. You can remember that." When she returned the butcher quickly and confidently greeted her, "Mrs. Butler, here is your meat."

A lady with a somewhat defective memory was introduced to the eccentric Miss Hazel Browne. Meeting Miss Browne again she recognized the woman but had forgotten her name. She did remember that she had tried the association test and quickly said, "I am afraid that I don't remember your name, but I distinctly recall you as some kind of a nut."

Then there was the student in social science, who was preparing for an examination. Since the United Nations was then in the news with Madame Pandit he expected that there would be a question involving her, but thought her name would be difficult to remember. Then he hit on an idea. "Pandit sounds like bandit with a P." At the examination he found the question, "What is the name of Nehru's sister?" and quickly wrote, "Madame Purglar."

Dr. Willis R. Whitney reported that when he was trying to remember a name, he was likely to think of several wrong names first, the fourth one being the right one, the first three being related in one way or another to the one he was trying to recall. For example, in trying to recall the name of a certain senator, the name *Blutgut* came to mind, then *Carney*, next *Gormley*; and then he knew that *Kilgore* was right. Tracing the matter back, the ideas of blood and gore assumed a German form in Blutgut, were Latinized in Carney, and Anglicized as Gormley; then crystallized as Kilgore.

It is in politics that a memory for names is a great asset. If one

193

can remember a voter's name and use it in conversation with him at later meetings, the citizen is impressed, and his support is assured. Some politicians use a prompter, a local party functionary or office holder, who stands close to the visiting dignitary and whispers the names as they come up in the reception line. Salesmen who have the faculty of remembering names increase their commissions.

Estes Kefauver said that people had a hard time pronouncing his name. When campaigning for the Senate of the United States, he pronounced his name clearly, with a strong accent on the first syllable, and was encouraged to find that an odd name, once learned, is more easily remembered than a plain one. He won the election.

Impressive, appealing, glamorous, easy-to-remember names are *Bonnie Maginn, St. Clair McKelway, Helen Twelvetrees, Columbia Maypole, Viola Brothers Shore,* and *Edna St. Vincent Millay.*

See also COCKTAIL PARTY NAMESMANSHIP

ROMAN NAMES

In earliest times an individual was known by only one name, as *Romulus* and *Remus,* the legendary twin founders of Rome. Later another name was added, that of the father or husband in the genitive case. Still later the name indicating the family (*gens*), marked generally by the suffix *-ius,* was added. In time all free-born men possessed three names, the individual name, the "praenomen," the name of the gens, the "nomen"; and the name of the family, the "cognomen," in that order, as *Caius Julius Caesar* and *Marcus Tullius Cicero.*

The praenomen was conferred by the parents on the ninth day after birth in the case of boys and on the eighth day in the case of girls. When joined with the nomen and cognomen it was regularly represented by the initial, or abbreviated, indicating Roman citizenship. The popular praenomina were limited in number, only sixteen being in common use. They were *Aulus, Decimus, Gaius, Gnaeus, Kaeso, Lucius, Manius, Marcus, Publius, Quintus, Servius, Sergius, Sextus, Spurius, Tiberius,* and *Titus.* Of these *Kaeso, Manius, Servius,* and *Spurius* were the most uncommon. In addition *Appius, Mamercus,* and *Numerius* were used in certain special patrician families. Other families commonly used only certain praenomina. The names *Primus, Secundus, Tertius, Quartus, Quintus, Sextus, Septimus,* and *Octavius* were finally used without reference to their meaning. Thus *Quintus*

194

became more popular than some of the earlier numerals. Not all women had praenomina, but bore the father's nomen in the feminine. If there were more than one daughter, a cognomen in the feminine would be used. Where men had three names women had only the nomen and cognomen.

The nomina, about one thousand in number, denoted members of the same gens or tribe, presumably descended from a common ancestor, and were used by both men and women. Examples are *Aemilius, Aurelius, Cornelius, Flavius, Iulius, Manlius, Pompeius,* and *Tullius.* Some with different endings first appeared in different localities in Italy.

Originally the cognomen was appropriate to the individual and given only to adults in patrician families to distinguish them from others with the same name. It was at first merely a nickname and usually referred to some peculiarity of body or mind, or derived from the place of birth, as *Albinus* (white-haired), *Balbus* (stammering), *Crassus* (fat), *Longus* (tall), *Niger* (black), *Rufus* (red), *Felix* (happy), *Luparius* (wolf-hunter), *Norbanus* (from the place name Norba), and *Antiatinus* (from Antium). Its regular use started about 100 B.C. although there is evidence of it two centuries earlier, and it descended to succeeding generations, becoming a family name among both patrician and plebeian families. Among the Romans themselves it was usual to refer to a man by his nomen and cognomen only, as *Julius Caesar.* Sometimes the praenomen was used with the nomen and other times with the cognomen, as *Caius Julius* and *Marcus Bibulus.* Several emperors were commonly known by their *praenomina,* as *Tiberius, Caius,* and *Titus.* The poet Horace was known by his nomen, his full name being Quintus Horatius Flaccus.

Additional cognomina might be added, called agnomina. Military men often took an agnomen commemorating a victorious campaign, as *Africanus, Asiaticus,* and *Macedonicus.* The large-scale disappearance of the praenomen and nomen by the beginning of the fourth century A.D., due in part to their limited number and consequently their limited usefulness in identification, left the cognomen as the single name. Sometimes double cognomina were used.

The eighteen most popular cognomina, in order of frequency, were *Felix, Secundus, Saturninus, Fortunatus, Primus, Maximus, Ianuarius, Rufus, Severus, Victor, Sabinus, Proculus, Faustus, Priscus, Hilarus, Crescens, Tertius,* and *Vitalis.* These names designated more than one-fourth of the people. The intense desire for good luck, long life, fortune,

195

victory, joy, and strength, and belief that a name was an omen, was reflected in the wish-names of *Faustus, Felix, Fortunatus, Hilarus, Maximus, Severus, Victor,* and *Vitalis,* so prominent in this list of the most common cognomina.

The collapse of the three-name system into the single name, the cognomen, for each individual was caused by several factors other than the Christian idea of equality. The weakening of the ancient Roman census where everyone had been required to state his full official name probably started the decadence of the three-name system. The nomen decreased in importance with the weakening of the unity of the gens. The political and social value of the full three names which indicated Roman citizenship declined when Caracalla and other emperors extended Roman citizenship to all provincials and foreigners. Aliens had only one name and were not inclined to change to the old system when it no longer designated citizenship. The praenomen lost its distinctive function when sons were given the same praenomen as the father and freedmen the same as their former master's. The paucity of praenomina in use contributed to their extinction.

Originally women had praenomina followed by the nomen of the father or husband and the genitive case of his praenomen. Then *filia* or *uxor* was included. Later the praenomen disappeared from the inscriptions.

Names of slaves commonly terminated in *-por* from *puer* (boy), as *Publipor* and *Quintipor.* In later times the slave had an individual name, often of foreign origin, followed by the nomen and afterward the praenomen of his master, both in the genitive case, to which was attached the word *servus.* A freedman selected a praenomen and received the nomen of his patron, to which was sometimes added a cognomen.

See Lindley Richard Dean. A *Study of the Cognomina of Soldiers in the Roman Legions,* Princeton, 1916. Iiro Kajanto, *Onomastic Studies in the Early Christian Inscriptions of Rome and Carthage,* Helsinki, 1963; and *The Latin Cognomina,* Helsinki, 1965.
See also CLASSICAL NAMES

RUINED NAMES

Some men have ruined names for centuries by their deeds. Some of the most infamous are *Judas Iscariot, Nero, Benedict Arnold, Quisling,* and the fictional *Simon Legree.* The name of *Adolf Hitler* is forever spoiled. Alois Hitler of Hamburg, Germany, Adolf's half brother, changed his name to Hans Iller, in 1948, because of the stigma with which people regarded the name of Hitler. A survey in 1958 disclosed that not a single Vienna-born boy had been named Adolf since 1938, the year Hitler's Nazis took over Austria. *Mussolini* tarnished his name for a long time to come. *Oliver*, the name of the unpopular Cromwell, was one that no one would dare adopt in England for a century after the Lord Protector's death in 1658.

Cain, the first murderer, and Esau, who impetuously sold his birthright for bread and pottage, produced tainted names. *Adam Baum* was a good name until the atom bomb became a nightmare to people. Before Cervantes' *Don Quixote* became a popular classic, *Sancho* was an aristocratic and royal appellation borne by many early Spanish and Portuguese kings, but since then it has been thought to have a slightly comic sound.

The Fink family had a decent, respectable surname and lived a pleasant life. Then it is said that a man named Fink worked for management during an early Chicago streetcar strike in 1892, and his name became synonymous with strikebreaker. *Fink*, a new word, thus entered the American language, the most derogatory term in Labor's vocabulary, a very nasty word among workingmen if not among the titans of industry. The term may originally have been Pink, short for Pinkerton, the detective agency which specialized in labor troubles, or it may be a shortened form of the common colloquial German words, *Schmutzfink* and *Dreckfink* (dirty person). The meaning of fink was made worse when *rat fink* was bandied about on radio and television.

RUSSIAN NAMES

Russians have three names, a family name, a given name, and a middle name, the latter a patronymic designating the father. Thus *Ivan Ivanovich Ivanov* is John the son of John, Johnson; *Vyacheslav Mikhailovich Molotov* is Vyacheslav Molotov the son of Mikhail. For women the patronymic terminates in *-ovna* or *-evna*. The middle name is arbitrarily derived from the forename of the father. Brothers and sisters have the same middle name, taking into account the proper gender. Patronymics came into use some time before hereditary family surnames, which first appeared about the fifteenth century.

Common people in Russia in early times used only Christian names together with individual nicknames. At first the use of patronymics was the sole prerogative of the princes and later of the nobility. The Czar himself determined who could add -*ovich* to his father's name. Peter I, in 1697, specifically permitted a prince to add -*ovich* to his patronymic. In the time of the Empress Catherine it was decreed that only those in the first five grades of the civil service could employ patronymics with the terminal -*ovich*, while those in the sixth to the eighth grade could use -*ov* or -*ev*. Others were forbidden to use the patronymical element. Later the common people were allowed to use the endings -*ov* and -*ev*.

Now more than 70 per cent of all Russian names end in either -*ov* as in *Malenkov* and *Molotov*, -*in* as in *Pushkin*, *Lenin*, and *Stalin*, or -*ev* as in *Khrushchev* and *Brezhnev*. Others terminate in the patronymics -*ich* or -*ovich* as in *Kaganovich*. The ending -*sky* designates names derived mostly from places, and there is *Tschaikovsky* (from Czajkow) and *Dostoyevsky* (from Dostoyevo). The suffix -*oy*, found in nicknames and place names, gives us *Tolstoy* (fat) and *Polevoy* (goose). Names designating occupations often end in -*ik*, as *Popik* (priest) and *Kovalik* (smith). All of these endings have feminine forms, usually with the inclusion of an *a*, as -*eva*, -*ova*, -*aya*, -*ina*, and -*ikova*.

Russian surnames are found in the same four classes as other European names. The various fur-bearing mammals and domesticated and other animals, which are an important part of the economy and history of Russia, are the basis for many Russian names. Examples are *Barsov* (leopard), *Kotov* (tomcat), *Slonov* (elephant), *Volkov* (wolf), *Kozin* (goat), and *Lisin* (fox). Names of birds are especially common, such as *Voronov* (crow), *Sokolov* (falcon), *Zuravelev* (crane), *Orlov* (eagle), *Golubev* (dove), *Gusev* (goose), and *Lebedev* (swan). Names of insects are found as the basis of many Russian names. Besides *Khrushchev* (cockchafer), there are *Muravev* (ant), *Zukov* (beetle), *Bloxin* (flea), and *Klopov* (bug).

Names from landscape features are *Xolomov* (hill), *Kustov* (bush), *Ozerov* (lake), *Bolotov* (swamp), *Gorin* (mountain), *Morev* (sea), and *Kamenev* (stone). There are place names, as *Grekov* (from Greece), *Litvinov* (from Lithuania), *Krymov* (from Crimea) *Rostovcev* (from Rostov), and *Moskvin* (from Moscow). Some occupational names are: *Goncarov* (potter), *Tolmacev* (interpreter), *Djakov* (clerk), and *Popov* (priest), Nicknames may be observed such as *Belov* (white), *Ryzov* (red), *Borodin* (beard), *Golovin* (head), *Kosygin* (slant-eyed),

Nogin (foot), *Gorbatov* (hunchbacked), *Ljubeznov* (amiable), *Ugrjumov* (sullen), *Xitrov* (cunning), and *Krotkov* (docile). As elsewhere there are many patronymics: *Borisov* (Boris), *Fedin* (Fedor), and *Petrov* (Peter). Inanimate objects appear to be the basis of some names such as *Grobov* (coffin), *Lomov* (crowbar), *Korobov* (box), *Kljukin* (walking stick), and *Pushkin* (cannon).

Under Russian law, upon marriage each partner may retain his or her surname, or they both may take either surname, which is almost always the father's family name. If both surnames are retained, the parents will usually agree on which name the children will use. The official signature is the given name and the family name, never an initial for the patronymic. In ordinary use the initial of the forename and the family name is usually found. Official documents usually require all three names.

The most common surname in the Moscow telephone directory is *Ivanov* (the equivalent of Johnson), with *Petrov* (Peterson) second, and *Smirnov* (quiet) third. *Kuznetzov* (the son of the smith) is also quite common. Russian names have simple meanings which the ordinary person understands.

After the Communist revolution parents were urged to give their children names indicative of the new order of things and to avoid the old names of saints. Some Russian couples selected *Vladlen,* being the first syllables of the first and last names of Vladimir Lenin. Others named the baby *Ninel,* being Lenin spelled backward. For a while names indicative of science were popular. There were *Vitamin, Edison, Dynamo,* and *Differential.*

The Russians, in an effort to emphasize Russian nationality, have criticized parents for giving their children foreign-sounding names. The *Russian Gazette* claimed that such examples as *Isolda, Eldorada, Elonora, Azalia,* and *Ella* for girls and *Arthur, Alfred, Henry,* and *Emil* for boys were not Russian in spirit, and sounded strange and even comic. Nevertheless, a large number of Russian given names have their counterparts in English and other Western languages. Names of Greek, Latin, and Hebrew origin entered Russia through the medium of the church, which pressured the change from pagan to Christian names. Most masculine given names (other than nicknames and pet names) end in a consonant, while most feminine names end in *-a.*

After Khrushchev reduced Stalin's status, the names of the late premier and his disgraced faction were wiped off the map, and the

Soviet authorities were cooperative in helping boys named *Josef* or *Stalin* and girls named *Stalina* to change their names. Many Josefs selected the peasant version, *Osip*. *Trotsky* was a common name in Russia and a proud one until he bounced out of favor. Having the same name as a Russian official is dangerous because one never knows when the Communist line will shift and it will be advisable to change the name.

The most popular masculine names in medieval times, according to a study by Professor Astrid Bæcklund, were *Ivan, Vasilei, Grigorei, Fedor, Semen, Jakov, Stepan, Michailo, Jurii,* and *Esif.* These names produced numerous patronymical names popular today. Other common personal names were *Ondrei, Pavel, Sidor, Mikita,* and *Oleksandr.*

Pet or diminutive forms of Russian given names are very common. Diminutive forms are generally applied to children, while endearing or pet forms are used to communicate the speaker's attitude toward the person. Scornful or derogatory forms are used to indicate displeasure, as when a parent scolds a child. The full formal forename is seldom used in speech. Almost every Russian forename has one or more hypocoristic forms. Foreign readers of Russian literature are confused when the same character is referred to by several caritative forms. Many of the common forms are not easily recognized as related to their full names. *Súra* is from *Aleksandr; Njúša* is a hypocoristic form of *Ánna.* Other forms can refer to any one of several names. *Sláva* can be for *Vladisláv* or any of the many other popular names terminating in *-slav.* Morton Benson points out that one name can either be a full name with its own hypocoristica or a pet or endearing form of another name. As an illustration he gives *Dóra* as a recognized Christian name with such pet or diminutive forms as *Dorka, Dorocka,* and *Dóruška,* or it can serve as a pet form of *Isidóra* and *Mitrodóra.*

Several authorities have pointed out that the stress creates the greatest difficulty in pronouncing Russian names, as it may occur on any syllable, and may shift in various declensional forms. The same name may vary with the individual. Some men are called *Ivánov,* others *Ivanóv.*

Closely related to the Russians and Byelorussians are the Ukrainians, although they have their distinct Ukrainian language. Like other Eastern Slavs they use three names: a given name, a middle name (patronymic), and a family name. Thus *Petró Petróvych Petrív* means Peter, son of Peter, Peterson. *Tarás Hryhórovych Shevchénko* is Taras Shevchenko son of Hryhir (Gregory). For women the patronymic ends in *-ivna*, from original *-ovna* and *-evna*; for example, María Ivánivna Doroshénko is Maria, daughter of Iván Doroshénko. Many patronymics became family names. Some of them differ by accent only. Thus Antón Antónovych Antonóvych is Antony Antonóvych, Anton's son.

Very common in East Ukraine is the suffix *-enko*, a fifteenth century form of *-ovych*, in surnames. Thus Petrénko is son of Peter, Pavlénko is son of Paul, and Tymoshénko is son of Tymish. It is interesting to note that *-enko* is never used as a patronymic or middle name; *-ovych* is found instead: Petró Petróvych Petrénko is Petró Patrénko son of Peter.

A typical West Ukrainian ending is *-uk* or *-iuk*; it corresponds to *-enko* in forming the patronymic surnames such as Antín Antónovych Antoniúk (Antony Antoniúk son of Antony). There is historical and geographical differentiation in the above patronymical family names. The most ancient all-Ukrainian suffix is *-ovych*, as seen in Petróvych. Later formations are East Ukrainian *-enko*, as in Petrénko and West Ukrainian *-uk* and *-iuk*, as in Petrúk and Antoniuk. An obsolete West Ukrainian patronymical suffix is *-(ov)iat*, as in Petroviát (Peterson) and Khronoviát (son of Khron).

Several names are metronymics. Most of these end in *-yshyn*. Thus Petryshyn refers to the son of Petrykha (Peter's widow), Mykhaylyshyn is the son of Mykhaylykha (Michael's widow), Antonyshyn is the son of Antonykha (Anton's widow), and Ivanyshyn is the son of Ivanykha (Ivan's widow).

Names derived from places usually end in *-skyj* or *-ckyj*, as in Volynskyj (one from Volynia) and Rudnyckyj (one from Rudnyk). Many of these are old names of Ukrainian nobility. Women's names end in *-ska* and *-cka*, as in Volynska and Rudnycka. Other topographic derivatives are formed by such suffixes as *-ec*, such as in Volynec; *-iak*, as in Volyniak; *-ianyn*, as in Volynianyn—all meaning the same, that is, inhabitant of Volynia.

Early princes of Ukraine popularized such given names as Volodymyr (Vladimir), Jaroslav, Sviatoslav, and Myroslav, the element *-slav* meaning "glory, fame." The famous Ukrainian Cossack leader in the seventeenth century, Bohdan Chmelnyckyj, popularized the name Bohdan (given by God). The corresponding female names are in *-a*, as Volodymyva, Jaroslava, Sviatoslava, Myroslava, and Bohdana. The children are usually called by diminutives and nicknames: Volodko, Slavko, Slavcio, Danko, Danusio. Very popular in Ukraine is the name

201

Taras due to the name of the national poet, Taras Shevchenko. Diminutives are *Tarasyk*, *Tarasko*, and *Tarasio* which can function also as family names.

See also AMERICANIZATION OF NAMES

RYUKYUAN NAMES

The Ryukyuan chain of islands, known to most Americans because of the savage battle on Okinawa, the largest island, in 1945, employs a language which is a dialectal form of Japanese, although Ryukyuan and Japanese are as different as French and Italian. The names used are similar to Japanese names and are written phonetically with Chinese characters. Usually the characters were used as pronounced in Chinese but some were as pronounced in the Japanese style. At the present time there appears to be a growing tendency to select Japanese given names for children.

Japanese law, about 1870, required every family to take a surname in Ryukyu, as in all Japan. At this time many Japanese surnames were adopted. Then in 1880 the law provided that surnames be written first followed by the given name, which had not been the order of Ryukyuan names in the past. Names of places where a particular group lived were selected by many as their family name. These were not changed even though there was a move to another locality. Some surnames were derived from official appointments, and these would be retained only as long as the appointee lived. They were not hereditary. Many distinctly Japanese family names are current in the Ryukyus.

Before the general adoption of family names among commoners, the house names functioned as an important identifying device. When family names were adopted the old house names formed the basis of many Ryukyuan names. Households had for many years been important community units and the center of ritual activities. House names often included words which expressed location or hope, as *Iri Yama* (west hill), *Fukuji Joo* (lucky gate), and *Muutu Yaa* (main house). Branch houses or subbranch houses generally retained one element of the main house or parent household, as *Yunan Tuku Joo* (fourth son of the back gate). In such branch houses the location words lost their significance with reference to the position of the house. In recent years some surnames have served as new house names.

See *Ryukyuan Names*, ed. Shunzo Sakamaki, Honolulu, 1964.

SAME NAME FOR BOTH SEXES

Among the names which do not disclose the sex of the bearers clearly are *Leslie, Vivian, Shirley, Marion,* and *Lynn.* Others are *Clare, Evelyn, Florence, Garnet, Hilary, Jesse, Jocelyn, Joyce,* and *Sidney,* also the Francis-Frances and Marion-Marian couplets when pronounced. Some of the names that belie their sex come from other languages. For example, *Hyacinthe* is a popular man's name in Yugoslavia.

There were the two young actresses who were discussing show people of a generation past when Florenz Ziegfeld was mentioned. "Who was Florenz Ziegfeld? I never heard of her," said one.

"You haven't," cried her friend, "why Florenz Ziegfeld produced the original Ziegfeld Follies and was married to Billie Burke."

"Well, I never heard of *him* either," was the withering reply.

When Beverly Smith, Jr., the Washington editor of the *Saturday Evening Post,* was a boy in Maryland and Virginia, Beverly was a a boy's name, and several able-bodied men were so named. But from about 1908 to 1920 there was Beverly Bayne, a beautiful female movie star, who had many fans. Parents named their daughters Beverly in such numbers that the name moved over into the feminine column. Smith, who had previously been known as Beverly Smith, to keep his masculine identity added Junior to his name. Smith and his wife sent a gift subscription of the *Post* to a friend, ordering a card to be enclosed, "From Grace and Beverly." Whereupon the Curtis Publishing Company politely addressed a thank-you letter to—Misses Grace and Beverly Smith.

Two little boys adopted a kitten which they named *Ben.* Later discovering that they had made a mistake, they renamed it *Ben Hur.*

SCOTTISH NAMES

Scottish surnames consist of two groups: Highland and Lowland. Highlanders did not use fixed family names until a comparatively late date. Until the eighteenth century a man was often designated by his father's name, sometimes accompanied by the grandfather's or even more remote ancestor's name. In the Lowlands surnames developed on the same lines as those in England, but full development did not come until two centuries later than the English.

In the Highlands it was advisable for a man to join a large and powerful clan for protection, and he would take the clan surname, usually *Mac* (son) prefixed to the chief's name, although of no kindred to the chieftain. Small clans or septs sometimes allied themselves to greater ones or were enlarged by inducing oppressed peasants to join. Three hundred years ago many things were done to "please the lairds," and the adoption of his surname as an act of loyalty called for his favor and protection. Leaving one clan to fight for another generally involved a change of surname. Highland names are thus chiefly patronymics. Chieftainship is hereditary. When it passes to or through a female, her husband is chieftain "by the courtesy of Scotland." A proprietor of lands is entitled to add the name of the property to his surname. The chief of a landed family whose surname and lands are the same is known as "of that ilk," such as *Menzies of that Ilk* or *Macnab of Macnab*.

The Lowlands were chiefly populated by English-speaking people mostly from the north of England, together with some Normans and French. Many had fled from the armies of William the Conqueror crushing the rebellion. Many Lowland names are as Scottish as they are English, such as *Anderson, Crawford, Douglas, Gibson, Gordon, Grant, Henderson, Jackson, Lawson, Marshall, Robertson, Russell, Thompson,* and *Williamson*. Other Lowland names are from places, as *Carmichael* (in Lanarkshire) and *Rutherford* (in Roxburghshire). Lowland names are hardly distinguishable from the usual run of English names.

Margaret is the favorite girl's name in Scotland as it has been for more than a hundred years. *Elizabeth* has moved into second place, replacing *Mary*. For boys the names of *John, James,* and *William,* in that order, have headed the list for many years. *Douglas, Duncan, Donald, Kenneth,* and *Malcolm* are popular Scottish names as well.

The Scottish Privy Council in 1603 expressly abolished the name of *Mac Gregor* and commanded those who bore the name to take another surname on pain of death. Again, by act of the Council in 1613 death was declared to be the penalty for any who should call themselves *Gregor* or *Mac Gregor*. By act of Parliament, in 1617, these laws were continued and extended to the rising generation to prevent the children, then approaching maturity, from resuming the name of their parents. Upon the Restoration, King Charles, in 1661, annulled the various acts against the clan Mac Gregor, and full use of the name was restored.

Sandy McTavish took a traveling job. Toward the end of the week he composed a telegram to his wife. In reply to his question the girl at the desk said that there was no charge for the name. Quickly tearing up the telegram, Sandy said, "I have a long name as I am an Indian, although I may not look like one, and my name is," and he carefully wrote it out, "Iwillarrivehomefridaynight."

A Scottish traveling salesman had occasion to telegraph his office frequently. The Western Union clerk noticed that he signed his name variously spelled Douglas Wasuily, Wathily, Wasaily. Next time he came in, signing it Douglas Wamily, she confronted him. "See here, just how do you spell your name?" she demanded, showing him copies of his other wires.

"Oh that," he replied, "You see I am engaged to my boss's secretary, and she gets the telegrams. The letters WA stand for 'will arrive,' M means 'Monday,' SU 'Sunday,' TH 'Thursday,' and SA 'Saturday.' The ILY means 'I love you.'"

SENTENCE NAMES

Many primitive names of persons consist of complete sentences. Instances are found in many places, mostly with a religious meaning. The early Arabs had such personal names as *Te'abbataśarran* (he had mischief under his arm) and *Yazīd* (he augments). Among the Christian Syrians men were named *Slībhā Zākhē* (the cross conquers) and *Kāmīshō* (Jesus is risen). In Abyssinia there was *Takastabĕrhān* (the light has been revealed). The Hebrew *Hephzibah* (I have my pleasure in her) and *Azrikam* (my help has arisen) are complete sentences. Some of the long Puritan names in England and America are sentence names.

Frequently short names consist of a noun and a verb, even at the the present day, such as *Daniel* (God has judged) and *Joseph* (Yahveh added). Many early names consisted originally of a complete sentence, some of which were abbreviated or shortened to a word or a phrase.

See also NAMES AND ADDRESSES FORMING COMPLETE SENTENCES; PURITAN NAMES

SHORT NAMES

The shortest complete name found is *Ik Ek*, who lived in Brock-ton, Massachusetts, a few years ago. Some other two-letter surnames are *Ah, By, Co, Do, El, Eu, Ex, Fu, Go, Ho, Hu, Ju, Ko, Li, Lu, Ma, Mu, Ng, Ni, Os, Si, So, Sy, Ta, Tu, Um, Un, Uy, Wo, Wu, Wy, Yi,* and *Yu.* The Social Security Administration listed 253 different names in 1964 with only two letters and twenty-five different family names containing only a single letter—only Q was missing from their list. There are numerous three-letter names, most of them being in the uncommon classification.

When it is remembered that short, sharp names are generally not so easily recalled to mind, a very short name may not be an asset except to one who must sign his name many times. People with longer names who must affix them to numerous documents shorten them by the use of initials for the given names and often employ just an undecipherable scrawl for the surname. So even here very short names do not possess real advantages.

See also LONG NAMES

SIGN NAMES

Shop signs have been in use since very early times. Remains of shop signs were found in the buried cities of Pompeii and Herculaneum. During the Middle Ages in Europe, shop and house signs were particularly widespread. Signboards were a necessity then when few outside of the clergy could read or write. Even the ordinary clergyman's skill was most imperfect. The plan of numbering the doors did not come into vogue until the early part of the eighteenth century. In medieval times there were no elaborate shop windows where goods for sale could be displayed. Consequently the only available means of showing a prospective customer what the maker and seller of goods had for sale was a pictorial sign. Brewers and sellers of ale were compelled by law in England and France to erect a sign as early as the latter part of the fourteenth century. Borrowed from the early Romans, this was the bush, a bunch of ivy or evergreen tied to the end of a pole.

The earliest shop or inn signs were not the black swans and red lions so common in later times or the combinations *Angel and Glove, Adam and Eve, Bag of Nails,* but such simple objects or tools of their trade as a boot for a shoemaker, a hat for a hatter, a cleaver for a butcher, a pair of shears for a tailor, a saw or a plane for a carpenter. One did not need to be artist enough to draw or paint

206

a reproduction of the goods for sale. The item itself could be merely attached outside the door. Many signboards consisted of pictures of various animals, birds, or fish. Every conceivable sort of object could be put to use as a sign.

Many unusual names are clearly derived from house, shop, and inn signs. It is the most natural thing in the world to call a man by the object on the signboard at the place where he lived or worked. Most of the signs have disappeared but their memory remains as family nomenclature. Because simple signs failed to stand the erosion of time and weather and few were mentioned in contemporary manuscripts, there is little real evidence of surnames derived from them. The best proof of these sign names are such identifications as *atte swan, de la rose, a cok* (cock), and *del hat*. Many books printed before the middle of the seventeenth century have such recitations on their title pages as, "Printed by Thomas Harper, for John Waterson, and are to be sold at his shop in Pauls Church-yard, at the signe of the Crowne."

Perhaps the best-known completely authenticated sign name is the German *Rothschild*, derived from the red shield on the bearer's house in the Jewish quarter of Frankfort-on-the-Main.

SINGLE NAME

Several entertainment personalities have used only a single stage name to gain attention. The French-Canadian comedian Gratien Gelinas attained success as *Fridolin*. Fernand Joseph Désiré chose to act as *Fernandel*; this was the nickname applied to him by his mother-in-law. *Paderewski* achieved fame after dropping Ignace Jan. He advised *Liberace*, the pianist, then a young man in Milwaukee, to drop his given names of Wladziu Valentino if he wanted to be successful in music. *Fabian* dropped his surname of Forte. *Cantinflas*, the Mexican theatrical personality, was born Mario Moreno; he created Cantinflas to hide his clowning from his family. *Capucine*, the French actress, was born Germaine Lefebvre.

In the thirties Harry Einstein attained radio fame as *Parkyakarkus*. Hildegarde Loretta Sell became a star when she found out that *Hildegarde* was the only name she needed. The Parisian, Ann Carpentier, came to Hollywood studios simply as *Annabella*, and a publicity writer explained, "If the public hears everyone calling a star by her first name, they decide that she must be popular." Singer-actress Ann Margret Olsson dropped her surname to be known only as *Ann-Margret*.

Many writers have used single names as pseudonyms, such as *Ouida* (Louise de la Ramée), *Saki* (H. H. Munro), *Voltaire* (François Marie Arouet), and *Elia* (Charles Lamb).

Mr. and Mrs. Alanson Herbert Tifft had a baby son about 1889 but could not decide on a name; so they resolved to let the boy choose for himself. He never got around to making a choice, and remained simply *Tifft* in school and in his business life until his retirement and death. He found that the single name became an asset of peculiar value, giving trouble only to a few unimaginative persons. However, he gave his two sons usual forenames, and his grandchildren all have the ordinary collection of names. His wife gave him the only nickname he ever acquired—Tiffit.

SISSY NAMES

There is a small group of names for boys that is generally regarded, in most quarters, not everywhere, as not manly. They are good names, but have been labeled as "sissy." Most everywhere regarded as sissy are *Algernon, Cadwallader, Clarence, Cuthbert, Murgatroyd, Reginald,* and *Percy* or *Percival*. Others often so regarded are *Aloysius, Archibald, Cecil, Chauncey, Claude, Cyril, Egbert, Ethelbert, Harold, Hector, Horace, Jonah, Lancelot, Llewellyn,* and *Lloyd*. It is just not safe to acknowledge the possession of these names in some neighborhoods. Some of them will in the future grow out of this classification. Feminine names for boys also come within this anathema. Sissy names for boys are much worse than masculine names for girls, many of whom welcome masculine nicknames.

Two cowboys were drinking in a western bar. One stuck out his hand and said, "I'm Tex."

"You from Texas?" asked the other, shaking his hand.

"Nope, I'm from Louisiana, but who wants to be called Louise?"

Yet many of these so-called sissy names have been borne by fierce, tough, fighting men of times past. William de Perci, a follower of the Conqueror, founded the Percy family and died in 1096. For five hundred years his descendants carrying the name fought in England's wars. The Percys of Northumberland were fond of chasing the

Douglases of Scotland across the River Tweed. As a Christian name *Percy* was popularized by the poet Percy Bysshe Shelley. Others have been borne by famous saints. There were two St. Cyrils. Horace was a great Roman poet.

There really seems to be no valid reason why these names are labeled as sissy. Why they are so regarded is obscure. Some readers will consider some of them as perfectly good names—those not regarded as sissy in the locality when the person was reared. Dr. George R. Stewart has suggested that those from English surnames, or with a distinctive English flavor, were first given in cultured families with a pretension of an aristocratic association or noble descent, and not in the rougher, more illiterate families, and thus they came to be considered decadent and therefore effeminate.

Home from school, the little boy told his mother that the boy in front of him was the teacher's pet. "What's his name?" asked the mother.

"Alice."

"For a boy! That's strange. Are you sure?" asked the mother.

"Yes. Teacher keeps calling him 'Alice dear, Alice dear,'" complained the boy.

Angered that the teacher would prefer another over her precious one, the mother confronted the teacher, objecting to the favoritism, to be told that the boy sitting in front of her son was Alistair Campbell.

SLOVAK NAMES

The Slovaks are closely related linguistically to the Czechs. The languages are mutually intelligible. The names flaunt the same numerous diacritical marks so irritating to Americans. Also they are invariably accented on the first syllable, which adds to the difficulty English-speaking people encounter with them. Many diminutive and patronymical suffixes are used.

Slovak surnames follow the general pattern found in other European countries. Patronymics are common, such as *Kubaš* (Jacob), *Pafko* (Paul), *Péterka* (little Peter), *Siman* (Simon), *Toman* (Thomas), *Martinek* (Martin), *Greguška* (Gregory), *Matuščak* (son of Matthew), *Jelačič* (son of Jelak), *Kavulič* (son of Kavula), and *Belejčak* (son of Bela). Some descriptive nicknames are *Bilko* (white), *Krany* (short), *Buciač* (thick one), *Hudak* (blond, red

209

one), *Vargovič* (with big lips), *Kročka* (slow moving), and *Brlety* (one who searches). There are the occupational names of *Fleischacker* (meat cutter), *Krámoriš* (merchant), *Kušner* (furrier), *Pekar* (baker), *Supka* (soup-maker), *Hlinka* (lime burner), and *Molnar* (miller). Strangers from other districts are *Polak* (from Poland) and *Pruša* (from Prussia); and from villages are *Bištricky* (from Bistrica). *Lednicky* (from Lednice), *Vlčansky* (from Vlčany), and *Gorčiansky* (from Gorce). *Hrusosky* is the dweller near a pear tree.

See also CZECH NAMES

SMITH

This is the most popular surname in the English-speaking world. At a time when metal, especially iron, was increasing in importance, the work of the smith was most necessary and admired. The trade of the smith was said to be the only one that a free man might follow in ancient times without degrading himself. One smith was needed in every village, and as it was a most honorable calling the smith was glad to be so named.

Smith originally meant merely a craftsman, or worker, especially a skilled worker in metal, wood, or other material. The term was said to have been given to all who smote with the hammer, although the word is clearly not derived from the verb *smite* as some authorities have claimed. Gradually the word narrowed down to mean only the worker in metals and more particularly the worker who forged iron. In modern times the term *blacksmith* has absorbed the smith.

The Kenites, mentioned several times in the Bible, were a nomadic or seminomadic tribe of smiths who, as early as the thirteenth century B.C., made their living in various parts of Palestine as metal craftsmen. The name of the tribe means "belonging to the smith." In I Samuel 13:19, is the statement, "Now there was no smith found throughout all the land of Israel." The shortage of smiths in Israel was thus such an important fact as to be recorded in the Bible. The first man born on this earth was a smith. The name of Cain, the eldest son of Adam and Eve, is derived from an ancient word meaning "smith" or "worker in metal." After man and woman came upon this earth, the next person needed was a Smith!

When Margaret Chase Smith, the senator from Maine, indicated a willingness to be president of the United States, a wit asked her how one Smith could ever hope to run this country when it took two Smiths to make even a cough drop. When a Nebraska Republican delegate tried to nominate Joe Smith for vice president as a lark in 1956, the status of every Joe Smith in the country rose. For months after, the Joe Smiths of the country were haunted by gagsters.

Some like to jibe at the Smyths for the harmless "y" in their name, thinking it a modern affectation, but that is almost invariably the spelling in the early rolls and literature of England, although in the very earliest English writings it was generally spelled with an *i* as in *Beowulf* and the *Anglo-Saxon Chronicle*. Gradually the *i* replaced the *y* and Elizabethan Smyths became Victorian Smiths. A curious variation is *Smijth*, one that seems harsh both to the eye and the ear. This form arose from the spelling with the double *i*, which being written *ij*, as was the custom, became naturally *Smijth*, and an important family with this name is found during the reign of Henry VIII in England. In early times the final *e* in *Smithe* and *Smythe* was just the result of a terminal flourish by the scribes. *Smith*, no matter how spelled, was pronounced the same in ancient times as it is today.

The name of Smith is found in almost all the important languages:

Language	Smith
Arabic	Khaddad
Armenian	Darbinian
Assyrian	Nappakhu
Bulgarian	Kovác
Catalan	Ferrer
Cornish	Angove, Gof
Croatian	Kovač
Czech	Kovář
Cymric	Gof
Danish	Smed
Dutch	Schmidt, Schmitz
Estonian	Kalevi
Finnish	Rautio, Seppänen
Flemish	De Smet, De Smedt
French	Lefevre, Lefebvre, Le Fevers, Ferrier, Ferron, Faure
Gaulish	Gobannitio
German	Schmidt, Schmitz, Schmitt, Schmid, Smidt
Greek	Skmiton
Gypsy	Petulengro

Language	Smith
Hebrew	Zillai, Kharash
Hindustani	Lohár, Sumár
Icelandic	Smiđr
Irish Gaelic	Gough, Goff
Italian	Ferraro
Kurdistan	Hasinger
Lapp	Ravddé, Smirjo
Latin	Faber
Lettish	Kalejs
Lithuanian	Kálvis
Manx	Gawn, Gawne
Magyar	Kovács
Norwegian	Smid
Persian	Ahangar
Polish	Kowal
Portuguese	Ferreiro
Rumanian	Covaciu
Russian	Kuznetzov, Koval
Sanskrit	Karmara
Scotch Gaelic	Gow
Slovak	Kováč
Spanish	Herrera
Swedish	Smed ·
Turkish	Temirzi
Welsh	Goff, Gowan

There was the man who said that his name was known and spoken wherever the English language was spoken, and upon being asked his name admitted that it was Smith.

He said that the worst thing about being a bachelor was that one's name dies with one.

Smith went to the doctor's office and appealed, "Doctor, can you help me? My name is Smith," whereupon the doctor was forced to reply, "No, I'm sorry; I simply can't do anything for that."

SOUND OF NAMES

Charles D. Rice wrote that M. Fidelis Blunk was reminiscent of a heavy object dropping into a rain barrel. An Egyptian gentleman named Aziz Ezzet observed that his name could be pronounced by slowly opening a soda bottle.

The names that the orator or preacher can say in august, full, resonant tones with rising accents are Abraham Lincoln and Shadrach, Meshach, and Abednego. To these must be added John Fitzgerald Kennedy.

Disagreeable-sounding names can be coined from harsh and disagreeable words. Dickens's unpleasant character Scrooge possibly derives from *scrouge*, a colloquial term meaning to crowd or press. It has been suggested that one reason for the success of the Ku Klux Klan was the weird potency in the sound of the name, evocative of bones crunching. People liked to repeat the name just to hear the sound of its mysterious, sonorous, sinister syllables. The name is probably derived from an innocent Greek word meaning "circle."

Some great, foreign, musical names have an impressive and harmonious sound to us. *Beethoven* possesses an aristocratic, ringing sound, but it is just a democratic Dutch word for "beet field." *Brahms* merely designates the son of Abraham, while *Paderewski* is the descendant of Patrick. *Tschaikovsky* refers to one who came from Czajkow, the name of various towns in Poland and Russia. *Chopin* is a French fighting man. *Dvorak* was originally a vassal or attendant at a court. *Schubert* and *Schumann* were shoemakers. *Verdi* means green. *Mozart* descended from Muothart. *Strauss* originally dwelt at the sign of the ostrich.

SOUTH AMERICAN NAMES

South American names, outside of Brazil and the French, English, and Dutch colonies, pretty well follow the Spanish name customs. This is true even where the population is predominantly Indian. When Indian parents take their child to the Bureau of Vital Statistics for registation of birth, the authorities enter their names according to the traditional Spanish system.

A list of permitted Christian names has been compiled in Argentina. They are all Spanish forms of saints' names. When Americans and Britons in that country try to register their newborn babies with English names they are blocked by Argentine officials not disposed to give an inch. The *New York Times*, in 1943, reported that the Ar-

213

gentine Criminal Court had fined a couple for naming sons *Zoroaster* and *Jupiter* and ordered their renaming.

See also BRAZILIAN NAMES; SPANISH NAMES

SPANISH NAMES

Before the Spanish people adopted hereditary family names, it was the custom to use as a surname the father's name in the genitive case. This called for the termination *-es* or *-ez*, as *Estébanez* (son of Stephen). These surnames thus changed with each generation. *Diego Fernández* was the son of *Fernando Muñoz*, and Diego's son might be *Gonzalo Díaz*. Some took patronymics derived from the grandfather. Gradually many of these patronymics evolved into hereditary family names. A few names designated office or occupation, as *Herrera* (smith) and *Alcalde* (mayor). *Romero* designated one who made a pilgrimage to Rome.

Lords who owned feudal manors or other landed estates tended to take the names of their principal estates as surnames. As the estates descended to the son, the name also descended. In some cases the estate name was used instead of the patronymic; in other cases both surnames were used. More than one estate name could be used as surnames at the same time. In Spanish names the preposition *de* before a geographic name, as in the appellation Fernandez *de Córdoba*, never had any prestige value as it had in France. The definite article may also be used with the preposition as in *de los Ríos* (from the rivers), or they may be coalesced as in *Delmar* (of the sea).

In the last two centuries the custom arose of a child taking as a surname the father's surname plus the surname of the mother joined by *y* (and) or, occasionally, by a hyphen. The father's surname comes first. Thus *José* the son of *Fernand González* and *Josepha Martinez* would be known as *José González y Martinez*. José might marry *Manuela González y de la Guerra* and their son *Rafael* would be *Rafael Gonzalez y Gonzalez*. The father's name is the one that descends to the children. When a woman marries she adds her husband's family name to her own preceded by *de*. If she outlives her husband, she continues to use the male name of her father, but before the male name of her husband she inserts the expression *viuda de* (widow of).

Among the commonest Spanish family names are *Chavez, Fer-*

nandez, Garcia, Gomez, Gonzalez, Lopez, Martinez, Ramirez, Rod-riguez, and *Ruiz. Garcia* is the number-one name in Spain with *Fernandez* second.

Baptismal names are the well-known saints' names from the church calendar of saints, such as *Juan, Homero,* and *Julio.* Among women the great favorite is *María.* As a popular name this often causes confusion; and to solve the need for further identification, the name of some place or event associated with the Virgin's life is added, and combinations result, such as *María de los Dolores* (Mary of the sorrows) and *María de la Cruz* (Mary of the Cross). Thus a name like *María de la Cruz de Castro Rodriguez y de la Torre* can be most confusing to a stranger.

In Spain, where the cult of the Virgin is so very important, most girls receive either Maria as a given name or one of the numerous designations referring to the Virgin Mother such as *Dolores, Mercedes, Carmen, Concepción, Encarnación, Luz, Consuelo, Amparo, Rosario,* and *Maria of Mercies.*

Boys are often given the names of *Jesus* and *Salvador.* Women are seen now and then with the names of *Jesusa* and *Salvadora.*

The use of colloquial and pet forms of the baptismal name among Spanish people is common. For example, Francisco and José may be referred to as *Pacorro* and *Chepe.* There are many nickname or diminutive pet forms for each common name. José might be *Che, Chepe, Chepito, Josecito, Joseito, Pepe, Pepillo,* or *Pepito,* and Francisco might be called *Chico, Chicho, Chilo, Chito, Currito, Curro, Farruco, Francisquito, Frasco, Frascuelo, Paco, Pacorro, Pancho, Panchito, Paquito,* or *Quico.* Most of the same pet forms ending in -*a,* would designate the girls named *Francisca* and *Josefa.*

Contractions with María are sometimes found in Spain such as *Marines* (for Maria plus Inez), *Mariflor* (for Maria plus Flora), and *Maricruz* (for Maria plus Cruz).

See also Americanization of Names

SPELLING VARIATIONS

Until the advent of Webster's dictionaries in the early part of the nineteenth century, people spelled both words and names as the fancy of the moment dictated. Spelling of Old English was roughly phonetic. Even after the spelling of ordinary English words became uniform, writers spelled names as it was thought they were pronounced. Uniformity in orthography was not regarded as of any importance. The same name was frequently spelled several different ways in the same document. Due to differences in dialect throughout England, many names were pronounced differently in different parts of the country, and variant spellings were thus brought about. In the south there is the surname *Gates* with *Yates* or *Yeats* in the north, both from the Old English word for a gate or the gap in a chain of hills.

A name like *Raleigh* (from Raleigh, red meadow, in Devonshire) simply invites variant spellings, such as *Ralegh, Raleighe, Raley, Rallegh, Raughley, Raughlie, Raughly, Raugleigh, Rauleigh, Rauly, Rawle, Rawleghe, Rawlei, Rawleigh, Rawley, Rawleygh, Rawlie, Rawlighe, Raylie,* and *Raylye.* James Ricenbaw, living near Cordova, Nebraska, collected forty misspellings of his surname in a year. David C. Billyeald of Chicago collected thirty-seven misspellings of *Billyeald*. Many people with unusual names salve their wounded feelings by collecting misspellings. Allyn Cole, of Glenwood Springs, Colorado, a lawyer searching the title to a parcel of real estate which was owned by a man whose descendants said his correct name was Guiseppe Antonio Zarlingo, found the following variations in the various recorded instruments: Giospe Zarlengo, Guiseppi Antonio Zarlengo, Guiseppe Zarlengo, Joseph Zarlengo, Joseph Zarlingo, Gioseppe Zarlingo, Guseppe Zarlingo, Joe Zarlingo, Josepe Xarlingo, Guiseppe Zarlenga, Giusseppe Zarlenga, and Giusseppe Antonio Zarlenga; not one of the twelve instances being the correct name.

Roswell L. Gilpatric, the deputy defense secretary, always spelled his name without the terminal *k.* The Armed Forces Information and Educational Directorate in 1962 issued a sixteen-page pamphlet entitled *Our Department of Defense,* spelling the deputy secretary's name with a *k.* The error was discovered, and the publication was disposed of as waste paper.

When a name originating in a country not using our alphabet is bandied in all the newspapers of the Western world, the spelling is a bit altered to approximate the pronunciation as written in the original. Let us take *Khrushchev:* In France, it is *Kroutchev;* in Germany, *Chruschtschow;* Italy has *Krushuiov;* Netherlands, *Chroestjew;* Spain, *Kruschev;* Israel, *Khrushtsev;* Finland, *Hrushtshev;* Poland, *Chruszezow;* Czechoslovakia, *Chruscov;* Norway, *Khrusjtsjov;* Sweden,

Krustjev; and Yugoslavia, *Hruscov.* The Japanese use five phonetic signs—*Hu-ru-shi-cho-hu.* When Russians write it in the Latin alphabet they use *Khruschov.*

The Chinese newspapers in Formosa agreed to render John F. Kennedy with three characters pronounced *Kan Nai Dai,* which translates into English as "willing-endurance-bliss."

Sometimes the spelling of a name is thought to indicate religion. For example, in certain parts of West Virginia the names *Hennessee, Kelley, McCarty, Murphey,* and *Rian* are looked upon as "Protestant," while their counterparts *Hennessey, Kelly, McCarthy, Murphy,* and *Ryan* are considered to be "Catholic."

Names with unusual spellings, such as found in the Irish, the Italian, the French, and the Slavic tongues, create a multiplicity of surnames in America. One unusual spelling can give rise to twenty or more different names through inability or unwillingness of English-speaking people to grasp the spelling and pronunciation.

It was Lincoln who, when asked whether his wife's family name, *Todd,* was spelled with one *d* or two, observed, "One *d* is enough for God, but the Todds need two." Perhaps the man with a common name who has his name pronounced correctly but is most likely to have it misspelled is *Shafer.* Common spellings, in approximate order of frequency, are *Schaefer, Shaffer, Schaffer, Schaeffer, Schafer, Shafer, Sheffer, Scheffer, Shaefer, Scheafer, Schefer, Sheaffer,* and *Scheaffer.* Perhaps *Schaefer* is the most authentic, the name being the German word for a shepherd. The Sheaffer Pen Company, in Fort Madison, Iowa, found that about 9 per cent of its correspondents misspelled the name. In one day twenty-one variants were noticed.

A Belgian business man was Mr. *O.* In London he had trouble insisting that it was just O. In France they insisted on spelling it *Haut* or *Eau.* The Dutch referred to him as *Van O.* The English thought that he was an Irishman who had lost half of his name. But everybody remembered his name.

Variations in Spelling Girls' Names

Almost every girl at some time or other experiments with the spelling and appearance of her Christian name. The most common alteration is to insert a "y" or change an "e" or an "i" to "y." Thus she appears as *Caryl, Candyace,* or *Cleopaytra; Ellyn, Adyline, Brynda,* or *Karyn; Lynda, Edyth, Robyn, Alyson, Lydya, Sayra,* and

217

even *Sylvya*. Of course the normal "y" can always be turned back to "i" to produce *Rubi, Cathi, Lidia,* and *Ami.* In 1964, President Johnson's sixteen-year-old daughter let it be known that she prefers her name to be spelled *Luci,* not Lucy. Others add the Old English "e" in an attempt to give chic and unusual effect to the name; and *Ruthe, Edithe* and *Debrae* are some of the results. Some names are just respelled, as when Alice turns out as *Alysse* or *Elys.* A letter in the middle of a name can be capitalized to make it distinctive, as *ArLene, JoAnn.* An extreme example is *ViViAnn.* Boys are seldom tempted to these wild displays to attract attention.

See also INFLUENCE OF NAMES

SUPERSTITION

Names enter into the superstitious beliefs of all primitive societies in one way or another. In both ancient Hebrew and Babylonian thought nothing could exist unless it had a name. To be and to have a name was the same thing. To eliminate the name was to terminate completely the existence of the bearer in this world and the next. A name was more than a means of identification. It sustained a very close relationship to the person; it was his very self, his soul. To insure the identification of the medicine with the sick man in ancient times, Chinese doctors wrote the name on paper, burned it, and then mixed the ashes with the medicine provided. Cursing a man by name would destroy his soul. Even using the name of the dead would bring his spirit back and was strictly avoided in many savage communities. Dogmas of this nature are found throughout the world.

In Venice in olden times if a man's name was the same as the candidate's, he was not allowed to vote even though there were no ties of kinship between them. Such was the dread with which the Venetians regarded the influence of that feeling which identifies the name with the individual, a feeling that prevents one from looking upon a man as a stranger if he bears the same name.

The Egyptian *Book of the Dead,* in 106 chapters, informs the deceased of the many names he must know in order to avoid the lower world's torments. As the deceased enters the Hall of Judgment he must know the name of the great god and the forty-two gods that exist with him in that hall. Then he is not allowed to pass into the next hall until he has identified correctly the names of the bolts, lintels, threshold, fastenings, socket, door leaves, and door posts. As he passes through the different gates the various doorkeepers, watchers, and heralds block his way until he discloses his accurate knowledge of their names. Twenty-one hidden pylons of the house of Osiris must have their names and the names of the gods who are doorkeepers declared. Many other names are required of the deceased, and parts of the *Book of the Dead* were often buried with the dead to aid his memory.

In many primitive tribes scattered throughout the world it is forbidden to speak the name of certain relatives, or to pronounce common words which are parts of the names. A synonym or some awkward description of the word must be used. If a name includes the word for tooth, one might say biter; if hand, one might mention the lower arm. They believe that violation of the taboo will bring harm on them or on the one mentioned.

Among the Australian aborigines there is a taboo on speaking a dead man's name. With some, this taboo lasts until the totem poles above the grave rot and fall; with others it lasts until the dead native is reincarnated, as they believe that he comes back as an animal, bird, or fish within ten years. Breaking the taboo, even unwittingly, can damn a man for life. Others with the same name change their names rather than risk a friend's calling them and breaking the taboo.

The custom among many primitive peoples is to conceal the child's real name and call him by some nickname in order to prevent the spirits from harming the child. Others confer two names at birth, one the real name to be used only for ceremonial purposes and the other for ordinary use. In some tribes a secret name is conferred at puberty when the young are admitted to full membership in the group.

In some primitive societies there is no hesitation about communicating names to strangers so long as the names are not spoken by the owners. The name is felt to be a part of one's person, and when it is uttered, the breath of the owner goes with it, a living part of the owner. A name divulged by its bearer can be used to produce ill effects on the owner if it is possessed by an evil being. It is curious to note that young children in our civilization hesitate to speak their names before strangers.

In different sections of the United States there are various superstitions, beliefs, and folk sayings concerning names, most of which are also found elsewhere. For example: A child named before it is born will die; unbaptized children who cry are calling for a name; a child named after its parents will not live long; giving the child the name of one recently deceased is bad luck; if initials form a word, the child will have bad luck, but others believe this will bring wealth; changing one's name is unlucky; if you answer when you hear your name called by a ghost, you will probably die; and repeating a certain number of times the name of one you wish to marry will bring about the desired result. Many others have customs directly contrary to these beliefs which they follow avidly.

Among many savages a very common custom is for boys and girls to take a new name at puberty and give up their old one. They believe that in so doing they take a new identity, become an entirely different person.

In many primitive and undeveloped societies throughout the world a woman is not allowed to utter her husband's name. She must refer to him by such terms as "the master," "the man of the house," or "father of so-and-so." She cannot even use the words composing the husband's name in their ordinary sense. In some tribes the men are reluctant to use the name of their wives, and if prevailed upon to do so, pronounce them only in a low tone.

It is the custom among the peasants of Bulgaria to name children born after the death of a first child *Zhivko* (life) if a boy, and *Zhivka* if a girl, to insure the life of the second child. The Navaho Indians believe that there is just so much power in a name and when that is used up the name is exhausted. A child is therefore scarcely referred to at all when it is born. Certain North American Indians and peoples in Tibet believed that sickness was caused by names that "did not fit," the cure being to acquire a new name that would fit.

See Edward Clodd, *Magic in Names and in Other Things*, London, 1920.

See also JEWISH FORENAMES; MAGIC NAMES

SURNAME

A surname is an additional name or nickname added to other names for identification or for reasons of vanity. Surnames started as bynames, to-names, or added names, of less importance than the given name or Christian name. A surname is not necessarily a family name, although that is the connotation usually given it in English at the present time. The French make a distinction between *surnom* and *nom de famille*. In England and on the continent, clerks invariably noted the surnames as descriptive terms in Latin. The family names that have come down to us are the actual spoken words used.

Surname is derived from Old French *surnom* (*sur*, over, plus *nom*, name). It was originally written over the given name, not in a direct line with the Christian name but above it and between the lines. It is not derived from sirname (*sir*, a variant of *sire*, father) although that spelling is commonly found in English literature in the fourteenth and fifteenth centuries, but is now obsolete.

Walking with her mother little Flossie greeted a small boy they met. Mother asked, "What is his name?"

"It's Johnnie, and he's in my class in the first grade," replied the girl.

"What is his last name?" inquired the mother.

"It's Johnnie Sitdown," said Flossie, "that's what the teacher calls him."

Little three-year-old Robert was asked his name by a neighbor. "Robert," he replied.

"Robert what?" she queried. Robert looked puzzled. "What does your mother say after Robert?"

Robert's eyes lit up. "She says, 'Robert Stop It.'"

See also SURNAMES IN COMMON USE

SURNAMES AS SYMBOL OF STATUS

From very early times in many countries it has been possible to ascertain the status of a person from his name. In early Scandinavian runic inscriptions, dating from about 200 to 800 A.D., it has been noted by Assar Janzén that people of prominent families bore dithematic or compound personal names while monothematic or simple names, often just nicknames, were borne by the middle and lower classes.

Throughout the history of the world the continuous reaching by the lower classes for aristocratic names, and the gradual abandonment by the noble families of their names to take others, has brought about an almost imperceptible change in types of names. In America, since anyone can adopt any name he chooses, no name, separate from the family name, sets the bearer apart from anyone else.

In many countries one name or another is felt to denote a slightly higher status. In Norway farm names are considered a little better from the standpoint of rank. In Sweden certain names such as *Hammarskjold* and *Palmstjerna* are the superior ones, while names ending in *-berg, -strom, -gren, -in, -lund, -man,* and *-kvist* rank definitely higher socially than those terminating in *-son*. Priest names in Sweden and Greece are highly respected. Polish names terminating in *-ski* are preferred by many in Poland. To many, territorial names seem to indicate a past possession of landed estates and are thus accorded slight hat-tipping deference. Some who dropped the German *von*, the Dutch *van*, or the French *de* resumed it for that reason. The English *à* (as in Thomas à Becket), *by*, or *atte* (at the) never appeared to indicate any superior status, however.

As the nobles were the first to be known by surnames, their use became a symbol of status, a badge of noble birth. In medieval times it seemed a disgrace for a gentleman to have but a single name. Camden tells of the reply, in the early part of the twelfth century, made by the daughter and heir of Fitz Hamon, a great lord, when King Henry I would have married her to his illegitimate son, Robert: "It were to me a great shame, to have a lord without'n his twa name." Recognizing the truth of the young lady's assertion the king thereupon gave his son the to-name of FitzRoy.

SURNAMES IN COMMON USE

In 1957 the Social Security Administration of the Department of Health, Education, and Welfare made a machine count of the common surnames in the Social Security Account Number File, containing 117,358,888 accounts, and another count in 1964, when the list contained 152,757,455 accounts. Data used by the machine took into account only the first six letters. Thus the names *William*, *Williams*, and *Williamson* were counted as only one name; no distinction was made between such names as *Robins* and *Robinson*, and *Peterson* and *Petersen*. From this machine information it is possible, with other statistics, to insert names like *Williams* and *Williamson* in their approximately correct order. Following is the list of the two hundred most common surnames with estimated numbers of each in the United States (the estimates being calculated from the number counted by machine in the Social Security Accounts):

1. Smith	1,872,400	
2. Johnson	1,416,100	
3. Brown	1,061,400	
4. Williams	1,058,200	
5. Jones	1,029,800	
6. Miller	895,300	
7. Davis	809,800	
8. Martin	723,800	
9. Anderson	619,300	
10. Wilson	615,700	
11. Taylor	538,500	
12. Moore	538,100	
13. Thomas	528,100	
14. Thompson	494,700	
15. White	494,300	
16. Jackson	485,300	
17. Harris	472,000	
18. Clark	426,000	
19. Lewis	380,900	
20. Walker	374,700	
21. Hall	362,100	
22. Allen	354,300	
23. Robinson	354,100	
24. Young	352,160	
25. Nelson	336,900	
26. King	335,100	
27. Wright	334,400	
28. Baker	322,300	
29. Hill	320,600	
30. Green	315,700	
31. Scott	315,300	
32. Adams	313,500	
33. Lee	294,500	
34. Mitchell	286,400	
35. Campbell	281,900	
36. Roberts	279,600	
37. Phillips	279,400	
38. Carter	266,700	
39. Evans	262,500	
40. Turner	253,500	
41. Murphy	252,400	
42. Rodriguez	251,300	
43. Collins	251,200	

44. Parker	247,000
45. Stewart	240,800
46. Edwards	239,800
47. Peterson	238,300
48. Cook	231,100
49. Rogers	230,100
50. Morgan	211,300
51. Gonzalez	210,000
52. Cooper	208,200
53. Kelly	208,100
54. Reed	206,900
55. Bell	205,800
56. Bailey	203,300
57. Wood	201,700
58. Garcia	200,600
59. Ward	199,700
60. Cox	196,500
61. Howard	190,900
62. Sullivan	189,100
63. Bennett	188,500
64. Brooks	187,500
65. Watson	186,000
66. Gray	185,200
67. Hughes	182,100
68. Griffin	181,500
69. Ross	180,300
70. Myers	180,100
71. Long	178,100
72. Price	174,700
73. Russell	173,100
74. Fisher	172,800
75. Foster	171,900
76. Nichols	171,400
77. Henderson	169,600
78. Sanders	167,500
79. Butler	164,000
80. Powell	163,800
81. Perry	162,800
82. Richardson	162,300
83. James	159,200
84. Jenkins	159,100
85. Barnes	158,400
86. Stevens	157,300

87.	Morris	157,200	130.	Palmer	121,700
88.	Reynolds	155,800	131.	Meyer	121,200
89.	Patterson	153,900	132.	Perez	121,150
90.	Coleman	150,300	133.	Stone	121,140
91.	Graham	150,000	134.	Freeman	120,900
92.	Hamilton	149,700	135.	Robertson	119,800
93.	Simmons	148,800	136.	Rice	118,900
94.	Lopez	148,700	137.	Henry	118,700
95.	Murray	148,600	138.	Hunter	118,500
96.	Williamson	148,100	139.	Fox	117,450
97.	Rivera	148,000	140.	Holmes	117,400
98.	McDonald	145,000	141.	Black	116,900
99.	Morrison	144,600	142.	Carlson	116,400
100.	Alexander	144,500	143.	Kelley	115,300
101.	Wallace	143,900	144.	Warren	114,800
102.	Cole	143,500	145.	Hunt	114,500
103.	Hayes	143,100	146.	Boyd	113,900
104.	West	142,290	147.	Harrison	113,300
105.	Kennedy	140,300	148.	Hicks	112,850
106.	Ellis	139,500	149.	Hansen	112,830
107.	Snyder	138,700	150.	Richards	112,700
108.	Olson	138,600	151.	McCarthy	112,500
109.	Marshall	138,500	152.	Dunn	112,400
110.	Ford	137,500	153.	Elliott	112,300
111.	Jordan	136,500	154.	Rose	112,000
112.	Burns	136,100	155.	Mills	111,300
113.	Gibson	135,600	156.	Arnold	109,750
114.	Bryant	131,900	157.	Daniels	109,670
115.	Wells	131,400	158.	Carr	109,340
116.	Porter	129,700	159.	Dixon	109,100
117.	Wagner	127,700	160.	Hoffman	108,550
118.	Hernandez	126,800	161.	Cunningham	108,500
119.	Owens	126,600	162.	Gardner	108,480
120.	Gordon	124,500	163.	Pierce	108,340
121.	Crawford	124,400	164.	Ferguson	108,100
122.	Tucker	123,700	165.	Little	107,400
123.	Mason	123,500	166.	O'Brien	107,390
124.	Schmidt	123,300	167.	Washington	107,380
125.	Ryan	122,900	168.	Hart	107,200
126.	Simpson	122,840	169.	Spencer	105,300
127.	Woods	122,750	170.	Johnston	105,250
128.	Shaw	121,800	171.	Andrews	105,100
129.	Webb	121,750	172.	Burke	104,900

173.	Weaver	104,700	187.	Grant	98,200
174.	Knight	104,200	188.	Stephens	97,500
175.	Berry	104,100	189.	Hudson	97,200
176.	Payne	104,000	190.	Wheeler	96,800
177.	Armstrong	103,400	191.	Lynch	96,400
178.	Lane	102,300	192.	Chapman	96,100
179.	Cohen	102,100	193.	Willis	95,600
180.	Duncan	100,750	194.	Walsh	95,300
181.	Larson	100,700	195.	Sanchez	95,200
182.	Riley	100,400	196.	Matthews	95,100
183.	Bradley	100,300	197.	Oliver	94,600
184.	Perkins	99,250	198.	Hawkins	93,950
185.	Carpenter	99,200	199.	Greene	93,900
186.	Ray	98,500	200.	Lawrence	93,390

All the nations have contributed to the common American names. For example: German *Muellers* and *Müllers* and Czech *Mylnářs* have become Millers; *Schmidts* have become Smiths; Irish *McShanes*, Swedish *Jansens*, Danish *Hansens*, have all become Johnson; Welsh *Davies* changed to Davis; *Bruns* from several nations have become Browns; Scotch *Muirs* and German *Mohrs* have changed to Moore; German *Weiss* translates to White; Scandinavian *Andresens*, *Anderssons*, and *Andriessens* have become Anderson; Czech *Kovářs* have become Smith, to name only a few.

Almost everyone thinks of his name as annoyingly common or pleasingly uncommon. The 2,200 most popular surnames in the United States are borne by half of the people. But to name the other half the Social Security Administration found that more than 1,100,000 uncommon names are in use.

Why Certain Surnames Are Common

The question as to just why some surnames are so much more common than others sometimes arises. A few surnames are explained here to help throw light on many others.

Smith, because every village needed one smith, and only one, so it became a surname in every village in England.

Miller, ditto; also in America because many German and other foreign millers changed to English *Miller*.

Jones, because John, pronounced *Jone*, was the most popular name in Wales at the time family names became fixed.

King, because of the many May Day, Christmastide, Easter,

225

and Whitsuntide revels and processions in each village that required one to play the king; many also came from being the king's man, that is, serving him in some capacity in the numerous manors he personally owned.

Brown, because many more men are dark-complexioned than light-skinned; *Brun* was also a popular given name.

Williams, because of the popularity of William as a given name in England and Wales at the time family names became fixed.

Johnson, because of the popularity of John in England and Johansson in Sweden.

Martin, because Martin, the saint, was a favorite subject of medieval art, and a popular given name at the time surnames became fixed; Martin is the most common French surname.

SWEDISH NAMES

Until late in the nineteenth century most Swedes had a given name followed by the given name of their father in the genitive case, to which was added *-son* or *-dotter* (daughter). If Johan *Eriksson* had a boy and a girl, they might be Karl *Johansson* and Greta *Johansdotter.* Karl's children might be Gustav *Karlsson* and Dora *Karlsdotter.*

To put an end to this chaotic situation a law was passed in 1901 which stabilized the family names as they were at that time. Thus Erik Johansson's son Karl became Karl *Johansson* and not Karl *Eriksson.* This law provided that thereafter names could not be changed except with the king's permission, which could be obtained only through a very complicated and expensive procedure. Then in 1946 a royal decree transferred the king's power to grant new names to the National Bureau of Statistics and provided for a simplification of the procedure.

The ten most common Swedish surnames are, in order of popularity, *Andersson, Johansson, Karlsson, Nilsson, Eriksson, Larsson, Olsson, Pettersson, Svensson,* and *Persson. Jansson, Johannesson, Jonasson,* and *Jonsson* are also quite common. The early efforts of the government made names like *Berglund, Bergström, Eklund, Engström, Forsberg, Lindberg, Lindgren, Lindkvist, Lundberg, Lundgren, Lundkvist Sandberg,* and *Sjöberg* within the fifty most common names. The termination *-ander* is popular. It is from the Greek word for "man."

Sweden's Family Name Committee and Royal Patent Registration Board has recommended that people who wish to adopt a less common name choose one with the same initial. In Stockholm, IBM machines were fed more than two thousand first syllables such as *Dahl, Ek, Rot, Ros,* and *Skog* together with about the same number of logical last syllables such as *Berg, Dal,* and *Lund* and the machine came up with 900,000 potential new names. Thus an Andersson might change his name to *Apelalm, Apeldal, Askede, Askskog,* or *Asklund.*

From time to time there was issued a list of names not in use which were considered to be appropriate and attractive family names. Many included words which suggested the love of nature, so much a part of the Swedish people. Combinations like *Berggren, Blomkvist, Dahlgren, Holmgren,* and the like were recommended.

The Family Name Committee has certain discretionary powers with respect to the adoption of new names. While it has been approving about 1,500 new names each year, it may reject one already in extensive use, or one that sounds ridiculous or is in any way offensive. Such names as *Blondi, Cactus,* and *Minsting* (smallest) have been turned down.

The list issued by the Family Name Committee in 1964 included about 56,000 recommended names, and provided that the nature words would only be used as final elements. The plant and topographical terms which compose the elements of these so-called civil names are easily recognized. Some of the most common final elements are: *-alm* (elm), *-asp* (aspen), *-berg* (mountain), *-blad* (leaf), *-blom* (flower), *-ceder* (cedar), *-dahl* (valley), *-fors* (waterfall), *-ek* (oak), *-gran* (pine), *-gren* (branch), *-holm* (river island), *-hult* (copse), *-lind* (linden tree), *-ljung* (heather), *-löf* (leaf), *-lund* (grove), *-kvist* (twig), *-ros* (rose), *-sjö* (sea), *-strand* (shore), *-ström* (stream); and the combinations with other pronounceable elements are endless.

In Sweden a person's last name, especially the last syllable, definitely influences his social standing. People whose surname ends in *-berg, -ström, -gren, -in, -lund, -man,* and *-quist* enjoy a higher social standing than persons whose surname terminates in *-son.* Citizens with such socially accepted names have easier access to the many public jobs. They almost monopolize the commissions in some regiments and in parts of the navy. Consequently, those with names ending in *-son* are stimulated to change them.

Another large class of surnames is the soldier names. When a

Swede was conscripted into the army he usually took a soldier name for his period of service. These were short, warlike names such as *Modig* (brave), *Stark* (strong), *Rapp* (fast), *Rask* (daring), and *Tapper* (courageous). Although this was a temporary name many soldiers and descendants of soldiers adopted the names as their permanent family names, or later changed back to their old soldier names.

Popular Swedish names for boys are: *Anders, Anton, Artur, Bengt, Erik, Ernst, Göran, Gustaf, Henrik, Hjalmar, Ivar, Johan, Josef, Karl, Knut, Magnus, Mikael, Niklas, Otto, Paul, Per, Peter, Rudolf, Stefan, Teodor, Tomas, Wilhelm,* and *Ulrik.* For girls there are: *Anna, Barbro, Blenda, Birgitta, Debora, Dorotea, Edit, Elisa, Ester, Frederika, Gertrud, Hedvig, Helfrida, Ida, Josefina, Karin, Katarina, Kristina, Lena, Margareta, Maria, Paulina, Rakel, Rosa, Rut, Sofia, Teresia, Ulla,* and *Vilhelmina.*

See also AMERICANIZATION OF NAMES

SWISS NAMES

Swiss names, corresponding to the multilingual composition of the Swiss population, are of German, French, Italian, or Romansh origin. The very common names are all of German derivation. There are a few originating, however, in Switzerland, such as *Zuercher* and *Zurcher* (one from Zurich), *Marti* (diminutive of Martin), and *Fritschi* (pet form of Friedrich). *Müller* is the most popular surname in Switzerland. Next most common are *Schmid, Weber, Meier* (a farm manager), found throughout all of Switzerland. Both *Schmid* and *Meier* have several variant spellings which are prevalent. Other common family names are *Huber* (tenant of a hide of land), *Beck* (brook), *Baumann* and *Bauer* (peasant, farmer), *Suter* or *Sutter* (shoemaker), *Pfister* (pastry baker), *Studer* (dweller by a bush), *Schneider* (tailor), *Schweizer* (a Swiss), and *Marti* and *Marty* (Martin). Many derivatives of *Johannes* or its shortened form *Hans,* became family names.

Many German-Swiss family names are typical male Christian names such as *Adam, Albert, Albrecht, Anton, Berchtold, Dietrich, Eberhard, Ernst, Franz, Karli, Kaspar, Klaus, Mathis, Niklaus, Ott, Otto, Reinhard, Richard, Rudolf, Ulrich,* and *Werner.*

The Swiss-French names are not much different from the family names in nearby France. Many of the Swiss-Italian names are similar to those current in the Lombardy area dialects, generally of a patronymical origin.

The most typical Romansh names are house names, beginning *de Ca* plus a given name. In modern use the *de* has usually been dropped and there are such names as *Cahannes, Capaul, Capol, Cadalbert* (of the house of Albert). *Ca* is also used with toponymical words, such as *Casura* (upper house), Casut (lower house), and *Caprè* (priest's house). *De* is also used with place names, as *de Curtins* (of the gardens), and *de Gonda* (of the stony slope).

Officers in charge of vital statistics rigidly limit the Christian names that may be bestowed on children. Common first names are *Karl, Joseph*, and *Maria*. *Maria* is often used for men in combination with masculine names, especially by the Catholic population.

See also FRENCH NAMES; GERMAN NAMES; ITALIAN NAMES

TEKNONYMY

This is the custom current among many savage tribes of the father and mother taking the name of the first-born child, called in English literature a teknonym. Thus if the child is named *Soa*, the male parent will be called *Father of Soa* and the female parent will be *Mother of Soa*. In a loose family culture this was an acknowledgment by the father that the child is his, a change from the primitive system of reckoning descent in the female line alone.

Ernest Crawley, in *The Mystic Rose*, explains that this custom arises from the desire of the parents to take the child under their protection by taking its name, that vital part of its soul or personality, thus protecting it from those who might attempt to work mischief against it. They thus profess in the most material way their responsibility to the child and their relation to it. This custom usually pertains only to the first child, although if it dies, the name of the next living child or the next-born child may be so adopted. Teknonymy has been found in Africa, among American Indians, in Australia, in Melanesia, among the Malays, and in Siberia.

THAILAND NAMES

Formerly a Thai was known in private and public only by his personal name. On his return from Europe in 1916, King Rama VI decreed that all persons should have a surname which was bestowed officially. These surnames are now becoming family names by law. Thus some modern names are (surname last): *Vadhana Isarabhakdi, Phun Phanko, Somboon Rochanakorn, Swasdi Bhotiwihok.* There is now a move to encourage abbreviation of the forename.

If a person becomes a priest, even temporarily, he acquires a new name, and on withdrawal from the priesthood he may introduce it as the middle word in his name. Thus in the name Vichitra Agravichitra Krairiksha, *Agravichitra* is the priestly name. A title or courtesy word implying respect may be prefixed to the name. Telephone directories are indexed by the individual name, not the surname or family name.

THEOPHOROUS NAMES OF MEN

Throughout the known history of the world men everywhere, in all eras, have borne names which contained the name of a god as one element. Primitive gods and their attributes are sometimes kept in the memory of man only through the names of men. The use of the names of God, or of gods, in men's names is a universal principle of naming. To bear the name of a deity is to sustain a special and very real relationship with that god, and be under that god's protection. Literally thousands of illustrations can easily be adduced. *Jesus* (Yahveh saves) is today the most widely known theophoric name.

Among the ancient Sumerians, who came into recorded history by 4000 B.C., the use of theophoric names was common. Some of them are: *Ur-Ninā* (dog, figuratively servant, of Ninā), *Subar-Bau* (pig, figuratively servant, of Bau), *Amar-Enzu* (calf of Enzu, the moon-god), and *An-al-šág* (Anu is kind). The early Babylonians included the patron deity or deities of a city in their names, such as *Selim-Bēl* (Bel, be merciful), *Iltamar-Adad* (he will worship Adad), *Lultamar-Sin* (may I worship Sin), and *Abednego* (servant of Nebo).

In ancient Egypt we find *Amenhotep* (he is united to Amen), *Phtahmiri* (beloved of Phtah), and *Thotmas* (fashioned by Thoth). In early India there is *Indrapālita* (protected by Indra), and *Agnidatta* (given by Agni). Hebrew names in the Bible referring to *El* and *Yahveh*, such as *Eliel* (El is God) and *Jeremiah* (exalted of Yahveh), are numerous. The Muslims use *Abd-Allāh* (slave of Allah), and are encouraged to use *Abd* with any of the ninety-nine names of Allah, such as *Abdorrahman* (merciful) and *Abdulaziz* (powerful). There are Norse names such as *Asmundr* (protection of Os) and *Thorvald* (strength of Thor). Some of our present-day names which include a god's name are *Thurstan* (Thor's stone) and *Osmund* (protection of Os).

In many ancient names just the name of the god is used, some of these being merely shortened forms of longer names. Many names among many peoples refer to God without naming Him, such as the Babylonian *Báši-ilu* (God exists), the Arabic *Atâallah* (God's gift), the Hindi *Devadatta* (God-given), the German *Gottschalk* (God's servant), and the English *Theodore* and *Dorothy* (gift of God).

TITLES

Mister, now abbreviated to *Mr.* is derived from the Latin *minister*, a servant. The word died out after 1600. About 1700, *mister* was revived to describe a tradesman as distinguished from a nobleman and became a symbol of respectability. As an abbreviation, *Mr.* first represented *Master*, a word which goes back to the Latin *magister*, "chief," "head," or "superior," but when *mister* was revived, the abbreviation *Mr.* was applied to it. The want of a plural for Mr. is supplied by *Messrs.*, an abbreviation for *Messieurs*, the plural of the French *Monsieur*. *Dan* is a title of honor, now archaic, equivalent to *master*, *don* or *sir*, surviving chiefly in Dan Cupid.

Mistress is originally from the feminine of *magister*. The abbreviation *Mrs.* for *Mistress* arose about 1600, but was switched to *Missis* or *Missus*, a slang substitute for *Mistress* from about 1850. In the seventeenth and eighteenth centuries *Mrs.* was prefixed to the name of an unmarried woman or girl. *Miss* arose from *mis.*, another abbreviation for *mistress*. As a title for an unmarried girl, *Miss* is of recent origin. In some places *miss* is still used for a young married woman and *missis* or *missus* for an older spinster. *Mrs.* has no real plural although *Mesdames*, a plural for the French *Madame*, is sometimes used. The plural of *Miss* is *Misses*. Various persons have suggested that the title *Ms.* be adopted for a woman to avoid revealing whether she is married or single. It would be pronounced *Miss*. The plural would be *Mss.*, pronounced *missez*. The suggestion appears to be a good one, but has not had any wide acceptance.

Mr., Mrs., and *Miss* are now just terms of respect for persons past the age of puberty. The term *Mr.* in England in the last century was usually used for a man with city property while *Esq.* was popular for one with country property. In America *Esquire* is applied to professional men (mostly to lawyers), literary men, and others of some importance, although the term is tending to become obsolete. It originated as the shield bearer or armor bearer in attendance on a knight, and became in Great Britain a title of dignity next below a knight for younger sons of the nobility, officers of the king's court, justices of the peace, sheriffs, and army officers, now only a courtesy title. Coke ruled that "everyone is entitled to be called esquire if he has the legal right to call himself a gentleman." Modern custom prevents the use of *Mr.* when *Esquire* is appended, and it is not used after *The Hon.*, but is sometimes used after *The Rev.*, when the Christian name is not included.

Some persons continue to use a title before their names which is no longer correct or appropriate, as *Colonel* John W. Baker after he has been discharged from the army. This, where it is not just a local custom, indicates insecurity, a vain desire to display past accomplishments, and to call attention to status and position. No one clings to the original army rank of private or corporal. Other titles most used in America in this way are *Captain, Major, General, Senator,* and *Judge.* The persistent use of titles is more common in professional and academic circles. The self-use of purely courtesy titles, such as *Honorable* and *Esquire,* is considered to be lacking in good taste. Such titles are for use by others. In Europe there is a much more frequent use of titles and ranks than in more democratic America; in Germany even the wife of a doctor is addressed as *Frau Doktor.*

Correct usage of British titles of nobility and honor, originating as it did over centuries, is too complicated for the rules to be fully outlined here. The peers in descending order are the duke and his wife the duchess, the marquis and his wife the marchioness, the earl and his wife the countess, the viscount and his wife the viscountess, and the baron and his wife the baroness. In everyday British usage for titled persons, there is *Lord* for a man and *Lady* for his wife regardless of exact rank. *Lord* is sometimes followed by the surname and sometimes by a territorial designation, as Lord *Halifax* (whose family name is Wood), and Lord *Derby* (whose surname is Stanley). There is a distinction between *Lord* for a peer followed by the surname or territorial designation and *Lord* for the courtesy title of the younger sons of peers linked with the Christian name and surname. In the same way *Lady* is used for all daughters of peers. Baronets and knights prefix *Sir* to their Christian names, or their full names, but not to their surnames alone; their wives prefix *Lady* to their surname. If the old saying that every Englishman loves a lord is true, it is only slightly less true of Americans.

Titles in the Moslem world present problems in the Western world. The Turkish title *Pasha* is an honorary title applied because of high position. Originally it was a military title bestowed on the highest officers. *Bey* was the next appointive rank below a pasha; now it is also just a courtesy title. *Afandi* or *Effendi* indicate the ordinary clerk or civil servant. These titles have now been abolished by law. In early times, since they had numerous wives, the wives of *beys* and *khans* had no title. In more modern times, with monogamy more common, the wives are known as *begums*.

Khan is a royal title, originally Turkistan, meaning "ruler." Lesser potentates adopted it, mainly in Persia and Afghanistan. In many cases those bearing it have dropped their family names, if they ever existed, and these therefore present a problem. With some it is now a last name; with others it is a title. Ali Mohammed Khan, the Afghan statesman, is usually listed under K. Liaquat Ali Khan, former prime minister of Pakistan, is found under L. The late Ali Khan, once married to Rita Hayworth, is under *Ali*, but Ali Khan, a notorious bandit in Iran, is *Khan*, possibly under the theory that a robber is not entitled to an honorary suffix. The Aga Khan is found under A, but *Aga* is also a title and means "chief."

Pandit, in India, refers to a learned man, with a religious connotation. *Pandita* is the feminine form. *Singh* is a military title from *simla*, meaning "lion." *Shaikh* often designates a Hindu converted to Islam. *Nawab*, meaning "nobleman," corrupted to *Nabob*, was sometimes adopted by men knighted by the English. In the Arab countries titles are being abolished. *Sayyed*, with the connotation of Mr., is being applied to all ranks and individuals alike.

The deterioration of titles caused by the efforts of man to increase prestige is well illustrated by the Spanish *Don*, now a title with little more meaning than our *Mr*. Forms of *Dominus* first were used as a title for God, then as a title for Christ and his apostles in the early Middle Ages. Next *Don* was adopted by the nobility and the aristocratic classes. After that anyone who wished to indicate some connection with the aristocracy did so by appropriating this title. Indiscriminate use led to its rejection by many noble families. In 1664, the Spanish government in reply to the constant demand offered it for sale. In Spanish America even some of the Indians began using *Don.*

When men achieve extraordinary eminence in their profession, titles are often dropped, especially after their death, and surnames alone are used. One seldom speaks, for example, of Mr. Washington, or Mr. Shakespeare, except perhaps in a jocular mood. Some Scottish clan chiefs consider it disrespectful if they are addressed as *Mr.*, as that title may be applied to anyone; the surname only is to be used.

TOM, DICK, AND HARRY

This is a convenient term for a group of ordinary men, taken at random, particularly men of no note, or persons unworthy of notice. It is often used contemptuously, particularly in the phrase commencing, "Every Tom, Dick, and Harry . . ." The idea of the use of common pet forms of popular Christian names to designate a number of insignificant men is found since Elizabethan times. Shakespeare in *Henry IV*, Part I, II, iv, 9 (1597), called the leash of drawers at the tavern *Tom, Dick,* and *Francis.*

The earliest example mentioned by the *Oxford English Dictionary* is from *The Farmer's Almanack* of 1815, published in Boston. In *The Vocal Miscellany* (1734, i, 332) the first line of a stanza reads, "Farewell, Tom, Dick and Harry." Archer Taylor regards the term as very probably an Americanism and suggests that its development from earlier English phrases is speculative. The French say *Pierre et Paul* while with the Germans it is *Heinz und Kunz.*

One of Samuel Goldwyn's associates became a proud father, and Goldwyn asked, "What did you name your son?"

"John," was the reply.

"Now why did you name him John?" declared the perturbed Goldwyn. "Every Tom, Dick, and Harry is named John!"

TRIPLETS' NAMES

San Diego triplets in 1959 were named Janet A, Jo-anne B, and Jean C, the initials designating the order in which they were born. In

Corona, California, triplets were named Faith, Hope, and Charity, a common English practice in the case of girl triplets. Triplet girls born to Mr. and Mrs. Cardwell at Elm Mott, Texas, in 1899, were named Faith, Hope, and Charity on the suggestion of Mrs. Grover Cleveland, the nation's First Lady at that time. On their sixty-sixth birthday, in May 1965, they each received a telegram of congratulations from President Johnson, together with a picture of the President. The names helped. Several parents of triplet boys have named them Tom, Dick, and Harry. The *New York Times* in 1965 reported triplets born in the Western Highlands of New Guinea named Namba Wan, Namba Tu, and Namba Tri.

Some have facetiously suggested *Dan, Nan,* and *Fan* to avoid changing but a single letter; or *Ada, Ava,* and *Asa*; or *Cara, Dara,* and *Sara*; or *Ita, Iva,* and *Isa*. One wag, not the father of triplets, suggested *Kate, Duplicate,* and *Complicate* to which another chimed in that if four came along the last could be designated *Climax*.

TURKISH NAMES

The given name, in Turkey, called the umbilical name, is bestowed when the midwife cuts the umbilical cord in the presence of a male relative, father or grandfather, who pronounces the name chosen. In some regions the maternal grandmother selects the name. The usual source of the names is the Koran. Some common names are *Mehmet, Ali, Hasan, Osman, İbrahim,* and *Suleyman*. Male names could change or merely increase in number several times during life as when circumcision names, school names, teknonyms, and nicknames are employed. Girls' names tended to remain more fixed.

Nicknames or bynames were often employed for purposes of more definite identity. These relate to place of birth, occupation, or some personal or physical characteristic. Thus *Adanalı Ali* would be Ali of the town of Adana; *Demirci Müzaffer* would be Müzaffer the smith; *Topal Kâmil* refers to Kâmil the lame. There is now a marked tendency to exchange Arabic names for "pure" Turkish names.

In 1934, under Mustapha Kemal Pasha, Turkey, striving for Westernized status and to facilitate taxation and military conscription, passed a law requiring all Turks to adopt and register surnames by January 1, 1935. This deadline was extended to January 1936 and then to January 1937. Names denoting professions or ranks, as *Doctor* or *Major* were prohibited, nor could names indicating race, nation, tribe, or clan be adopted. Existing titles of *Aga*, *Effendi*, *Bey*, and *Pasha*, formerly used extensively, were abolished; and *Bay*, equivalent to the English *Mr.*, was adopted. This was to be inserted between the given names and family name.

Mustapha Kemal, the benevolent dictator, requested the Grand National Assembly to confer on him a surname and on November 24, 1934, they gave him the name *Atatürk* (Father Turk), and his family and descendants were to receive the name *Atadan* (of the father). Atatürk then conferred the family name İnönü on his chief lieutenant, İsmet Pasha, commemorating the battle at İnönü against the Greeks. The social elite and urban dwellers in the republic quickly selected names; but the country people, not understanding the implications of the law, resisted the idea of assuming family names. Turkish-sounding surnames were not required by the law, and many ethnic minorities registered non-Turkish names.

Professor Robert F. Spencer of the University of Minnesota has classified these new Turkish family names in six categories: (1) occupational names, (2) place names, (3) heroic and tribal eponyms, (4) names of objects, (5) *lâkap* or ancient nicknames referring to lineage, and (6) attractive or euphonic names. There are occupational names often ending in *-cı*, as *Bakırcı* (coppersmith), *Civici* (nail maker) and *Halici* (rug weaver). The suffix *-li* often indicates a surname derived from a place name, as *Konyalı* (from Konya) and *Köylü* (from the village). Other place names are *Dağ* (mountain) and *Deniz* (sea). Some heroic names chosen by Turks with some knowledge of ethnic history are *Selçük*, *Osmanlı*, *Osmanoğlu*, *Karaosman*, *Yuvuz*, and *Teoman*. Object names used are *Bozkurt* (gray wolf), *Arslan* (lion), *Duman* (smoke), *Buğday* (wheat), *Özüt* (pure milk), *Deve* (camel), and *Karga* (crow). The *lâkap* or old names designating a family, subtribe, or other social unit were sometimes retained as individual family names, such as *Seli Kemal* (from Silleli, those of Sille), and *Karnibüyük* (lineage of Konya). Some chose a word with a pleasant meaning or because of its euphony, as *Yücel* (sublime), *Onan* (prosperous), and *Sevilen* (beloved).

Today there is a large number of surnames in Turkey, as many people have chosen distinctive names. In 1950, for the first time, the telephone directory for the city of Istanbul listed subscribers by surname whereas before individuals were designated by given name, and the city district had to be known in order to locate the person desired.

TWINS' NAMES

Twins generally are given similar or related names. Often the parents are so excited at the time of the twins' birth that they give little thought to the effect of the names in future years. One problem a twin faces, more than the single-born, is the acquisition of his or her own distinct personality. A name closely related to another with whom he is brought up tends to aggravate the problem. A study made by Robert Plank disclosed that 62 per cent of twins have names with the same initials, 17 per cent have names with some other strong similarity, while only 21 per cent have dissimilar names. He further found that this pattern was more pronounced now than formerly.

Twins are generally relegated to alliterative combinations, as *Pamela and Penelope, James and John, Ivette and Ivonne, Jack and Jill,* and *Jacqueline and Josephine.* Or the letters can be rearranged, as *Edan and Edna* or *Arno and Rona.* Providing that a girl twin does not lisp they could be yclept *Selma and Thelma.* Pairs can be made by changing the initial letter only. For girls there might be *Delia and Celia, Carla and Marla, Cora and Dora, Rita and Riva, Cara and Sara;* and for boys, *Byron and Myron, Duke and Luke, Giles and Miles, Joel and Noel,* and *Ronald and Donald.* For mixed twins there are *Willy and Milly. Harry and Carry, Boris and Doris, Ira and Ora, Roy and Joy.* Other pairs of names for mixed twins that are the same except for the change of a letter other than the first are: *Adam and Adah, Clark and Clara, Carl and Cary, Francis and Frances, Frederick and Frederica, John and Joan, Marion and Marian, Mark and Mary.* For double twins there are *Jay, Ray, May,* and *Fay,* plus *Gay* for good measure.

Facetious suggestions for names of twin boys are: *Edward and Re-Edward, Max and Climax,* and *Pete and Repeat;* and for girl twins, *Kate and Duplicate.* The British press reported in 1946 the case of a London clergyman who refused to baptize the other twin *Duplicate.* While the press argued the point as to whether parents have the right to bestow any name they choose on their offspring, the mother went ahead and registered her daughter as Duplicate and persuaded another minister to perform the ceremony. Suggestions made

237

in a humorous vein are sometimes taken seriously. One suggested that twins be named *Jeru* and *Salem* so that both of them could be summoned by hollering "Jerusalem."

Dick Gregory, the comedian, who fought so much in the South and elsewhere for integration, gave twins born March 18, 1964, the middle names of *Inte* and *Gration*. Mr. and Mrs. Harry Evans of Dubuque, Iowa, named their twins *Bing* and *Bang* in 1962. Some have named mixed twins *Romeo* and *Juliet*.

When the priest asked the parents what names had been selected for the twins, the nervous father stammered, "Steak and Kidney."

"What kind of names are those?" exclaimed the surprised clergyman, whereupon the calm mother cut in,

"Forgive him, Father—he means Kate and Sidney."

Twins were born to a couple in England about midnight. The eldest was named *Tuesday* and the youngest, *Wednesday*.

TYPES OF CHRISTIAN NAMES

Girls' names are of ten principal types:
1. Common Biblical names, such as *Mary* and *Elizabeth*
2. Uncommon Biblical names, such as *Bithiah* and *Hagar*
3. Flower names, such as *Daisy, Myrtle, Pansy* and *Violet*
4. Character names, such as *Faith* and *Charity*
5. Jewel names, such as *Opal, Pearl, Ruby,* and *Sapphire*
6. Month names, especially *April, May,* and *June*
7. Nicknames or diminutives, such as *Jennie, Peg,* and *Sally*
8. Masculine pet forms, such as *Bobbie* and *Billie*
9. Foreign forms, such as *Olga* and *Bianca*
10. Artificial or invented names, as *Jiola* and *Uana*

Boys' names are of seven principal types:
1. Common Biblical names, such as *John, Joseph,* and *Samuel*
2. Uncommon Biblical names, such as *Chelub* and *Jabez*
3. Family names, such as *Bradford, Grant, Scott,* and *Sanford*
4. Common Teutonic names, such as *Robert, Walter,* and *William*
5. Nickname or diminutive forms, such as *Billy, Bob, Hal,* and *Sam*
6. Foreign forms, such as *Arne* and *Giuseppe*
7. Titles, such as *Colonel, Duke,* and *General*

See also CHRISTIAN NAME; PATTERNS IN CHRISTIAN NAMES

UKRAINIAN NAMES *See* Russian Names

UNFORTUNATE NAMES

Some names through no fault of their bearers have proved to be most unfortunate, and have been the cause of loss of life. After World War II many people were arrested by the Russians at checkpoints in Germany and Austria because they had the same name as someone the Russians were looking for.

Flavius Valens, emperor over the eastern parts of the Roman Empire in the latter part of the fourth century A.D., was told by his favorite astrologers that the crown would devolve upon the head of an officer whose name began with *Theod.* He interpreted this as Theodorus and had everyone of that name killed. In 379 A.D. he was succeeded by the Roman general Theodosius the Great.

Leontius (the lion) and Apsimarus (the adder) replaced Justinian II as emperors of the Eastern Roman Empire. After ten years in exile Justinian regained the throne in 705 and had the two emperors who had succeeded him trussed up and used them as footstools. Justinian II thus followed the Biblical injunction (Psalms 91:13), "Thou shalt tread upon the lion and the adder."

Hippolytus (torn by horses), in Greek legend a son of Theseus, was killed by Poseidon who frightened the horses of his chariot, causing it to overturn and drag Hippolytus to his death. The Catholic church venerates St. Hippolytus, a Roman soldier who was converted by St. Laurence, tried by the Emperor Valerian, and sentenced to be torn in pieces by wild horses as in the myth of his namesake.

Po-Yen, minister to Emperor Tohan Timur of China, is reported to have ordered the execution of every Chinese named *Chang, Wang, Liu, Li,* and *Chao,* but the dynasty was overthrown before the order could be carried out.

When King Bossa Ahadi ascended the throne of Dahomey in French West Africa several centuries ago, he made sure that no one pronounced his name, even by accident. He had everyone killed who was named *Bossa.*

When Fidel Castro acquired so much ill fame, Bernard Castro, the president of the Castro Convertible Couch Company in New York, a large manufacturer of couches for thirty years, became apprehensive lest people associate his business with Cuban troubles and seriously considered a change of name. He found, however, that people felt sorry for him and would introduce him as "the good Castro," and thus remember his name.

USE OF FIRST NAMES

People with an inferiority complex will sometimes try to lift themselves by intimating equality with their superiors through quickly using first names. Social climbers try to join the company of old, aristocratic families by the use of first names. They feel that anything that will suggest equality with another will boost them up a notch in the social scale. It usually irritates an executive to have the office boy call him by his given name. The practice may elevate the prestige of the office boy, but it usually lowers the standing of the executive. Employees do well to refrain from calling their bosses by their first name until they are sure that the practice is not resented, even though the bosses or superiors use first names. Between two workers more nearly equal in status the resentment is not so great.

By the same token people are proud to have a superior greet them in public by their given name or nicknames. Persons of more or less equal status often feel drawn to those who use their names frequently in intercourse with them. Salesmen have observed this and quickly progress to the point where they appear to be on most intimate terms. Some people go so far as to pay the headwaiter or the orchestra leader in a prominent restaurant or night club to nod and greet them by their first names when they enter with a party of friends.

Until the latter part of the eighteenth century even siblings did not use first names but preferred to say "sister" or "brother." In the nineteenth century young men called each other by their surnames. Husbands and wives did not even dare to use Christian names in ordinary speech. Wives referred to their husbands only as *Mr.* A young lady of marriageable age was always *Miss* with the surname. Toward the end of the eighteenth century society leaders began to call each other by their Christian names, but the practice quickly subsided. In the reign of Edward VII (1901–10) the use of first names became fashionable, but there still existed many restrictions. With the beginning of the twentieth century, the use of Christian names gradually became fashionable, first in the United States and slightly later in England. Today to use one's surname is almost a slight—at best a very stiff, formal gesture.

Extroverts, people who are good mixers, breezy, friendly, good-natured, politically alert, are the ones who will call people by their first names on short acquaintance. This is a warm and friendly gesture which irritates some people. Introverts are less likely to make many close friends. They are cold and formal and insist on adding *Mister* to the surname. Even though the indiscriminate use of first names did not originate from second-string radio, newspaper, and political personalities trying to imply that they were equal to the best, such use was greatly stimulated through these entertainers.

Many elderly people, and some not so elderly, deeply resent strangers calling them by their given names or nicknames. They consider it rude and undignified. Some write to authorities on etiquette, asking, "What can I say?" The reply is generally a disapproval of the indiscriminate use of first names together with such weak, suggested responses, as "Please call me Miss Baker," or "I'm sorry, but I prefer to be called Miss Green."

Some feel that the formal use of full names by children in referring to parents is stiff and shocking. They then generally assert that there are no names more beautiful than mother and father. In England, cooks are usually called *Mrs.* by their employers, and they address their employers as *Sir* and *Madam*. In America, domestics are usually called by their given name or a nickname. Office girls, receptionists, typists, and secretaries used to be called *Miss*, but now they are referred to by their first names except for an older one now and then.

In 1954, after the newspapers reported that President Eisenhower's grandson, David, called him *Ike*, a wave of disrespect swept the country, as evidenced by youngsters calling their grandparents by their first names. Mrs. Dwight D. Eisenhower liked the use of first names. In a letter to a newspaper columnist she wrote, "Actually, I have always felt flattered when the American people, with typical informality, speak of me as 'Mamie'. I know they do it from a feeling of warmhearted friendliness."

Even Pope John XXIII did not hesitate to take advantage of first names. In 1962, when Jacqueline Kennedy went to visit, the Pope asked his secretary how he should address the President's wife and was told to say "Mrs. Kennedy" or just "Madame." When the First Lady arrived at the Vatican, it was reported that he extended his arms and cried, "Jacqueline."

Some plead for the "genteel interval" which they define as the lapse of time between the moment one is introduced to a stranger and the time it is decent to call him by his nickname. Some have suggested, as an intermediary step, one might first proceed to the full Christian name before the nickname. Thus *Robert*, still a name of some slight dignity, might be a step between *Mister* and *Bob*.

The custom of calling even casual acquaintances by their first names is widespread among American businessmen and others. Yet many in America deplore the custom after asserting that they are not themselves formal and stuffy. The custom is also common in Ireland but not in other European countries.

Emily Post, in 1956, let herself get trapped into approving *Mr.* with the first name when a sensitive waitress disliked hearing other waitresses call their boss in his early thirties by his Christian name. Referring to him as "Mr. John" is more than a little stiff; it is most prissy today.

Women in Reno, Nevada, waiting for their divorces, call other women immediately after introduction by their first names. They avoid the *Mrs.* title, and in response to an introduction say, "Hello, Susan." They want company, and this gives them a sense of togetherness. A pet gripe is the person at the other end of the telephone line who cheerfully announces, "This is Mary." Mary who? Or one who signs a postcard from an exotic vacationland as "Linda." Comedians are fond of saying that girls who are in a hurry to call you by your first name are probably seeking after your last.

Then there was the very prim and proper lady who spoke to her chauffeur, "Thomas, I do not like calling my chauffeurs by their Christian names. What is your name?"

"Darling, Madam."

"Drive on, Thomas."

VANITY

People think that if their name is an old one, they are more important and better than the unsophisticated masses. People now want to prove that they come from an old Anglo-Saxon family. And many desire to confirm that their ancestors came to England with William the Conqueror. The list of the Conqueror's officers and adherents who fought with him at Hastings is known as the Battel Abbey Roll. Certain families whose ancestors were not present have been able to induce the monks of Battel to insert their names in the roll to prove the antiquity of their surnames. Various early copies of this list contain the majority of the names, but many names are found in only one or two copies.

An old Scottish Earl of Seafield is said to have attempted to show that his family name of Grant went back to Biblical times. By altering a single letter in *Genesis* 6:4, he made it read, "There were Grants [giants] in the earth in those days." When an unfeeling skeptic pointed out that they were swept away by the flood, he haughtily maintained that the verse had been misplaced in error and should have come after the deluge.

VARIATIONS IN SPELLING GIRLS' NAMES *See under* SPELLING VARIATIONS

VIETNAMESE NAMES

A Vietnamese name usually consists of three words, first a family name, a middle name (of minor importance), and an individual name. The family names are only about two hundred in number and mostly of Chinese origin. Some illustrative names are: *A, Au, Bao, Bien, Bu, Chu, Chung, Dieu, Dinh, Do, Gan, Ha, Huynh, Ke, Khuong, Kim, La, Le, Linh, Ly, Ma, Minh, Nga, Ngo, Nguyen, Nhan, Nhu, Nong, On, Ong, Pham, Phuong, Quan, Roan, Sam, Si, Su, Ta, Tao, Thanh, Thuong, U, Ung, Vay, Vi, Vuong.* Others are similar to these names. Some family names contain two of these words hyphenated. The middle word or name may indicate sex similar to our titles, *Mister* and *Miss.*

Pretty girls' names of the Vietnamese are illustrated by the names of the ten daughters of Ngo Dinh-Luyen, the ambassador to Britain in the early 1960s. In English translation they are: *Cherry Bud, Harmonious Music, Beautiful Cloud, Pure Diamond, Jade Orchid, Luminous Cherry, Cherry Branch, Swallow of the Cloud, Bright Dawn,* and *Golden Orchid.*

WELSH NAMES

The great bulk of Welsh surnames has been directly derived from given names either by their use without alteration or with the addition of *-s* to signify "son" or the possessive case. The Welsh did not completely adopt fixed family names until the latter part of the nineteenth century when the Norman and Biblical Christian names had almost completely ousted some of the more resonant Welsh names such as *Blethyn, Cadwaladr, Caradoc, Gronwy, Idris,* and *Llewarch.* The Welsh patronymical names are therefore derived almost entirely from the common Norman and Biblical given names, and are thus limited in number. An inquiry for Mr. Jones in a Welsh village would be futile. In early times a Welshman, for identification, might be known as Llewelyn ap Dafydd ap Ieuan ap Griffith ap Meredith ap Eynon ap Morgan ap Owen ap Llywarch, although his neighbors might know him only as Llewelyn ap Dafydd ap Ieuan. When one knew a person's name he knew the whole family and the genealogy.

The common Christian names, *Adam, David, Edward, Evan, Harry, James, Jone* (the Welsh form of John), *Lewis, Philip, Robert, Roger, Thomas,* and *William,* and about forty more given names have been the favorites in Wales as disclosed by the very common surnames derived from them by the addition of -s. The ancient Welsh personal names of *Griffith, Howell, Llewelyn, Lloyd, Madoc, Meredith, Morgan, Owen,* and *Rhys* have also produced many Welsh family names. For some reason the Welsh name *Arthur* did not produce Welsh surnames; as a surname, *Arthur* is mostly English.

Mag, an earlier form of the Gaelic *Mac,* became *Map* and *Mab* with the Welsh branch, and with the falling away of the M we have *ap* and *ab.* These Welsh patronymics *ap* and *ab* have coalesced with Christian names to produce numerous surnames beginning with B and P. For example, ap Ellis easily becomes *Bellis;* ap Evan becomes *Bevan;* ap Eynon turns to *Beynon;* ap Owen is *Bowen;* ap Rees turns to *Breese;* ap Harry or Henry can become *Parry* or *Penry;* ap Howell becomes *Powell;* ap Hugh is *Pugh;* ap Rhys turns to *Price* or *Pryce;* while ap Richard becomes *Prichard.* In other cases it is included in full, as *Apjohn* and *Upjohn.*

Lloyd, from *llwyd* (brown or gray), is the best-known native Welsh surname. Other color names are *Gwynne* and *Wynne* (white), *Don* from *dwn* (dark or swarthy), *Glace* and *Lace* from *glas* (green or blue), *Moyle* (black), and *Gooch* and *Gough* from *goch* (red). Other common native Welsh names are *Vaughan* (little), *Anwyl* (beloved), *Teague* (fair), *Dew* (fat), and *Vane* (thin or slender). Some native Welsh personal names have become family names, as *Cadwaladr, Evan, Griffith, Idris, Llewellyn. Owen, Rees,* and *Tudor.*

244

Surnames from Welsh place names are *Arden, Blayney,* (head of a valley), *Cardif, Carew* (fortress), *Carne* (hill), *Glough* (crag), *Conway, Gwinnett, Lougher, Machen, Maysmor* (large field), *Mostyn,* and *Wales.* Surnames from occupations are rare; however, there is *Crowther* (fiddler).

In the past many natives of Wales have deliberately duplicated their surnames in the Christian name chosen for their sons. There are many called *John Jones, William Williams,* and *Owen Owens* in the land.

WHAT IS YOUR NAME?

In America, this question is meant to elicit one's full name. In Great Britain, witnesses testifying in court are asked, "What are your names?" In France, the query, "What is your little name?" means "What is your first name?" In several languages the question is, "How are you called?"

Among many primitive peoples this casual question is most indelicate—in the poorest possible taste. It is like asking one on a first meeting to tell the most sacred and secret things in his private life. When it is believed that there is power in a name to inflict injury, one is not going to give that power to a stranger to do possible harm.

Shakespeare, in *The Tempest,* III, i, 36, causes Ferdinand to say to Miranda, "I do beseech you,—chiefly that I might set it in my prayers,—What is your name?"

WHAT'S IN A NAME?

This is included in one of the most widely quoted phrases in English. Every casual writer about names feels that he must use the phrase at least once in his article if, indeed, he does not make it the title of his sketch. Numerous anonymous articles have appeared in magazines and newspapers under this title.

Shakespeare's assertion has had an influence on the thinking of many—that names really do not matter. But one wit observed that a rose by any other name might very well smell like a petunia. A schoolboy attempting to quote the bard said, "A nose by any other name would smell as much." It is possible to set out the gist of Shakespeare's announcement without being too blunt. One might

245

say: That which we denominate a flower of the genus *Rosa* by any other onomastic expression would possess the property of titillating the olfactory in an equally dulcet manner. This is undoubtedly what the bard meant in *Romeo and Juliet*, II,ii,43.

There is the quotation by James Russell Lowell (*A Glance Behind the Curtain*, I, 251), sometimes erroneously attributed to the Bard of Avon: "Let us speak plain: there is more force in names than most men dream of." A reference to Shakespeare's many allusions to names points up the fact that if he did not quote the exact words above, they nevertheless accurately reflect his thinking more than the words he put into the mouth of poor Juliet.

Gertrude Stein, in her fuzzy, repetitious, dream-like musing, seems to recognize that there is something in a name although, like others, she cannot put her finger on it. In discussing Wilbur Wright in her book, *Four in America* (pp. 83–84), she drones on in her characteristic manner: "Everybody has a name anybody has a name and everybody anybody does what he does with his name feels what he feels about his name, likes or dislikes what he has to have with having his name, in short it is his name unless he changes his name unless he does what he likes what he likes with his name."

WIVES' PET NAMES *See under* PET NAMES